M000110262

PROTEST and DEMOCRACY

UNIVERSITY OF CALGARY
Press

PROTEST and
DEMOCRACY

Edited by Moisés Arce and Roberta Rice

© 2019 Moisés Arce and Roberta Rice

University of Calgary Press
2500 University Drive NW
Calgary, Alberta
Canada T2N 1N4
press.ucalgary.ca

This book is available as an ebook which is licensed under a Creative Commons license. The publisher should be contacted for any commercial use which falls outside the terms of that license.

LIBRARY AND ARCHIVES CANADA CATALOGUING IN PUBLICATION

Title: Protest and democracy / edited by Moisés Arce and Roberta Rice.
Names: Arce, Moisés, editor. | Rice, Roberta, editor.
Description: Includes index.
Identifiers: Canadiana (print) 2019005316X | Canadiana (ebook) 20190053208 | ISBN 9781773850450 (softcover) | ISBN 9781773850467 (open access PDF) | ISBN 9781773850474 (PDF) | ISBN 9781773850481 (EPUB) | ISBN 9781773850498 (Kindle)
Subjects: LCSH: Protest movements—21st century. | LCSH: Civil rights movements—21st century.
Classification: LCC HM883 .P76 2019 | DDC 303.48/4—dc23

The University of Calgary Press acknowledges the support of the Government of Alberta through the Alberta Media Fund for our publications. We acknowledge the financial support of the Government of Canada. We acknowledge the financial support of the Canada Council for the Arts for our publishing program.

Printed and bound in Canada by Marquis
♻ This book is printed on Enviro paper

Cover image: Colourbox 11771867
Copyediting by Ryan Perks
Cover design, page design, and typesetting by Melina Cusano

To those who struggle to make the world a better place for all of us.

MA and RR

Contents

List of Tables and Figures

Tables

Figures

Abbreviations

ACN	Action Canada Network
APEC	Asia-Pacific Economic Cooperation
ART	Alliance for Responsible Trade
CAE	Credit with State Endorsement (Chile)
CASEN	National Socioeconomic Characterization Survey (Chile)
CSA	Community Supported Agriculture
CUSFTA	Canada-US Free Trade Agreement
EU	European Union
FECh	University of Chile Student Federation
GMO	Genetically Modified Organism
GNP	Gross National Product
IMF	International Monetary Fund
LAPOP	Latin American Public Opinion Project
LOCE	Constitutional Law of Education (Chile)
MERCOSUR	Southern Common Market
NAFTA	North American Free Trade Agreement
NDP	National Democratic Party (Egypt)
NGO	Non-Governmental Organization
NOFA-VT	Northeast Organic Farming Association of Vermont

OECD	Organization for Economic Cooperation and Development
OWS	Occupy Wall Street
POS	Political Opportunity Structure
PPD	Party for Democracy (Chile)
PSU	University Selection Test (Chile)
RMALC	Mexican Action Network against Free Trade
SPP	Security and Prosperity Partnership of North America
TPP	Trans Pacific Partnership
VPIRG	Vermont Public Interest Research Group
WTO	World Trade Organization

Acknowledgements

This project is based on a simple premise—that protest is good for democracy. Traveling from conceptualization to publication, however, was no simple route. Discussion of this collaborative endeavor between the co-editors began in 2003 in Lima, Peru where Roberta was conducting field research for her dissertation and Moisés was serving as a visiting professor at the Pontificia Universidad Católica del Perú (PUCP). We began the project in earnest in 2011 under the guidance and care of our editor, Jessica Gribble, at Lynne Rienner Publishers. Our original vision was something akin to a handbook of social protest and we counted on sixteen contributors and all manner of studies. We had our first inkling that perhaps we were overly ambitious in our vision during a panel presentation on the project at the 2014 Congress of the Latin American Studies Association (LASA) in Chicago, Illinois when one of the audience members stated: "I don't get it. How are these papers related?" It was not long afterwards that our dear editor and friend, Jessica, left Lynne Rienner (we hope it was not because of our book project!) and our volume collapsed.

In 2015, when Roberta finally landed a tenure-track position, the idea of relaunching the co-edited volume resurfaced. This time we narrowed our focus to understanding the political consequences of the 2011 global protest cycle. Fortunately, a core group of our initial contributors were willing and able to stick it out with us and reshape their contributions to fit this new emphasis. All of the wonderful contributors to this current edited collection have been with us since 2011. We are eternally grateful for their patience and generosity. We also want to acknowledge the contributions to our ideas on protest and democracy of those initial contributors who were unable to wait such a long time to publish their work: Prakash Adhikari,

José A. Alemán, Ronald A. Francisco, María Inclan, Cassilde Schwartz, and Susan Spronk. Our insights into the dynamic relationship between protest and democracy are that much richer for having worked with you.

We are very thankful to the anonymous reviewers of this manuscript for their helpful comments and recommendations. Their feedback has improved the manuscript a lot, yet all shortcomings remain our own. We would like to thank the University of Calgary Press for bringing this project to fruition. Special thanks to the amazing staff at the Press: Brian Scrivener, director; Helen Hajnoczky, editorial and marketing coordinator; Alison Cobra, marketing specialist; and Melina Cusano, graphic designer. Your words of encouragement and outstanding work ethic made all the difference. We are also grateful to the University of Missouri for providing copyediting and other support. Moisés would also like to thank the participants of several academic conferences where the papers of this book were shared. Roberta would also like to acknowledge the contributions to this project of the students in her POLI455 Protest, Rebellion and Revolution class at the University of Calgary for providing welcome feedback on all of the ideas in the book. This book is designed with them in mind.

Part I:
CONCEPTS AND EXPLANATIONS

1

The Political Consequences of Protest

Moisés Arce and Roberta Rice

In 2011, *Time* magazine declared "The Protester" its person of the year. Political protests sprang up throughout 2011 in the most unlikely places. The Arab Spring protests against authoritarian rule began in Tunisia and quickly spread to Egypt and much of the Middle East. Anti-austerity protests broke out in Greece, Spain, and Portugal. In Chile, students demanded the end of for-profit education. And in the United States, the Occupy Wall Street movement brought attention to income inequality. The most unlikely individuals sparked or led these massive protest campaigns, including Mohamed Bouazizi, a Tunisian fruit vendor; Khaled Said, an Egyptian computer programmer; and Camila Vallejo, a Chilean student organizer. The composite protester turned out to be a "graduated and precarious youth" (Estanque, Costa, and Soeiro 2013, 38). The protest actions of the so-called desperate generation revealed, in different ways, a crisis of legitimacy on the part of political actors—or a failure of political representation—inasmuch as they gave voice to widespread dissatisfaction with the state of the economy (Castañeda 2012; Hardt and Negri 2011; Mason 2013). In all cases, the protesters sidelined political parties, bypassed the mainstream media, and rejected formal organizations and traditional leadership structures. They relied instead on the Internet and local assemblies in public squares for collective debate and decision-making in an open-ended search for new democratic forms (Castells 2012).

What impact, if any, did the new global protest cycle have on politics and policies in their respective countries? Addressing this question is the central task of our volume. The objective is to advance our understanding of the consequences of societal mobilization for politics and society. The volume brings together emerging scholars and senior researchers in the field of contentious politics in both the Global North and Global South to analyze the new wave of protests relating to democratic reform in North Africa and the Middle East, the political ramifications of the economic crisis in North America, and the long-term political adjustment of Latin America after the transition toward market-oriented economic policies.

There has never been a more auspicious time for studying the relationship between protest and democracy. The so-called third wave of democracy that swept the Global South beginning in the mid-1970s has brought about the most democratic period in history (Hagopian and Mainwaring 2005; Huntington 1991). While much analytical attention has been paid to the role of protests in democratic transitions, more work is needed on protest dynamics in the era of free markets and democracy. In keeping with Goodwin and Jasper's definition, this volume uses the term "political or social protest" to refer to "the act of challenging, resisting, or making demands upon authorities, powerholders, and/or cultural beliefs and practices by some individual or group" (2003, 3). The term "protest or social movement" refers to organized and sustained challenges. We define political change as "those effects of movement activities that alter in some way the movements' political environment" (Bosi, Giugni, and Uba 2016, 4). The political consequences of social movements include policy, institutional, and even regime change. The global protest cycle of 2011 offered us a rare glimpse into the articulation of new issues, ideas, and desires that may have a profound impact on future political contests worldwide. They may also be the harbinger of things to come.

This introductory chapter establishes the stance of the volume. It begins by delving into the literature on the causes and consequences of the new global protest cycle. We examine the relationship between globalization and protest activity and find that by analyzing grievances, both material and ideational, and by putting them into context, we gain new insights into what might be driving contemporary protest events as well as their goals, objectives, and potential outcomes. The second section of

the chapter addresses the prominent debates in the social science literature concerning the rise of protests in the context of widespread democratization and economic liberalization throughout the world. One set of
arguments explores the effects of these protests on democracy, examining
whether protest undermines or enhances the quality and stability of democracy. Another set of arguments studies the impact of domestic political
institutions on protest, analyzing how the variation of parties and party
systems in democracies channels or absorbs social unrest. Generally, these
arguments emphasize the broader political environment or context in
which protests unfold, thus highlighting the salience of political conditions as central to the rise of mobilizations. In the final section, we seek to
advance the literature on the political outcomes of social movements by
proposing a new analytical framework, one that calls for more attention
to protesters' grievances, their global linkages, and the responsiveness or
"permeability" of domestic political institutions to movement demands.
We conclude with an outline of the plan for the rest of the book.

Understanding the New Global Protest Cycle

Globalization can be understood as the increasing integration of national
economies worldwide by means of foreign direct investment, trade liberalization, and other market-oriented economic reforms. The dominant
response to the international debt crisis of the 1980s in the Global South
has been a profound shift in development thinking, away from state-led,
inward-oriented models of growth toward an emphasis on the market,
the private sector, and trade (Nelson 1990; Willis 2005). The prevailing
policy approach has generated intense disagreements within scholarly circles over whether or not it is improving or exacerbating economic
well-being. Most economists agree that market reforms have increased
average income levels over time (Bhagwati 2004; Lora and Panizza 2003;
Walton 2004). However, critics counter that such reforms have resulted
in minimal economic gains at best, and exaggerated social inequalities
and poverty at worst (Berry 2003; Huber and Solt 2004; Wade 2004). The
dual transition to free markets and democracy that has occurred throughout much of the developing world begs the questions: What effect has

economic globalization had on protest activity? How does regime type affect this relationship?

The literature on political protest in the current democratic era is divided over whether or not economic conditions politicize or demobilize protesters.[1] Scholars operating within the demobilization (or depoliticization) school of thought suggest that there has been a substantial decline in the capacity of social actors to organize and mobilize politically as a result of the problems of collective action posed by free market contexts (Agüero and Stark 1998; Kurtz 2004; Oxhorn 2009; Roberts 1998). Market reforms are argued to undermine traditional, class-based collective action and identity through a reduction in trade-union membership and the greater informalization of the workforce, thereby weakening its obvious opponents, particularly the labor movement. According to this perspective, pervasive social atomization, political apathy, and the hollowing out of democracy have become the global norm.

By contrast, and following contributions from the literature on social movements—in particular, political process theory (e.g., Tarrow 1998; Tilly and Tarrow 2006)—scholars within the repoliticization school suggest that a new global tide of protest is challenging elitist rule and strengthening democracy in the process (e.g., Arce and Bellinger 2007; Bellinger and Arce 2011; Arce and Kim 2011). To these observers, social protests appear to be occurring with greater frequency and intensity. As Simmons explains in chapter 2 of this volume, political process theory emphasizes the salience of political conditions as central to explaining the emergence and development of protest movements. Likewise, the repoliticization perspective emphasizes the importance of national-level political conditions as central to explaining anti-market mobilizations. Specifically, these conditions capture the formal dimensions of political opportunities (McAdam 1996), which allow one to examine the variation of protest activity across geography and time (e.g., McAdam 1982; Tarrow 1989).

The focus on political conditions, which originates from political process theory in general, and the formal dimensions of political opportunities in particular, downplays the role of economic conditions, such as inequality generated by economic liberalization, which existing literature portrays as the common source for mobilization (e.g., Kohl and Farthing 2006). To be clear, both the depoliticization and repoliticization schools of thought agree that these economic conditions impose severe material hardships on popular sectors, such as lower wages, employment insecurity, higher prices, cuts in social programs, and regressive land reform, among other examples. The question, then, is: What role do these economic conditions, which could also be interpreted as grievances or threats, play in mobilizing social actors? Following the depoliticization perspective, these grievances or economic-based threats all but demobilize social actors. And the presence of political conditions as put forth by democracy is not expected to revitalize protest activity.

Other authors, in contrast, argue that these grievances or threats were pivotal for the mobilization of social actors. In Silva's analysis, for instance, episodes of anti-neoliberal contention were "Polanyian backlashes to the construction of contemporary market society" (2009, 266). And neoliberal reforms "generated the *motivation*—the grievances—for mobilization" (Silva 2009, 43; italics in original). Following Tilly (1978), Almeida (2007) also emphasizes the salience of negative inducements or unfavorable conditions as threats that are likely to facilitate various forms of "defensive" collective action. Harvey (2003) would characterize the claims of civil-society groups in opposition to economic liberalization as "protests against dispossession." To some degree, these works mirror what political scientist James C. Davies called the "J-curve of rising and declining satisfactions" (Davies 1962; 1969). Davies's theory suggests that protest will break out when conditions suddenly worsen and aggrieved groups seek someone to blame for the disturbing course of events (see Simmons, chapter 2 in this volume). The transition to a market economy implied an erosion of social citizenship rights (e.g., access to basic social services and publicly subsidized benefits), and thus made things worse for popular sectors of civil society (Almeida 2007). Similarly, the expansion of the natural resource extractive economy, as a consequence of the deepening of economic liberalization policies, entailed a greater need for water and land, and consequently it affected both urban and rural populations. Accordingly, conflicts over the extraction of natural resources have increased in Latin America in recent years (Arce 2014).

However, following political process theory (e.g., Tarrow 1998), and emphasizing the formal dimensions of political opportunities (McAdam 1996), the repoliticization perspective argues that an approach based solely on grievances—such as those generated by globalization—does not explain collective action very well. In brief, grievances are abundant, and we do not always see social movements rise to challenge them (Tarrow 1998). For this reason, as Simmons explains in chapter 2, McAdam, McCarthy, and Zald (1988) spoke of the "constancy of discontent." Instead, political opportunities have been argued to explain protest activity based on four factors external to the movement, beginning with institutional access to the state and including the presence of elite allies and divides as well as declining state repression (McAdam 1996), which play a key role in shaping incentives for protest activity. Recent research by Goodwin and Jasper (2012), however, casts considerable doubt on the explanatory power of political opportunities for the emergence of contention. The authors found that political opportunities are more likely to shape protest activity in nondemocratic than democratic societies. According to Goodwin, "the widespread assumption among scholars that political opportunities are *necessary* for the emergence of contention is clearly mistaken" (2012, 294; italics in original). In short, the time is ripe to rethink the formal dimensions of political opportunities to better understand contemporary protest movements.

Democracy and Protest

Given the global scope of the chapters presented in this volume, it is worth restating the context in which protests are unfolding throughout the world. For instance, in some regions of the world, as in the Middle East (e.g., Kingston, chapter 6), protests are central to the spread of democracy. In other regions, as in Latin America (e.g., Donoso and Somma, chapter 7), protests are unfolding where democracy has already taken root, and are not necessarily seen as a direct challenge to democratic rule. The social science literature advances different arguments about the pros and cons of mobilizations, depending on whether a transition to democracy has or has not taken place. While the chapters in this volume address both scenarios, greater attention is paid to the dynamics of protest after democratic transitions and in the context of widespread economic liberalization. In this section—and to better understand the significance of protest in the current era of democracy and free markets—we examine three interrelated questions: Does protest endanger or advance democracy? How do political institutions shape protest? And finally: Why do some individuals protest, while others do not?

With regard to the first question, the existing social science literature portrays protest movements as both threats to and as promoters of democracy. The "disaffected radicalism" thesis, for instance, is based on the assumption that protesters reject conventional channels of representative democracy. Widespread political protests are viewed from this perspective as constituting a danger to the legitimacy and stability of the political system (Crozier, Huntington, and Watanuki 1975; Gurr 1970; Muller 1979). It has also been suggested that strong and sustained social mobilization, such as the protest episodes that toppled successive national governments in Argentina (2001, 2002), Bolivia (2003, 2005), and Ecuador (1997, 2000, 2005), contribute to institutional weakening by altering political systems through unconstitutional means (Mainwaring, Bejarano, and Pizarro Leongómez 2006). These intense mobilizations, however, did not result in an outright regime breakdown, but rather in changes to democratic regimes (Hochstetler 2006).

In sharp contrast to the view of social protests as a threat, the "normalization" thesis suggests that protest movements can complement or reinforce conventional political participation by offering a measure of direct representation for those who perceive mainstream politics to be unresponsive to citizen concerns (Johnston 2011; Meyer 2007; Norris 2002). From this perspective, protest movements foster greater democratic openness and responsiveness. They make decision-making processes more democratic and hold governments to account through their mobilizational campaigns. The concept of the "movement society" reinforces the notion that social protest has become a standard feature of democratic politics (Meyer and Tarrow 1998). In the same way that social movements cannot be fully comprehended without an examination of their political context, public policy and the inner workings of government cannot be fully understood without examining social movement pressure tactics (Goldstone 2003).

Turning to the second question—the way in which political institutions shape protest—the relationship between partisan and protest politics has been a matter of serious debate, and the existing social science literature also advances a couple of different perspectives. On the one hand, the literature on democratic transitions assumes that democratization and partisan politics lead to civil-society demobilization as the struggles of social movements are subsumed within or displaced by formal political institutions, such as parties and legislative chambers (O'Donnell and Schmitter 1986; Oxhorn 1994). According to O'Donnell and Schmitter (1986), societal mobilization increases at the early stages of the democratization process, and then decreases as the political dynamic shifts toward electoral contestation and political parties rise to the forefront of social struggles. On the other hand, social movement scholars have suggested that democratization creates new opportunities and incentives for protesters as state tolerance of dissent and the availability of potential allies generate institutional conditions that are relatively open to collective action (McAdam 1982; Tarrow 1989). For this group of scholars, the presence of democracy, in particular, enhances the opportunity for mobilization. And democratic settings guarantee such opportunities better than nondemocratic regimes (Tilly and Tarrow 2006).

While it is intuitively clear that democracies should be prone to mobilization, existing research has also shown that there is substantial variation in the level of protest activity across democracies (Kitschelt 1986) and over time (Arce 2010). On this subject, a number of studies have pointed to party systems, and the quality of representation embedded within them, as crucial intervening variables that condition democracy's effects on protest (Arce 2010; Mainwaring, Bejarano, and Pizarro Leongómez 2006; Rice 2012). Where party systems are strong and institutionalized, they tend to invite assimilative strategies—that is, protest movements attempt to work through the established political institutions as the latter offer multiple points of access to shape policies (Kitschelt 1986). These assimilative strategies ultimately put downward pressure on the scale and intensity of mobilizations. In contrast, where party systems are weak and poorly developed, parties do not serve as effective transmission belts to connect citizens with the state, and thus parties fail to channel or aggregate the demands of the popular sector. Weak or inchoate party systems create a "representation gap" that encourages disruptive, confrontational strategies. In such systems, mass political participation has a tendency to become radicalized and to overwhelm the weak institutions of the state (Huntington 1968).

Thus far, we have reviewed some of the general arguments concerning the effects of protests on democracy. Whereas the "disaffected radicalism" thesis portrays protests as a danger to democracy, the "normalization" thesis views protests as a social force that advances it. Moreover, we have examined the interaction between partisan and protest politics. Generally, some scholars expect partisan politics to outbid protest politics, particularly after democratic transitions. Other scholars, in contrast, suggest that protest politics prevail under democratic settings even when partisan politics becomes routinized. The final question we examine in this section seeks to explain why some individuals are more likely than others to protest.

Previous scholarship had suggested that protesters were radicals or extremists suffering from some form of social alienation (Kornhauser 1959; Gurr 1970; Smelser 1962), or that protest was a weapon of the poor and downtrodden (Piven and Cloward 1979). Contemporary studies based on individual-level survey research carried out mainly in the advanced industrialized democracies reveal the opposite to be the case. For example, Norris, Walgrave, and Van Aelst's study of Belgian protesters found that, "people who demonstrate are also significantly more likely to be civic joiners, party members, and labor organization members, not less" (2005, 201). In a similar vein, Schussman and Soule (2005) found that among Americans, being registered to vote had a positive and significant effect on one's likelihood of participating in protest activities. Outside advanced industrialized democracies, and confirming the balancing between traditional forms of political participation and protest, survey research in Argentina and Bolivia has also shown that "individuals who protest are generally more interested in politics and likely to engage in community-level activities" (Moseley and Moreno 2010, 5). Because these protesters are actively engaged in political life, these studies support the notion that social protest has become another legitimate expression of political demands in democratic states.

Beyond individual-level survey research examining the traits and political attitudes of protesters, several chapters in this volume provide rich examples of popular actors and organizations engaged in mobilizations across several regions (see Ayres and Macdonald, chapter 3, and Goertzl, chapter 8). In the current era, in fact, protest movements have joined together numerous groups from civil society, including Indigenous peoples, women's organizations, students, human rights groups, landless small farmers, informal and unemployed workers, as well as the traditional labor unions. These movements have also displayed a broad repertoire of contentious activity, such as attacks on government buildings and politicians' houses, national and provincial roadblocks, the banging of pots and pans, the establishment of camps in civic squares, and urban riots. These changes involving actors and types of protest actions are examples of the shifting nature of anti-government mobilizations in the context of widespread economic liberalization (Arce 2008; Arce and Bellinger 2007; Bellinger and Arce 2011; Rice 2012). Social media has also enabled mobilizations to spread very quickly (see Larson, chapter 4), and possibly contribute to the formation of coalitions that cut across classes, the urban and rural divide, and environmental and nationalistic discourses. Having discussed the individual socioeconomic and attitudinal characteristics associated with protest behavior, we now turn to our framework of analysis.

A New Framework of Analysis

Social protest plays an important role in democracies. Understanding the political consequences of such protest is the main goal of this volume. In the social movement literature, protest is considered mainly as a dependent variable in need of explanation. In contrast, we treat protest as an independent variable by assessing how social protest is realigning politics around the globe. Much of the literature on this emerging topic suggests that the political effects of social movements are contingent and conditioned by political opportunity structures and limited largely to the agenda-setting stage of the policy-making process (Amenta 2006; Bosi, Giugni, and Uba 2016; Cress and Snow 2000; Soule and Olzak 2004). In a review of the literature, Amenta et al. (2010) stated the importance of moving scholarship beyond a focus on the policy-agenda-setting stage to address movement influences on institutional processes. To do so would require a comparative research design. Specifically, the authors suggest that, "without scholarship comparing across movements, the demonstrated

Moisés Arce and Roberta Rice

influence of individual movements over specific outcomes is difficult to place in perspective. One way to do so is to compare a small number of historically similar movements with greatly different results in political influence" (Amenta et al. 2010, 302). The 2011 global protest cycle offers us the opportunity to assess a diverse array of protest movements occurring almost simultaneously across vastly different political contexts and with dramatically different results.

Our volume advances three major claims that, if taken together, constitute a new framework for studying protest and democracy. We argue that protest movements are more likely to influence political and institutional change when: a) they are part of a global cycle of protest; b) the content of the claims or grievances resonate with society; and c) the political system is responsive to the demands of protesters.

We are currently witnessing a global uptick in protest activity, with some of the largest protests in world history (Ortiz et al. 2013). The similar timing, demands, and characteristics of these protest movements suggest that they are part of a global cycle of protest. Sidney Tarrow defines a protest cycle as

> a phase of heightened conflict across the social system: with a rapid diffusion of collective action from more mobilized to less mobilized sectors; a rapid pace of innovation in the forms of contention; the creation of new or transformed collective action frames; a combination of organized and unorganized participation; and sequences of intensified information flow and interaction between challengers and authorities. (1998, 142)

It is clear from the social movement literature that protests ebb and flow. Yet, at certain times in history, protests seem to coalesce around a particular set of ideals, which may make them more effective at inducing political and institutional change. For instance, the 1960s saw a dramatic surge in protest movements in the advanced industrial democracies, including the civil rights movement, the women's movement, the gay rights movement, and the environmental movement (Keck and Sikkink 1998; Kitschelt 1986; McAdam 1982; Tarrow 1998). Each, to varying degree, changed public policies and institutions in their respective countries. The political effects of contemporary protest movements may also be heightened by their inclusion in a global protest cycle.

The extent to which the content of protesters' claims or grievances resonates within the larger society in which they are embedded can also impact movement outcomes. Collective action frames are the mobilizing ideas and meanings that mediate between structure and agency (Snow and Benford 1992). While social movement theorists have come to view shared meanings and ideas as mechanisms or processes that legitimate and motivate collective action, less attention has been paid to the ways in which they might influence political and institutional change (McAdam, McCarthy, and Zald 1996). As our contributors will show, material and ideational grievances have been at the forefront of the new global protest cycle. Social media has enabled today's protesters to transmit grievances to much larger audiences than in the past. If the content of these messages resonates with a significant portion of the public, this may not only draw out more protest participants, but potentially influence future political agendas and electoral contests, as many of the case studies in this volume demonstrate.

Finally, the degree to which a political system is open or closed to protest demands may condition protest impacts. It is clear from the findings of social movement studies that institutions matter to protest behavior. Institutions create incentives for social actors to behave in certain ways by structuring the rules of the game (March and Olsen 1989; Rothstein 1996). Open and responsive political systems that provide wide formal access to the state encourage citizens to seek change by way of existing institutional mechanisms. Strong and well-institutionalized party systems are argued to channel political demands and dampen political conflict (Mainwaring and Scully 1995). While patterns of collective action are conditioned to a certain extent by the quality of representation embedded in party systems, so, too, are the political and institutional consequences of those actions. In the course of absorbing and channeling discontent into the party system, the political system may become altered to better reflect the demands of protest movements. In the words of Jasper: "Nothing is more disastrous than trying to climb through a closed window" (2014, 24). The extent to which the new global protest cycle will impact domestic politics and policies depends on the permeability of political institutions to protest demands, as well as the willingness of protesters to engage with democratic institutions.

In the course of developing our framework of analysis, a number of new insights into social movement dynamics were revealed. First, political opportunity structures (POS), a central concept in the social movement literature, may be more important to explaining movement outcomes than they are to explaining movement emergence. Second, social mobilization may be able to pry open or create a POS where none existed or were previously latent. Third, the presence of a POS may be necessary for social movements to produce meaningful institutional and political change. These findings are especially pertinent at a time when the POS concept has come under increasing academic fire for its fuzziness, lack of dynamism, and limited causal importance in explaining social movement formation (Goodwin and Jasper 2012). The secondary task of our project, then, is to repurpose the POS concept to better understand the political consequences of social protest.

Plan of the Book

The volume is organized into four sections. Part I (chapter 2) is dedicated to the origins of social protest. It presents the theoretical debates in the literature concerning the basic question of why people protest. Part II (chapters 3, 4, and 5) look at contemporary protest mechanisms and processes. These chapters advance the literature significantly by directly addressing key themes in the study of protest movements, including the transnational arena, social media, and civil society and other nongovernmental organizations. Part III (chapters 6, 7, and 8) addresses movement outcomes. The chapters present theoretically-informed case studies from the latest global protest cycle, including the Arab Spring, the Chilean Winter, and the Occupy Wall Street protests. Part IV concludes the volume with a collective essay (chapter 9) that highlights the various chapters' key themes, issues, and contributions in an effort to advance our understanding of the political consequences of social movements.

In chapter 2, Erica Simmons explores competing theoretical explanations of and approaches to the emergence of social movements. She calls for renewed analytical attention to grievances, both material and ideational, in social movement theorization. Simmons suggests that the content of the claims that people make can have an impact on movement emergence and dynamics. By analyzing the grievances that are at the core of a movement, and by putting them into context, we gain new insights not only into what might be driving contemporary protest events, but also why they succeed or fail to meet their objectives.

In chapter 3, Jeffrey Ayres and Laura Macdonald focus on protest movements that cut across national borders to challenge economic globalization. Based on an analysis of the Vermont food sovereignty movement, alongside the example of North American activists opposed to the Trans Pacific Partnership, they argue that sustained and coordinated transnational protest movements are rare. Instead, activists tend to borrow from messages, claims, and strategies developed elsewhere, which are then adapted to local realities. Rather than "going global," activists engage in "scale-jumping" by making strategic use of transnational methods without abandoning local and national pursuits.

In chapter 4, Jennifer M. Larson takes up the question of how social media influences protest events and outcomes. Based on her analysis of the uses of social media during the recent global protest cycle, Larson maintains that its impact on contentious politics is contingent and contextual. While social media allows protesters to broadcast grievances in immediate, emotionally charged, and provocative ways, it is unclear if such technology plays a causal role in spurring protest actions and enabling protesters to achieve their desired goals. Nevertheless, governmental attempts to shut down or regulate the Internet suggest that there is a correlation between the use of social media and increased protest activity.

In chapter 5, Carew E. Boulding analyzes the influence of nongovernmental organizations (NGOs) on protest activity in emerging democracies. Throughout much of the Global South, NGOs are an important component of associational life. The expectation in the literature is that NGOs are schools for democratic citizenship. Using quantitative analysis, Boulding finds that in the context of weak and unstable political institutions, NGOs tend to boost protest activity rather than electoral participation. Her findings support the notion that effective democratic institutions tend

Moisés Arce and Roberta Rice

to dampen social conflict. In the absence of strong, well-institutionalized political parties, NGOs facilitate protest activities.

In chapter 6, Paul Kingston examines the Arab Spring protests in support of democratic reform in the Middle East. He suggests that political opportunity structures can ebb and flow with protest waves. The Arab Spring protests occurred in the absence of a window of opportunity. Arbitrary acts of state violence against predominantly nonviolent civil-society actions served as a catalyzing agent or trigger for widespread mobilization. These actions, in turn, managed to generate genuine opportunity structures. Stated differently, social actors were able to open windows of opportunity for themselves. Nevertheless, Kingston's chapter highlights the fact that windows of opportunities are temporary and can quickly close, placing firm limits on the possibilities for change in some cases.

In chapter 7, Sofia Donoso and Nicolás M. Somma analyze the Chilean Winter protests against the privatization of secondary and postsecondary education. The chapter details the push for education reform in Chile and the successful policy outcomes of this movement. The authors highlight how protest movements both shape and are shaped by institutional politics. In so doing, they shed much-needed light on the interactive relationship between social movements, policy change, and political opportunity structures. Donoso and Somma argue that social movements are a vital element of routinized politics in contemporary democracies through the way in which they introduce new demands into the policy agenda and affect the political process.

In chapter 8, Ted Goertzel analyzes the Occupy Wall Street movement as well as the Tea Party protests and their implications for US politics. He adopts a micro-level, grievance-based approach to explain the surge of protest activity in the country following the financial crisis of 2007–08. The chapter argues that dashed expectations following a period of economic advancement gave rise to two highly distinct yet effective protest movements. As Goertzel demonstrates, the incorporation of protest demands into the polity changed the political climate in the country. Whereas the conservative Tea Party movement managed to force the Republican Party further to the right, much of the agenda of the Occupy movement was co-opted by the second (2012) Obama campaign. This dynamic produced a highly polarized political party system, the implications of which are still being felt. In short, in the course of absorbing and channeling discontent into the party system, the political system was altered to reflect emerging realities.

The volume concludes with chapter 9, in which Moisés Arce, Roberta Rice, and Eduardo Silva examine what happens once a protest cycle has ended. In other words, we aim to assess how protest politics are realigning political systems around the world. We do so by elaborating on our original framework of analysis on the basis of the findings of our contributors. The chapter challenges students of contentious politics to take up the task of studying when and how protest movements promote the greater democratization of social and political life. We encourage scholars to develop a diverse theoretical and methodological toolkit, and to keep a close eye on the drama as it unfolds on the global stage.

Notes

1   The depoliticization/repoliticization debate draws on Arce (2008), Arce and Bellinger (2007), Bellinger and Arce (2011), and Arce and Kim (2011).

References

Agüero, Felipe, and Jeffrey Stark, eds. 1998. *Fault Lines of Democracy in Post-Transition Latin America*. Miami: North-South Center Press.

Almeida, Paul D. 2007. "Defensive Mobilization: Popular Movements against Economic Adjustment Policies in Latin America." *Latin American Perspectives* 32, no. 3: 123–39.

Amenta, Edwin. 2006. *When Movements Matter: The Townsend Plan and the Rise of Social Security*. Princeton, NJ: Princeton University Press.

Amenta, Edwin, Neal Caren, Elizabeth Chiarello, and Yang Su. 2010. "The Political Consequences of Social Movements." *Annual Review of Sociology* 36: 287–307.

Arce, Moisés. 2008. "The Repoliticization of Collective Action after Neoliberalism in Peru." *Latin American Politics and Society* 50, no. 3: 37–62

———. 2010. "Parties and Social Protest in Latin America's Neoliberal Era." *Party Politics* 16, no. 5: 669–86.

———. 2014. *Resource Extraction and Protest in Peru*. Pittsburgh: University of Pittsburgh Press.

Arce, Moisés, and Paul T. Bellinger Jr. 2007. "Low-Intensity Democracy Revisited: The Effects of Economic Liberalization on Political Activity in Latin America." *World Politics* 60, no, 1: 97–121.

Arce, Moisés, and Wonik Kim. 2011. "Globalization and Extra-Parliamentary Politics in an Era of Democracy." *European Political Science Review* 3, no. 2: 253–78.

Bellinger, Paul T. Jr., and Moisés Arce. 2011. "Protest and Democracy in Latin America's Market Era." *Political Research Quarterly* 64, no. 3: 688–704.

Berry, Albert. 2003. "Who Gains and Who Loses? An Economic Perspective." In *Civilizing Globalization*, edited by Richard Sandbrook, 15–25. Albany: SUNY Press.

Bhagwati, Jagdish N. 2004. *In Defense of Globalization*. New York: Oxford University Press.

Bosi, Lorenzo, Marco Giugni, and Katrin Uba. 2016. "The Consequences of Social Movements: Taking Stock and Looking Forward." In *The Consequences of Social Movements*, edited by Lorezno Bosi, Marco Giugni, and Katrin Uba, 3–37. New York: Cambridge University Press.

Castañeda, Ernesto. 2012. "The Indignados of Spain: A Precedent to Occupy Wall Street." *Social Movement Studies* 11, no. 3–4: 309–19.

Castells, Manuel. 2012. *Networks of Outrage and Hope: Social Movements in the Internet Era*. Cambridge, MA: Polity Press.

Cress, Daniel M., and David A. Snow. 2000. "The Outcomes of Homeless Mobilization: The Influence of Organization, Disruption, Political Mediation, and Framing." *American Journal of Sociology* 105: 1063–1104.

Crozier, Michael, Samuel P. Huntington, and Joji Watanuki. 1975. *The Crisis of Democracy: Report on the Governability of Democracies to the Trilateral Commission*. New York: New York University Press.

Davies, James C. 1962. "Toward a Theory of Revolution." *American Sociological Review* 27, no. 1: 5–19.

———. 1969. "The J-Curve of Rising and Declining Satisfactions as a Cause of Some Great Revolutions and a Contained Rebellion." In *Violence in America*, edited by Ted R. Gurr and H. D. Graham, 690–730. New York: Praeger.

Estanque, Elísio, Hermes Augusto Costa, and José Soeiro. 2013. "The New Global Cycle of Protest and the Portuguese Case." *Journal of Social Science Education* 12, no. 1: 31–40.

Goldstone, Jack A. 2004. "More Social Movements or Fewer? Beyond Political Opportunity Structures to Relational Fields." *Theory and Society* 33: 333–65.

———, ed. 2003. *States, Parties, and Social Movements*. New York: Cambridge University Press.

Goodwin, Jeff. 2012. "Conclusion: Are Protestors Opportunists? Fifty Tests." In *Contention in Context: Political Opportunities and the Emergence of Protest*, edited by Jeff Goodwin and James M. Jasper, 277–94. Stanford, CA: Stanford University Press.

Goodwin, Jeff and James M. Jasper, eds. 2003. The Social Movements Reader: Cases and Concepts. Oxford: Blackwell Publishers.

———. 2012. *Contention in Context: Political Opportunities and the Emergence of Protest.* Stanford, CA: Stanford University Press.

Gurr, Ted. 1970. *Why Men Rebel.* Princeton, NJ: Princeton University Press.

Hagopian, Frances, and Scott Mainwaring, eds. 2005. *The Third Wave of Democratization in Latin America.* Cambridge: Cambridge University Press.

Hardt, Michael, and Antonio Negri. 2011. "The Fight for 'Real Democracy' at the Heart of Occupy Wall Street: The Encampment in Lower Manhattan Speaks to a Failure of Representation." *Foreign Affairs.* http//www.foreignaffairs.com (accessed 13 March 2016).

Harvey, David. 2003. *The New Imperialism.* New York: Oxford University Press.

Hochstetler, Kathryn. 2006. "Rethinking Presidentialism: Challenges and Presidential Falls." *Comparative Politics* 38, no. 4: 401–18.

Huber, Evelyne, and Fred Solt. 2004. "Success and Failures of Neoliberalism." *Latin American Research Review* 39, no. 3: 150–64.

Huntington, Samuel P. 1968. *Political Order in Changing Societies.* New Haven, CT: Yale University Press.

———. 1991. *The Third Wave: Democratization in the Late Twentieth Century.* Norman: University of Oklahoma Press.

Jasper, James M. 2012. "Introduction: From Political Opportunity Structures to Strategic Interaction." In *Contention in Context: Political Opportunities and the Emergence of Protest*, edited by Jeff Goodwin and James M. Jasper, 1–33. Stanford, CA: Stanford University Press.

Johnston, Hank. 2011. *States and Social Movements.* Cambridge, MA: Polity Press.

Keck, Margaret E., and Kathryn Sikkink. 1998. *Activists Beyond Borders: Advocacy Networks in International Politics.* Ithaca, NY: Cornell University Press.

Kitschelt, Herbert P. 1986. "Political Opportunity Structures and Political Protest: Anti-Nuclear Movements in Four Democracies." *British Journal of Political Science* 16, no. 1: 57–81.

Kohl, Benjamin H., and Linda C. Farthing. 2006. *Impasse in Bolivia: Neoliberal Hegemony and Popular Resurgence.* London: Zed Books.

Kornhauser, William. 1959. *The Politics of Mass Society.* New York: Free Press.

Kurtz, Marcus J. 2004. "The Dilemmas of Democracy in the Open Economy: Lessons from Latin America." *World Politics* 56, no. 2: 262–302.

Lora, Eduardo, and Ugo Panizza. 2003. "The Future of Structural Reform." *Journal of Democracy* 14, no. 2: 123–37.

Mainwaring, Scott, Ana María Bejarano, and Eduardo Pizarro Leongómez, eds. 2006. *The Crisis of Representation in the Andes.* Stanford, CA: Stanford University Press.

Mainwaring, Scott, and Timothy R. Scully. 1995. "Introduction." In *Building Democratic Institutions: Party Systems in Latin America*, edited by Scott Mainwaring and Timothy R. Scully, 1–34. Stanford, CA: Stanford University Press.

March, James, and Johan P. Olsen. 1989. *Rediscovering Institutions: The Organizational Basis of Politics.* New York: Free Press.

Mason, Paul. 2013. *Why It's Still Kicking Off Everywhere: The New Global Revolutions.* New York: Verso.

McAdam, Doug. 1982. *Political Process and the Development of Black Insurgency, 1930–1970.* Chicago: University of Chicago Press.

———. 1996. "Conceptual Origins, Current Problems, Future Directions." In *Comparative Perspectives on Social Movements: Political Opportunities, Mobilizing Structures, and Cultural Framings*, edited by Doug McAdam, John D. McCarthy, and Mayer N. Zald, 23–40. New York: Cambridge University Press.

McAdam, Doug, John D. McCarthy, Mayer N. Zald. 1988. "Social Movements." In *Handbook of Sociology*, edited by Neil Smelser, 695–737. Beverly Hills: Sage.

McAdam, Doug, John D. McCarthy, and Mayer N. Zald. 1996. "Introduction." In *Comparative Perspectives on Social Movements: Political Opportunity, Mobilizing Structures, and Cultural Framings*, edited by Doug McAdam, John D. McCarthy and Mayer N. Zald, 1–20. New York: Cambridge University Press.

McAdam, Doug, Sidney Tarrow, and Charles Tilly. 2001. *Dynamics of Contention.* Cambridge: Cambridge University Press.

Meyer, David S. 2007. *The Politics of Protest: Social Movements in America.* New York: Oxford.

Meyer, David S., and Sidney Tarrow, eds. 1998. *The Social Movement Society.* Lanham, MD: Rowman and Littlefield.

Moseley, M., and Moreno, D. 2010. "The normalization of protest in Latin America." *Americas Barometer Insight Series*, 42. https://www.vanderbilt.edu/lapop/insights/Insights_Compilation_Volume_II_2010-2011_V4_W_08.04.16.pdf (accessed 10 November 2018).

Muller, Edward N. 1979. *Aggressive Political Participation.* Princeton, NJ: Princeton University Press.

Nelson, Joan M, ed. 1990. *Economic Crisis and Policy Choice: The Politics of Adjustment in the Third World.* Princeton, NJ: Princeton University Press.

Norris, Pippa. 2002. *Democratic Phoenix: Reinventing Political Activism.* Cambridge: Cambridge University Press.

Norris, Pippa, Stefaan Walgrave, and Peter Van Aelst. 2005. "Who Demonstrates? Antistate Rebels, Conventional Participants, or Everyone?" *Comparative Politics* 37, no. 2: 189–205.

O'Donnell, Guillermo, and Philippe C. Schmitter. 1986. *Transitions from Authoritarian Rule: Tentative Conclusions about Uncertain Democracies.* Baltimore, MD: Johns Hopkins University Press.

Ortiz, Isabel, Sara Burke, Mohamed Berrada, and Hernan Cortes Saenz. 2013. "World Protests 2006–2013." Working paper, Initiative for Policy Dialogue and Friedrich-Ebert-Stiftung, New York.

Oxhorn, Philip. 1994. "Where Did All the Protesters Go? Popular Mobilization and the Transition to Democracy in Chile." *Latin American Perspectives* 21, no. 3: 49–68.

Oxhorn, Philip. 2009. "Beyond Neoliberalism? Latin America's New Crossroads." In *Beyond Neoliberalism in Latin America? Society and Politics at the Crossroads*, edited by John Burdick, Philip Oxhorn, and Kenneth M. Roberts, 217–33. New York: Palgrave Macmillan.

Piven, Frances Fox, and Richard A. Cloward. 1979. *Poor People's Movements: Why They Succeed, How They Fail*. New York: Vintage Books.

Rice, Roberta. 2012. *The New Politics of Protest: Indigenous Mobilization in Latin America's Neoliberal Era*. Tucson: University of Arizona Press.

Roberts, Kenneth M. 1998. *Deepening Democracy? The Modern Left and Social Movements in Chile and Peru*. Stanford, CA: Stanford University Press.

Rothstein, Bo. 1996. "Political Institutions: An Overview." In *A New Handbook of Political Science*, edited by Robert E. Goodin and Hans-Dieter Klingemann, 133–66. Oxford: Oxford University Press.

Schussman, Alan, and Sarah A. Soule. 2005. "Process and Protest: Accounting for Individual Protest Participation." *Social Forces* 84, no. 2: 1083–1108.

Silva, Eduardo. 2009. *Challenging Neoliberalism in Latin America*. New York: Cambridge University Press.

Smelser, Neil. 1962. *Theory of Collective Behavior*. New York: Free Press.

Snow, David A., and Robert D. Benford. 1992. "Master Frames and Cycles of Protest." In *Frontiers in Social Movement Theory*, edited by Aldon D. Morris and Carol McClurg Mueller, 133–55. New Haven, CT: Yale University Press.

Soule, Sarah A., and Susan Olzak. 2004. "When Do Movements Matter? The Politics of Contingency and the Equal Rights Amendment." *American Sociological Review* 69: 473–97.

Stahler-Sholk, Richard, Harry E. Vanden, and Glen David Kuecker. 2007. "Globalizing Resistance: The New Politics of Social Movements in Latin America." *Latin American Perspectives* 32, no. 2: 5–16.

Tarrow, Sidney. 1989. *Democracy and Disorder: Protest and Politics in Italy, 1965–1974*. Oxford: Oxford University Press.

———. 1998. *Power in Movement: Social Movements and Contentious Politics*. New York: Cambridge University Press.

Tilly, Charles. 1978. *From Mobilization to Revolution*. Reading, MA: Addison-Wesley.

Tilly, Charles, and Sidney Tarrow. 2006. *Contentious Politics*. New York: Oxford University Press.

Wade, Robert Hunter. 2004. "Is Globalization Reducing Poverty and Inequality?" *World Development* 32, no. 4: 567–89.

Walton, Michael. 2004. "Neoliberalism in Latin America: Good, Bad, or Incomplete?" *Latin American Research Review* 39, no. 3: 165–83.

Willis, Katie. 2005. *Theories and Practices of Development*. New York: Routledge.

2

How Do We Explain Protest?
Social Science, Grievances, and the Puzzle of
Collective Action

Erica S. Simmons

How and why social movements emerge, develop, strengthen, and fade has long intrigued social science scholars.[1] In particular, three frameworks have emerged that dominate the social movement literature: resource mobilization, political opportunity, and the framing process (McAdam, McCarthy, and Zald 1996, 7). They are now largely understood to constitute one approach—the political process model (e.g., see Piven and Cloward 1977; McAdam 1982). Even as the dynamics of protest shift in the face of marketization, globalization, and rising democratization and inequality, questions about why people protest continue to return to the core tenants of political process theory. Many current explanations for protest either seek to refine and further specify how and when we might expect to see particular elements of the political process model at work, or to encourage scholars to push the model towards increased interactivity and attention to social construction (e.g., McAdam, Tarrow, and Tilly 2001). The question remains, however, whether we are theoretically equipped to explain protest in what Arce and Rice in chapter 1 of this volume call "the era of free markets and democracy."

This chapter offers an overview of contemporary theorizing on social movements, focusing largely on the political process model and the contributions made by scholarship tied to the "cultural turn."[2] The chapter is divided into four sections. The first section introduces social movement theorizing that emphasized "strains" or "breakdowns." The second section turns to the political process model and outlines both its central components and a number of contemporary critiques. The chapter then addresses the "cultural turn" in social movement theory and offers the broad contours of its central contributions. The chapter concludes by proposing that scholars would do well, once again, to pay attention to the content of a movement's claims. By focusing on the claims that people make when they protest—the grievances at the core of a movement—we enhance our answers to old questions and suggest new avenues for future research.

Strains and Breakdowns: Early Theorizing on Social Movements

Early approaches to theorizing social movements are heavily rooted in the idea that rapid social transformations would lead to intense periods of collective action (Smelser 1963). Scholars developed variations on the general theory, focusing on "strains" or "breakdowns."[3] Davies (1962; 1969) advocated for the power of the "J-curve of rising expectations" (1962, 14). He argued that revolutions are most likely when long periods of economic and social development are followed by a quick downturn. If expectations form in response to perceptions that conditions are improving and they instead decline quickly, revolution will result. Building on Davies's emphasis on expectations and "state of mind," Geschwender (1968) proposed a more general theory, one applicable to social movements as well as revolutions, arguing that conflicting perceptions of social and economic reality could help explain the rise of the civil rights movement. Black Americans had experienced rising living standards throughout the 1930s and '40s only to find "the doors closed as tightly as ever" (Geschwender 1968, 134) at the close of the Second World War. Gurr (1970) followed closely on Davies's and Geschwender's heels when he enjoined scholars to focus on relative deprivation, arguing that collective action could be explained by the intensity with which deprivation is experienced. In these accounts, social movements are largely seen as reactive to social crises and can be explained by attention to individual cognitive processes or breakdowns in social relationships.

Critiques of breakdown, strain, or relative deprivation approaches abound (e.g., McCarthy and Zald 1977; McAdam 1999; Tilly, Tilly, and Tilly 1975). The "constancy of discontent," as McAdam, McCarthy, and Zald (1988) call it, is at the core of many objections to grievance-centered approaches.[4] Tarrow offers a clear articulation of this line of reasoning: "Even a cursory look at modern history shows that outbreaks of collective action cannot be derived from the level of deprivation that people suffer or from the disorganization of their societies; for these preconditions are more constant than the movements they supposedly cause" (1998, 81). In short, grievances exist everywhere but we do not always see social movements emerge to address them. While some defenders continued to voice support for strain or breakdown theories (e.g., Piven and Cloward 1992), the idea that grievances consistently outnumber social movements, and therefore cannot provide the variation necessary for a convincing explanation, has gone largely uncontested. Indeed, by the late 1990s, it appeared as though the heavy criticism of grievance-centered approaches had relegated them to "the dustbin of failed social science theories" (Snow et al. 1998, 2).

The Political Process Model

With the rise of the political process model, social movement theory took a sharp and decisive turn away from grievances. Proponents of a political process approach focused not on the claims movements made, but rather on the context in which they operated; the "world outside a social movement" became key to understanding movement dynamics (Meyer 2004, 126). Resource mobilization and political opportunity approaches emerged first (e.g., Eisinger 1973; Tilly 1978; McCarthy and Zald 1977; McAdam 1982), with frames (Snow et al. 1986) quickly on their heels. While all three are now often understood to be part and parcel of the political process model, it is useful to start by taking each in turn.

For resource mobilization theorists, the rise of a movement can be understood with reference to resources external to the movement organization as well as the movement's organizational structure itself (McAdam,

McCarthy, and Zald 1996, 7). McAdam defines the resources and structures relevant to this approach as "those collective vehicles, informal as well as formal, through which people mobilize and engage in collective action" (1999, xi). Organizations, financial resources, and connective structures (networks, relationships, etc.) are treated as critical ingredients in a social movement's ability to organize. The resource mobilization approach challenges scholars of social movement emergence to understand the importance of mobilization processes to sustained collective action. The result is a "focus on [the] groups, organizations, and informal networks that comprise the collective building blocks of social movements" (McAdam 1999, ix).

Attention to the resources available to movements has improved our understanding of the dynamics and trajectories of important moments of political protest. For example, Clemens (1997) shows how the associations women made through clubs, parlor meetings, and charitable organizations served as critical foundations to social-reform movements in the early twentieth century. My own research in Cochabamba, Bolivia, details how activists drew on strong networks of neighborhood associations, unions, and irrigator organizations to recruit participants for the water wars in the winter and spring of 2000 (Simmons 2016c). Without the relationships formed and cultivated through these kinds of associations, both the social-reform movement in the United States and the movement against water privatization in Bolivia may never have gotten off the ground. Wickham-Crowley (1992) shows how the concept is useful not only for understanding peaceful social movements, but efforts at armed resistance as well. We cannot, he argues, explain the success of guerrilla movements in Latin America without taking into account access to military equipment. Here, Wickham-Crowley draws our attention not to organizational networks, but rather to material resources. More recently, we can point to the ways in which social media served as a mobilizing structure for the Egyptian protests of 2011 (see Gerbaudo 2012; Kingston, chapter 6 in this volume). While we should not treat social media as an agent that acts independently of the activists and social movement participants that use them, we should nonetheless understand them as tools for social mobilization.

Although attention to mobilizing structures and resources has added much to our understandings of social movements, the concept has not gone without critique. Goodwin and Jasper note that the definition is so broad that "no analyst could possibly *fail* to uncover one or another mobilizing structure 'behind' or 'within' a social movement. . . . The concept thus begs the question of how and when certain of these 'structures,' but not others, actually facilitate collective protest" (2004b, 20). McAdam, Tilly, and Tarrow argue that resource mobilization approaches "exaggerate the centrality of deliberate decisions" and "downplay the contingency, emotionality, plasticity, and interactive character of movement politics" (2001, 15). Some scholars have worked to further define and specify the types of resources available to movements, and how they might work to help explain social movement dynamics and trajectories. Most recently, Edwards and McCarthy (2004) have developed a typology of social movement resources, outlining the importance of what they call moral, cultural, social-organizational, human, and material resources.[5]

Yet challenges with the concept remain. First, it is not always clear whether a particular mobilizing structure helps to build or undermine a movement—the same structure could work both ways depending on the context (e.g., see Cloward and Piven 1984). Strong organizations can work to build a movement just as easily as they can undermine the movement's ability to achieve its goals by making the movement available for co-optation. Second, movements may capitalize on existing structures or networks, but they can also consciously and purposefully build their own. Returning to the example of the Bolivian water wars mentioned above, while activists drew on powerful preexisting local networks throughout the protests, the most important organization in the movement's growth, a multisector association called the Coordinator for Water and Life, was a product of the movement itself. Attention to political opportunity structures, the next approach outlined below, does not address these particular flaws in resource mobilization theories, but it does begin to draw scholars' attention to the context in which a movement operates.

As its name suggests, the political opportunities approach focuses on changes in political opportunities (McAdam, McCarthy, and Zald 1996, 7). When scholars look to political opportunities to help explain social movement dynamics, they are usually looking at large-scale changes that create openings or windows to which a movement can respond. Specifically, scholars may look to "changes in the institutional structure or informal power relations of a given national political system," or "differences in the political characteristics of the nation states in which [movements] are embedded," to explain movement emergence (McAdam, McCarthy, and Zald 1996, 3). Political opportunity theorists remind scholars that political context and long-term processes can be critical to understanding variation in social movements across geography and time.

Political context can advantage some claims, close off possibilities for others, make some strategies more attractive or successful, and influence who participates in protest politics and how. McAdam's (1982) emphasis on newly enfranchised northern black voters as an important causal factor in the emergence of the civil rights movement offers a classic example of how political opportunities shape movement emergence. With more black voters to appease, northern politicians began to see support for civil rights legislation as potentially working to their advantage. As politicians responded to and advocated for the movement's claims, the movement was able to grow. Political opportunities may also emerge out of specific events. The shooting at an elementary school in Newtown, Connecticut, in December 2012 arguably created a political opportunity for the gun-control movement in the United States, as many American citizens expressed an interest in stricter gun measures in the wake of the violence. The possibilities for what can work as a "political opportunity" are seemingly endless. The concept can refer to everything from formal domestic political institutions to the international context to economic or social cleavages.

However, political opportunity scholars often fail to describe exactly which kinds of change will be most conducive to contentious political action. Scholars who emphasize political opportunities rarely suggest causal trends or hypothesize that a certain change in political opportunity structure will have a similar effect on a variety of social movements.[6] Instead, scholars often show how particular political opportunities work in particular moments without theorizing how they might work in a different time or place. Among scholars who use the concept, a debate rages over whether expanding or contracting structures are most conducive to mobilization (McAdam 1982; 1999, xi). This distinction offers limited leverage for scholars seeking to better understand the mechanisms and processes at work. Furthermore, it introduces ambiguous terminology into an already poorly defined debate. An "opportunity" in some circumstances might be a constraint in others. One need only consider the impact of repression on protest politics to understand how context-dependent the concept of "political opportunity" is. The threat of violence against members of the opposition arguably helped to keep many Chileans at home during the early years of the Pinochet dictatorship, while perceived acts of repression during the Bolivian water wars may very well have encouraged bystanders to join the protests.

Yet, as the introduction to this volume suggests, attention to political institutions, and particularly those that often accompany democratic politics (e.g., party systems, freedom of the press, etc.) may provide important explanatory leverage in our understandings of when and where social movements emerge and why they take the forms they do. While scholars do not agree on which political institutions might be most conducive to political protest and why, further research on how different systems of representation might "open" or "close" opportunities for dissent could offer a useful parsing of the political opportunity concept.

Ultimately, the concept risks becoming a catchall framework that can play a role in the development of almost any social movement and can only be determined post hoc. This is not to say that political possibilities do not matter—indeed, any study of contention must also pay careful attention to the "political horizons" (Gould 2009) of the moment. We cannot simply look at the structural conditions during a given moment in political history and designate that moment a "political opportunity."

Furthermore, even with the most felicitous conditions of "political opportunity," some movements begin only after a so-called catalyzing event. Contingency appears to have remained central to our explanations for movements as influential as the Yellow Revolution in the Philippines, where the assassination of Benigno Aquino arguably played a critical role, and the antinuclear movement, which is difficult to explain without reference to the incident at Three Mile Island. As Gamson and Meyer note, "used to explain so much, [political opportunity structure] may ultimately explain nothing at all" (1996, 275).

As the importance of perceptions surfaced as a central critique of a purely structural approach to political opportunities, scholars began to think systematically about the ways in which movement leaders help to shape those perceptions. In the mid-1980s, Snow et al. (1986, 464) developed the concept of frame alignment, arguing that for a social movement to resonate with individuals and, as a result, create a base of participants and support, the frames through which individuals understand the world must somehow align with a movement's goals or activities. McAdam, McCarthy, and Zald offer a succinct definition—"the conscious strategic efforts by groups of people to fashion shared understandings of the world and of themselves that legitimate and motivate collective action" (1996, 6). Movements may emerge or grow because leaders frame or reframe messages in ways that can attract a new or broader constituency. Or, potential participants may shift their own beliefs or expectations as a result of a movement's repackaging, bringing an audience into closer alignment with a movement's objectives.

Attention to frames can help us to understand movements as varied as the student mobilizations in China in 1989 and the white separatist movement in the 1990s in the United States. Craig Calhoun (1994) shows us how Chinese students changed the frames deployed throughout their movement from articulations that appealed specifically to students' conceptions of the role of intellectuals in Chinese society to broader appeals to patriotism and self-sacrifice. As the movement expanded, its leaders both responded to and helped to encourage increased participation by deploying frames that would resonate outside of the student community. In his study of white separatists in the United States, Berbrier (1998) shows how frame-transformation and frame-alignment processes worked not to appeal to new constituents, as they did in China, but rather to adapt to changing cultural practices. Movement leaders changed movement rhetoric from a language of hate to one of cultural pluralism, calling on love, pride, and heritage preservation to motivate their members.

While these two examples suggest a tight control over frames by movement leaders, other studies reveal that framing processes are highly contested and rarely controlled (e.g., see Babb 1996). Furthermore, while many studies take the meaning-making processes at the core of concepts like frame resonance as both given and coherent, theoretically there is room in frame analysis for movement participants to alter the meaning-making processes in which they are engaged. Through attention to frames, we can see how movements themselves produce and reproduce "culture."

An initial difficulty with much scholarly discussion of the framing and reframing process is that it often implies the exteriority of language, symbols, and historical memory. Frames often appear to come from outside of the social world of movement participants. This exteriority suggests an elite-mass dichotomy in which elites manipulate masses through the framing process. The approach often forgets that the language, symbols, and memory of both leaders and participants are embedded in the same context—movement-framing processes cannot exist outside of the social world in which the movement takes place (Mueller 1992, 5). As a result, frames themselves are a product of their context. The work that a frame does (or fails to do) to help motivate political protest can only be understood when we analyze the frame's meanings in the contexts in which it is deployed.

Part of the challenge with much of the framing literature is that all of the relevant dynamics of meaning can be black-boxed by terms like "resonate."[7] The term is often deployed—particularly in the context of the literature on collective action—to refer to sympathetic or positive emotional responses to something. If a frame "resonates" we understand it to have evoked emotions, images, or memories. Yet even the metaphor of the frame suggests problems with the concept of frame resonance. A frame is something outside of something else—it is a border designed to enhance the appearance of a picture inside, or a basic structure designed to bear a load. The ways in which scholars deploy the frame metaphor places meanings somehow on the outside, while simultaneously insisting on a frame's embeddedness. It is difficult to reconcile the two, and this may be at the root of many of the challenges inherent in using the concept of a frame to better understand processes of political contention.

The "Cultural Turn" and "New Social Movements"

The recent "cultural turn" in social movement theory encourages scholars to move beyond frames when incorporating culture into their analyses (e.g., see Goodwin, Jasper, and Polletta 2001; Gould 2004; Johnston, Laraña, and Gusfield 1994). Responding largely to the rise in identity- and rights-based movements in the mid-1960s, much of this literature challenges the ways in which culture and emotions have been incorporated into—or ignored by—the political process model. Goodwin and Jasper (2004a) highlight many of the same drawbacks to approaches emphasizing political opportunities and mobilizing structures outlined above. They take the critique one step further, however, by arguing that political process theorists often incorporate culture in problematic ways. Cultural dynamics, they argue, are not all "captured by framing" (Goodwin and Jasper 2004a, 28). Furthermore, adherents to the political process model, they argue, often treat culture as a bounded "thing" instead of practices that are always changing and can have multiple significations. Goodwin and Jasper call on social movement scholars to "recognize that cultural and strategic processes define and create the factors usually presented as 'structural,' " and to treat culture as "ubiquitous and constitutive dimension of *all* social relations, structures, networks and practices" (2004a, 23).

Emotions have received particular attention among adherents of the cultural turn, inspiring an edited volume on the subject (Goodwin, Jasper, and Polletta 2001) and multiple chapters in other volumes (e.g., Gould 2004; Aminzade and McAdam 2001). Many contend that the emotional dimensions of social movements should not be simply subsumed into frame analysis. Goodwin, Jasper, and Polletta go so far as to argue that "much of the causal force attributed to [mobilizing structures, frames, collective identity, and political opportunities] comes from the emotions involved in them" (2001, 6). Gould reminds us that, "analytical attention to the power of emotions . . . can provide us with important insights, illuminating, for example, participants' subjectivities and motivations, and helping us to build compelling accounts of a movement's trajectory, strategic choices, internal culture, conflicts, and other movement processes and characteristics" (2004, 157).

While political process theorists might be inclined to analyze emotions as part of an intentionally deployed mobilization strategy via resonant frames, an approach that sees emotions as *only* strategic overlooks a myriad of other roles that emotions can play in social movement dynamics. Gould (2004) encourages scholars to "bring emotions back in," and argues in particular that by paying attention to the experience of feelings we can both shed light on questions central to mainstream social movement research agendas and bring new subjects of inquiry to the fore. For example, Wood (2001; 2003) helps to explain participation in rebellion in El Salvador through attention to "process benefits." Protest itself becomes an end goal as participants derive pleasure and pride from the experience. Jasper (1997) focuses our attention on the power of "moral outrage," arguing that "moral shocks" can help to motivate movement participation. In her study of gay and lesbian activism around the AIDS crisis, Gould (2009) shows how emotional utterances (for example, expressions of grief or rage) can actually help to produce the very emotions articulated. The claim "we are angry" not only calls a particular "we" into being, but can also help to produce anger itself.

Insofar as the "cultural turn" emphasizes an approach to culture that treats culture as semiotic practices, its theoretical foundations open the door for renewed attention to grievances—to the moral and material claims that people make. But scholars tied to this "turn" also shy away from the explicit theorization of movement claims. In 1994, Johnston, Laraña, and Gusfield described grievances as a "forgotten theoretical issue," and argued that "new social movement" research had revived attention to grievances (1994, 20). Yet while some of this literature draws attention to connections between shared feelings of injustice and strong attachments to collective identity, it does not offer a systematic theorization of different kinds of grievances and how they might work differently to prompt resistance.

Jasper's (1997) work on "moral shocks" appears to be one of the few analyses that attempts to systematize how we think about grievances and the ways they work. But Jasper does not thoroughly explore why a threat to one issue or good might be understood as a "moral" shock in some times and places and not in others, or why different grievances might come together as common claims in some moments and fail to do so in others.[8] In their critique of Jasper, Polletta and Amenta correctly observe that "virtually any event or new piece of information can be called in retrospect a moral shock," and they enjoin scholars to "ask what it is about certain events that create such anger, outrage, and indignation in those exposed to them that they are driven to protest" (2001, 307). They go on to ask, "Are some *kinds of issues* more likely to generate moral shocks than others?" (Polletta and Amenta 2001, 307; emphasis in original). In the next section of this chapter, I articulate a first step towards taking up Polletta and Amenta's call.

Proposing a Meaning-Laden Approach to Grievances

I propose that attention to grievances—understood to be constituted by not only material, but also ideational claims—can deepen our analysis of the dynamics of contention (see also Simmons 2014; 2016c; 2016b; 2016a). I begin with the idea that social movement theory needs to bring the role of the grievance back in. While efforts that focus on strain, breakdown, or relative deprivation (discussed at the beginning of this chapter) may have been rightly sidelined, they should not be thrown out entirely. The content of a movement's claims can influence movement emergence, trajectory, and composition, and should therefore play a central role in our analyses. Indeed, as Arce and Rice show in the introductory chapter to this volume, different kinds of grievances may have different effects on protest and in particular its impact. The key is to create useful categories of analysis—for Arce and Rice, disaggregating "economic threat" into "globalization" and "inequality" added important leverage to their analysis. While discontent may be constant (McAdam, McCarthy, and Zald 1988) different types of discontent may have different effects on social movement emergence, growth, and decline.

I argue that a potentially fruitful approach to categorizing griev- ances is through a focus on what certain events or sets of claims *mean*. For example, inequality will take on different meanings across different times and places (and even within those times and places), and it works to produce protest (or not) differently as a result. I would take Arce and Rice's analysis in chapter 1 a step further to say that the economic condi- tions that have accompanied globalization should not be lumped together without a corresponding analysis of what those conditions mean to the people who experience them. Social movement theory would do well to focus its lens on the meaning work done by grievances—understood as meaning-laden claims—and how that work can help to explain the timing and composition of political protest.

Resources, political opportunities, and frames are critical to our understandings of social movements. But I propose that adherents to the political process model should pay careful attention to *how* resources, opportunities, or frames become available and *why* they are available to some movements and not to others. Here, attention to the grievance—understood as constituted by material and symbolic claims and conceptions—can enhance our analysis, serving as a moving part that contributes additional explanatory power to existing approaches (Simmons 2014; 2016c). By incorporating the meanings of grievances, we can deepen our understandings of these three processes as well as the broader dynamics of social movement emergence and development.

Grievances are most usually treated as objectively identifiable claims. Grievances are things we can easily observe, compare, and quantify, even without local knowledge. Grievances at the core of social movement activity have included everything from property taxes, to racial discrimination, to abortion, to climate change. They can make claims relevant at the international, national, or highly local levels. A meaning-laden approach to grievances recognizes that these claims are both materially and ideationally constituted—that to understand the grievance at, for example, the center of the gay marriage movement, we have to understand what marriage means in different times and places and to different people, and how those meanings work to shape both support for, and opposition to, the movement. Furthermore, a meaning-laden approach suggests that the ideas with which some claims are imbued might be more conducive to motivating political resistance than others.

The approach is inherently grounded in context—scholars begin by understanding the meanings that grievances take on in particular times and places. But it is also potentially generalizable; as scholars uncover the ways in which apparently different grievances may represent similar ideas across time and place, those grievances can be categorized similarly, and their potential relationship to social mobilization explored. The approach does not focus on the deliberate work that social movement activists do to articulate grievances and construct resonate frames or, more generally, how people "do things" with culture (Williams 2007). Nor does it treat systems of symbols as static, coherent, or fixed, in the way that some scholarship suggests.[9] I seek, in other words, to take neither an agentive nor a structural approach to culture.

Instead, I draw on an anthropological conceptualization of culture as "semiotic practices" to look behind the agency-oriented approaches that dominate the cultural social movement literature. This approach pays particular attention to "what language and symbols *do*—how they are inscribed into concrete actions and how they operate to produce observable political effects" (Wedeen 2002, 714; emphasis in original), as opposed to what actors do with them. These meanings are constantly contested, both by chronologically linear processes of change and by the multiple significations that may exist within social groups. When we look at how symbols operate in the world, understanding them as dynamic and conflicted, we can begin to ask questions about why and how meanings might work to help generate moments of collective political protest.

I propose that a close parsing of the work that symbols do can give us analytical leverage over questions of movement emergence and composition. By focusing our analytic lens on the ways in which different grievances are imbued with similar or different meanings in different contexts, we can come to think of grievances as more than just the relative gain or loss of a material "thing" or a set of political privileges. Williams encourages us to think about "*socially and culturally available* array of symbols and meanings from which movements can draw" (2007, 96; emphasis in original). These symbols and meanings inform our understandings of what a grievance "is." By understanding grievances as embedded in cultural context, we can productively engage with the ways in which the claims themselves shape social movement outcomes, not simply how movement entrepreneurs articulate those claims.

The framing literature recognizes that grievances take on meanings and that these meanings matter for how people are mobilized. Certain issues in certain communities will be more easily translated or constructed in such a way as to have enough motivational power to become a rallying point for collective action. Whether there is a systematic, cross-contextual relationship between the meaning of the grievances and the power of a particular frame goes relatively ignored, even in an approach as attentive to grievances as the framing one is. Which frames resonate and when may indeed be highly contingent: similar grievances in a physical sense could resonate with different ethnic or national identities, different myths or historical experiences, and take on different meanings as a result. Which frame is developed and how becomes a secondary concern. Instead, the question is whether there is something systematic about the way the *problems themselves* are understood that is likely to generate collective action frames irrespective of the context.

It is theoretically possible that certain *categories* of grievances, where the meaning of the grievance and not its physical attributes produces the category, are likely to have more frame resonance than others. The framing literature helps us understand how frames work but not whether there is something systematic about the meanings that make those frames possible and potent. The potential for systematic similarities between grievances with "potent" frame resonance is left unexplored.

The basic argument proposed here is that while grievances maintain material power, their ideational aspects, as well as the reciprocal relationship between the two, play a critical role in developing understandings of what the grievance "is." The meanings with which grievances are imbued should be considered a product of what we might understand to be their materiality. At the same time, those meanings themselves help to determine and define how we understand that very material value. As Wedeen has argued, "material interests might be fruitfully viewed not as objective criteria but as being discursively produced: in other words, what counts as material interest is mediated through our language about what 'interest' means and what the material is" (2008, 183). Furthermore, the relationship is not static. Instead, the "ideational" and the "material" continually work in ways that are "reciprocally determining, that is, mutually implicated in the changes that each undergoes through time" (Wedeen 2008, 49). Voting is not simply the act of putting a marked piece of paper in a ballot box to select a political leader, though we might understand the action to be part of the material component of voting. Instead, it has a host of different meanings for different actors in different contexts. As a result, restricting or expanding voting privileges may mean different things in different times and places to different people. In addition to the material aspect of the reform—the restriction or expansion of voting—it might symbolize, for example, freedom, democracy, dictatorship, or revolution.

But even as this chapter proposes a move towards cultural context, it is also explicitly focused on the potential for developing analytical categories of grievances with generalizable purchase. Apparently different claims in decidedly different contexts may take on similar meanings and, as a result, generate protest through similar mechanisms. We would then want to think about the processes through which those meanings are produced and reproduced, trying to identify why and how apparently different material goods take on similar meanings. We could then create a broader analytical category for the type of grievance (for example, market-driven subsistence resource threats) and do systematic research to understand the ways in which similar moments in which the grievance (defined materially and ideationally) is present might produce similar patterns of resistance in different contexts. Through this analysis we could generate causal accounts of social mobilization where the meanings that the grievances take on are part of the causal story.

A comparison of protests against water privatization in Cochabamba, Bolivia, and appeals for affordable tortillas in Mexico City, Mexico, provides a useful illustration (see Simmons 2016c for a full elaboration). In both places, the grievances at stake (water in Cochabamba and corn in Mexico) had come to mean community to many of the people participating in the movements. The marketization of water or corn not only put patterns of material consumption at risk, but also threatened understandings of self, neighborhood, region, or nation. To threaten access to water in Cochabamba was to threaten ancestral *usos y costumbres* (roughly translated as "traditions and customs"); to tap into a legacy of cultivation and regional scarcity; to undermine irrigation and water-collection practices, as well as the community organizations that had developed to maintain these practices; and to challenge a pervasive belief that water belonged to the people. In Mexico, tortillas, and corn more generally, are not only a cornerstone of both urban and rural diets, but also a foundation of mythology, a centerpiece of daily ritual and social interaction, and a part of how many conceive of themselves as Mexican. In each of these contexts, to threaten water or corn was to threaten not only a material relationship with a material good, but perceptions of community as well. When we understand both grievances as meaning-laden, we can better understand the movements that emerged to defend them.

Erica S. Simmons

Conclusion

The central objective of this chapter has been to provide an overview of the dominant approaches to the study of social movements. The chapter began with a look at early theorizing on collective action that emphasized externally induced sociostructural strains and grievances as the principal causes of social discontent and mobilization. This approach gave way to alternative explanations that emphasized internal factors, such as networks and resources, as well as broader political and contextual factors that facilitate or inhibit movement emergence. The chapter also examined the recent "cultural turn" in social movement theorizing and its emphasis on meaning and identity as important variables in generating and sustaining collective action. Drawing on this body of literature, the chapter called for renewed analytical attention to the content of social movement claims through a meaning-laden approach to grievances.

The key to future research in this vein is to pay attention to the meanings these grievances take on in the particular times and places in which they emerge. One need only think of the variety of claims that social movements voice to think of other potential objects of inquiry. For example, it seems obvious that electoral irregularities will be understood differently in different contexts. Perhaps an understanding of what elections have come to mean can help us explain why, in some cases, electoral fraud leads to widespread unrest while in others we see little or no social response. Yet social scientists can, and often do, code electoral fraud similarly, and come to general conclusions as a result.[10] Attention to other types of claims may yield similar results. For example, if we understand repression as a meaning-laden claim—the same kind of physical punishment may take on different meanings in different times and places—we may be able to shed light on the variation in the ways in which repression can work both to put out the flames of resistance in some moments and fan those very flames in others. All repression should not be coded similarly as it is likely to work differently depending, at least in part, on the meanings it takes on. By looking at the meanings with which various acts of repression are imbued, we might think systematically about when we expect them to work a certain way, and when we expect the opposite effect.

The implications of the theory developed here is that when we code a movement's claims based on strictly material considerations, we lose the variation in the grievance produced by the meanings it takes on. An understanding of what elections *mean*, for example, will help scholars better explain and predict when their violation is likely to create opposition. When we understand grievances as meaning-laden, we may shed light on patterns in how opportunities emerge, resources are built, and frames become available. Grievances can be a "moving part" of analysis, which can deepen existing understandings of the dynamics of contention.

NOTES

1 See McAdam, McCarthy, and Zald (1996) and Tarrow (1998) for an overview of the social movement literature. See McAdam, Tarrow, and Tilly (2001) for the most recent iteration of dominant frameworks in the field.

2 For further elaboration see Simmons (2016c; 2016b; 2014).

3 Snow et al. (1998) categorize "breakdowns" as a subset of the "strain" theory.

4 An additional line of critique focused assumptions of irrationality and disconnection embedded in strain theories (McAdam 1999). The movements of the 1960s suggested that participants could be both rational actors and highly embedded in dense social networks.

5 Edwards and McCarthy draw heavily on Cress and Snow (1996).

6 See Skocpol (1979) and Goodwin (2001) for exceptions.

7 Thanks to Elisabeth Clemens for helping to bring this to my attention.

8 Thanks are due to Sidney Tarrow for helping to clarify the second half of this observation.

9 Here I am drawing on a widely accepted critique of Clifford Geertz's work on Indonesia (Geertz 1973, 1980; Wedeen 2002). See also Goodwin and Jasper (2004a).

10 Joshua Tucker (2007) both supports my claim that the systematic study of electoral fraud should yield generalizable results and treats all electoral fraud as if it might have the same results. In fact, his argument, grounded in a rational-choice framework, suggests that electoral fraud should take on the same meaning across time and place, as long as citizens have "serious grievances against their government" (Tucker 2007, 537). Almeida (2003) also suggests that he understands fraudulent elections to function similarly across place and time when he states that fraudulent elections can serve as a particularly powerful motivator for threat-induced collective action.

References

Almeida, Paul D. 2003. "Opportunity Organizations and Threat-Induced Contention: Protest Waves in Authoritarian Settings." *American Journal of Sociology* 109, no. 2: 345–400.

Aminzade, Ron, and Doug McAdam. 2001. "Emotions and Contentious Politics." In *Silence and Voice in the Study of Contentious Politics*, edited by Ronald R. Aminzade, Jack Goldstone, Doug McAdam, Elizabeth J. Perry, William H. Sewell Jr., Sidney Tarrow, and Charles Tilly, 14–50. New York: Cambridge University Press.

Babb, Sarah. 1996. "A True American System of Finance: Frame Resonance in the U.S. Labor Movement, 1866 to 1886." *American Sociological Review* 61, no. 6: 1033–52.

Berbrier, Mitch. 1998. "Half the Battle: Cultural Resonance, Framing Processes, and Ethnic Affections in Contemporary White Separatist Rhetoric." *Social Problems* 45, no. 4: 431–50.

Calhoun, Craig. 1994. *Neither Gods nor Emperors: Students and the Struggle for Democracy in China*. Berkeley: University of California Press.

Clemens, Elisabeth Stephanie. 1997. *The People's Lobby: Organizational Innovation and the Rise of Interest Group Politics in the United States, 1890–1925*. Chicago: University of Chicago Press.

Cloward, Richard A., and Frances Fox Piven. 1984. "Disruption and Organization: A Rejoinder." *Theory and Society* 13, no. 4: 587–99.

Cress, Daniel M., and David A. Snow. 1996. "Mobilization at the Margins: Resources, Benefactors, and the Viability of Homeless Social Movement Organizations." *American Sociological Review* 61, no. 6: 1089–1109.

Davies, James C. 1962. "Toward a Theory of Revolution." *American Sociological Review* 27, no. 1: 5–19.

———. 1969. "The J-Curve of Rising and Declining Satisfactions as a Cause of Some Great Revolutions and a Contained Rebellion." In *Violence in America*, edited by Ted Robert Gurr, 690–730. New York: Praeger.

Edwards, Bob, and John D. McCarthy. 2004. "Resources and Social Movement Mobilization." In *The Blackwell Companion to Social Movements*, edited by David A. Snow, Sarah A. Soule, and Hanspeter Kriesi, 116–52. Malden, MA: Blackwell.

Eisinger, Peter. 1973. "The Conditions of Protest Behavior in American Cities." *American Political Science Review* 81:11–28.

Gamson, William A., and David S. Meyer. 1996. "Framing Political Opportunity." In *Comparative Perspectives on Social Movements*, edited by Doug McAdam, John D. McCarthy, and Mayer Zald, 275–90. New York: Cambridge University Press.

Geertz, Clifford. 1973. *The Interpretation of Cultures: Selected Essays*. New York: Basic Books.

———. 1980. *Negara: The Theatre State in Nineteenth-Century Bali*. Princeton, NJ: Princeton University Press.

Gerbaudo, Paolo. 2012. *Tweets and the Streets: Social Media and Contemporary Activism*. London: Pluto Press.

Geschwender, James A. 1968. "Explorations in the Theory of Social Movements and Revolutions." *Social Forces* 47, no. 2: 127–35.

Goodwin, Jeff. 2001. *No Other Way Out: States and Revolutionary Movements, 1945–1991*. New York: Cambridge University Press.

Goodwin, Jeff, and James M. Jasper. 2004a. "Caught in a Winding, Snarling Vine: The Structural Bias of Political Process Theory." In *Rethinking Social Movements: Structure, Meaning, and Emotion*, edited by Jeff Goodwin and James M. Jasper, 3–30. New York: Rowman and Littlefield.

———, eds. 2004b. *Rethinking Social Movements: Structure, Meaning, and Emotion*. New York: Rowman and Littlefield Publishers.

Goodwin, Jeff, James M. Jasper, and Francesca Polletta, eds. 2001. *Passionate Politics: Emotions and Social Movements*. Chicago: University of Chicago Press.

Gould, Deborah B. 2004. "Passionate Political Processes: Bringing Emotions Back into the Study of Social Movements." In *Rethinking Social Movements: Structure, Meaning, and Emotion*, edited by Jeff Goodwin and James M. Jasper, 155–76. New York: Rowman and Littlefield.

———. 2009. *Moving Politics: Emotion and Act Up's Fight against AIDS*. Chicago: University of Chicago Press.

Gurr, Ted Robert. 1970. *Why Men Rebel*. Princeton, NJ: Princeton University Press.

Jasper, James M. 1997. *The Art of Moral Protest: Culture, Biography, and Creativity in Social Movements*. Chicago: University of Chicago Press.

Johnston, Hank, Enrique Laraña, and Joseph R. Gusfield. 1994. "Identities, Grievances, and New Social Movements." In *New Social Movements: From Ideology to Identity*, edited by Enrique Laraña, Hank Johnston, and Joseph R. Gusfield, 3–35. Philadelphia, PA: Temple University Press.

McAdam, Doug. 1982. *Political Process and the Development of Black Insurgency, 1930–1970*. Chicago: University of Chicago Press.

———. 1999. *Political Process and the Development of Black Insurgency, 1930-1970*, 2nd ed. Chicago: University of Chicago Press.

McAdam, Doug, John D. McCarthy, and Mayer N. Zald. 1988. "Social Movements." In *Handbook of Sociology*, edited by Neil J. Smelser, 695-737. Beverly Hills, CA: Sage.

———. 1996. *Comparative Perspectives on Social Movements: Political Opportunities, Mobilizing Structures, and Cultural Framings*. New York: Cambridge University Press.

McAdam, Doug, Sidney G. Tarrow, and Charles Tilly. 2001. *Dynamics of Contention*. New York: Cambridge University Press.

McCarthy, John, and Mayer Zald. 1977. "Resource Mobilization and Social Movements: A Partial Theory." *American Journal of Sociology* 82, no. 6: 1212–41.

Meyer, David S. 2004. "Protest and Political Opportunities." Annual Review of Sociology 30: 125–45.

Mueller, Carol M. 1992. "Building Social Movement Theory." In *Frontiers in Social Movement Theory*, edited by Aldon Morris and Carol M. Mueller, 3–25. New Haven, CT: Yale University Press.

Piven, Frances Fox, and Richard A. Cloward. 1977. *Poor People's Movements: Why they Succeed, How they Fail.* New York: Pantheon Books.

———. 1992. "Normalizing Collective Protest." In *Frontiers in Social Movement Theory*, edited by Aldon Morries and Carol M. Mueller, 301–25. New Haven, CT: Yale University Press.

Polletta, Francesca, and Edwin Amenta. 2001. "Conclusion: Second That Emotion? Lessons from Once-Novel Concepts in Social Movement Research." In *Passionate Politics: Emotions and Social Movements*, edited by Jeff Goodwin, James M. Jasper, and Francesca Polletta, 303–16. Chicago: University of Chicago Press.

Simmons, Erica. 2014. "Grievances Do Matter in Mobilization." *Theory and Society* 43. No. 5: 513–36.

———. 2016a. "Corn, Markets, and Mobilization in Mexico." *Comparative Politics* 48, no. 3: 413–31.

———. 2016b. "Market Reforms and Water Wars." *World Politics* 61, no. 1: 37–73.

———. 2016c. *Meaningful Resistance: Market Reforms and the Roots of Social Protest in Latin America.* New York: Cambridge University Press.

Skocpol, Theda. 1979. *States and Social Revolutions: A Comparative Analysis of France, Russia, and China.* New York: Cambridge University Press.

Smelser, Neil J. 1963. *Theory of Collective Behavior.* New York: Free Press.

Snow, David A., E. Burke Rochford, Steven K. Worden, and Robert D. Benford. 1986. "Frame Alignment Processes, Micromobilization, and Movement Participation." *American Sociological Review* 51, no. 4: 464–81.

Snow, David A., Daniel Cress, Liam Downey, and Andrew Jones. 1998. "Disrupting 'the Quotidian': Reconceptualizing the Relationship between Breakdown and the Emergence of Collective Action." *Mobilization* 3, no. 1: 1–22.

Tarrow, Sidney G. 1998. *Power in Movement: Social Movements and Contentious Politics*, 2nd ed. New York: Cambridge University Press.

Tilly, Charles. 1978. *From Mobilization to Revolution.* Reading, MA: Addison-Wesley.

Tilly, Charles, Louise A. Tilly, and Richard H. Tilly. 1975. *The Rebellious Century, 1830–1930.* Cambridge, MA: Harvard University Press.

Tucker, Joshua A. 2007. "Enough! Electoral Fraud, Collective Action Problems, and Post-Communist Colored Revolutions." *Perspectives on Politics* 5, no. 3: 535–51.

Wedeen, Lisa. 2002. "Conceptualizing Culture: Possibilities for Political Science." *American Political Science Review* 96, no. 4: 713–28.

———. 2008. *Peripheral Visions: Publics, Power, and Performance in Yemen*. Chicago: University of Chicago Press.

Wickham-Crowley, Timothy. P. 1992. *Guerrillas and Revolution in Latin America: A Comparative Study of Insurgents and Regimes since 1956*. Princeton, NJ: Princeton University Press.

Williams, Rhys H. 2007. "The Cultural Contexts of Collective Action: Constraints, Opportunities, and the Symbolic Life of Social Movements." In *The Blackwell Companion to Social Movements*, edited by David A. Snow, Sarah A. Soule, and Hanspeter Kriesi, 91–115. Malden, MA: Blackwell.

Wood, Elisabeth J. 2001. "The Emotional Benefits of Insurgency in El Salvador." In *Passionate Politics: Emotions and Social Movements*, edited by Jeff Goodwin, James M. Jasper, and Francesca Polletta, 267–81. Chicago: University of Chicago Press.

———. 2003. *Insurgent Collective Action and Civil War in El Salvador*. New York: Cambridge University Press.

Erica S. Simmons

Part II:
MECHANISMS AND PROCESSES

Transnational Protest: "Going Global" in the Current Protest Cycle against Economic Globalization

Jeffrey Ayres and Laura Macdonald

In September 2012, a group of several dozen Vermont farmers and citizens gathered outside a Doubletree Hotel in the suburb of South Burlington to greet the attendees of the Vermont Feed Dealers Association conference with protest signs declaring their opposition to genetically modified organisms (GMOs). Holding signs emblazoned with such slogans as "NO GMO," "Sustainable Corporate Dominance," and "Friends Don't Let Friends Plant Monsanto," the protesters lined the access road to the hotel so the attendees—arriving to see a speech by the vice president for national affairs of the Monsanto Corporation—were faced with the show of opposition to genetically engineered crops and foods in the state of Vermont. In comments at a news conference following the protest, representatives of several small family farms that participate in Burlington-area community supported agriculture (CSA)—including Flack Family Farm and Full Moon Farm, as well as the director of Rural Vermont, a nonprofit food advocacy organization that opposes corporate industrial agricultural practices in the state—espoused a vision of an ecologically sustainable and diverse agricultural community, free of corporate control and GMOs. In articulating her stance against Monsanto and global corporate agribusiness, Rachel Nevitt of Full Moon Farm declared, "what is sustainable here folks is our voice of dissent . . . our desire for honest and just, moral and environmental action must be sustained" (Spring 2012).

Meanwhile, a contentious fall evolved into an early winter of discontent for North American activists opposed to the Trans-Pacific Partnership (TPP) negotiations taking place that December in Auckland, New Zealand. The TPP negotiations involved twelve Asia-Pacific states in talks designed to liberalize and promote trade and investment across the region; this included such controversial issues as changes to procurement rules to enhance corporate bidding rights, the creation of an investor-state provision to empower corporations to sue for purportedly lost profits, and the delaying of the introduction of and sale of generic drugs. Spearheaded by the social-activist organization the Council of Canadians, the Washington Fair Trade Coalition, and the US-based Citizens Trade Campaign, over two hundred people representing environmental, Indigenous, family-farm, seniors, and labor groups gathered in British Columbia's Peace Arch Park on the BC-Washington border to protest the New Zealand negotiations and to raise awareness of the launch of a tri-national campaign against the TPP by Canadian, American, and Mexican activists. Activists held a cross-border organizing summit and released what they called the "North American United Statement Opposing NAFTA Expansion through the Trans Pacific Partnership," with the goal of convincing over a thousand North American social-activist organizations to sign on to the statement opposing the TPP. In announcing the start of the tri-national campaign, the Council of Canadians trade campaigner Stuart Trew, an organizer of the cross-border event, predicted that "the people of all three countries will come together . . . at this symbolic moment to call for openness and democracy in trade agreements, and for a completely different vision of globalization that puts the interests of people above profits" (Council of Canadians 2012).

While these stories may seem to involve completely separate issues and events, we believe that they are in fact tied together in a long-running political drama of contentious protest against economic globalization.[1] An initial protest cycle spread largely across the developing world in the 1980s against structural adjustment, fed into anti-globalization protests more globally in the 1990s, and then reemerged with anti-austerity and Occupy protests in the second decade of the twenty-first century. This wave of

Jeffrey Ayres and Laura Macdonald

contentious protests affecting diverse regions of the world—what we characterize herein as the third global protest cycle against economic globalization—illustrates a number of transnational characteristics. In this chapter, we analyze several characteristics of the shifting and dynamic nature of transnational contentious politics and present two short case studies that display some of these characteristics. Our efforts directly respond to themes developed by Arce and Rice in the first chapter of this volume, including their provocative discussion of the connection between protest and democracy (or the lack thereof), as well as their concern with the political consequences of protest, including possible political realignments, and with what they characterize as the economic threats of globalization and inequality against protest activity. Our main goal is to analytically "unpack" protest activity that is often simplistically mischaracterized as "going global," and to provide examples of how people have employed diverse strategies of a transnational character to contest the negative effects of economic globalization.

Theorizing Transnational Contention: "Going Global" Unpacked

This chapter focuses on the transnational dimensions of contemporary social protest. As noted in chapter 1, some authors believe globalization has led to a broad acceptance of liberal-democratic norms and "the end of politics" (the "depoliticization" argument), while others argue that it has resulted in a dramatic increase in social movement activity and protest, with the increased transnationalization of contentious politics (the "re-politicization" thesis). Similar to Rice (2012), we believe that the picture is considerably more complex than either of these two extreme positions suggest.

Within this current global protest cycle, we are attracted to the concept of transnational contentious politics for several reasons. First, we find it analytically more helpful to focus on "contentious politics" as a broader phenomenon than social movements, because it allows us to include protest actions that seem transnational in some respects but lack a more sustained and organized cross-border character. Tarrow has defined contentious politics as "collective activity on the part of claimants or those who claim to represent them relying at least in part on non-institutional forms of interaction with elites, opponents and the state" (1996, 874). In his work with McAdam and Tilly (1996; 2001), Tarrow has emphasized the more long-term evolutionary character of contentious politics. McAdam (1982) has also argued, moreover, in his well-known study of the American civil rights movement—in which he developed the now ubiquitous political process model—that social protest is the result of long-term, historical sociopolitical upheaval and change. The two cases of various forms of collective claims-making with cross-border characteristics we briefly discuss in this chapter—the global food sovereignty movement and protests against North American trade politics—can be seen as part of a wider pattern of decades-long, variegated, and still-developing processes of contentious politics against economic globalization.

Second, as noted above, we are concerned about the common use of the term "transnational social movement," which fails to capture important features of a considerable amount of contemporary protest activity. Over the past two decades, there has been an evolution in research on transnational protest—some of which arguably got caught up in the heady days of global justice protests during the late 1990s, as seen at such meetings as the 1999 Seattle World Trade Organization Ministerial, the 2001 Summit of the Americas meeting in Quebec City, and the G8 meeting in Genoa—that has considered in different ways the role of the state and international institutions in shaping this protest. Some of the earlier research wrestled with the potentially paradigm-shifting character of global protest (Della Porta, Kriesi, and Rucht 1999; Khagram, Riker, and Sikkink 2002; Smith and Johnston 2002; Smith, Chatfield, and Pagnucco 1997). These authors have often suggested that the state was retreating as a site for social protest as power shifted to non-state actors such as nongovernmental organizations, multinational corporations, and international institutions such as the WTO, the World Bank, and IMF (Matthews 1997). Were transnational social movements emerging as the dramatic new corrective to transnational capital, replacing increasingly enfeebled labor unions and political parties that appeared to lose their ability or willingness to serve as countervailing powers against capital (Piven and Cloward 2000)? This perspective moved from the "methodological nationalism" characteristic of early social movement theorization toward a "methodological transnationalism" that failed to capture the complex and contradictory forms of interaction between local, national, and global scales. In some ways, this enthusiastic heralding of the emergence of global social movements mirrored the enthusiastic view of proponents of globalization who saw it as an implacable force that would inevitably erase national differences in a wave of harmonization and convergence. Both advocates and opponents of globalization thus tended to portray political and economic change as unilinear and uniform across the globe.

In the current context, we are struck by the more complex, multilinear, and diverse character of the interaction between protest and economic globalization. We also argue below that the dichotomies between national and transnational should be replaced with a multiscalar understanding of contemporary political changes. We emphasize the cyclical pattern of contentious political behavior against economic globalization that has evolved over the past several decades—as opposed to evidence of a consistent and sustained trajectory of growing cross-border collaboration between activists from multiple countries—in other words, what one would expect from a transnational social movement (Guidry, Kennedy, and Zald 2000; Moghadam 2005; 2013; Smith and Johnston 2002). As Oliver and Meyer (1998) have noted, "social movements come and go," with social unrest frequently coming in waves of widening distribution and diffusion of protest events or actions, organizations, frames, and beliefs across a population. Scholars have written of "contentious decades," such as the 1960s (Gitlin 1993; Isserman and Kazin 2011), and even "rebellious centuries" (Tilly, Tilly, and Tilly 1975). We find it more analytically helpful to see the examples of widespread protest against economic globalization since the global financial crisis of 2007–08 as one protest cycle in a longer-term pattern of contentious politics against economic globalization. We place the short case studies of transnational contentious politics within Tarrow's (2011) conceptualization of a cycle of contention.

The latest wave of protest that has been occurring in many different parts of the world over the past few years—from Occupy Wall Street and Black Lives Matter in the United States, to anti-austerity protests in Europe, to Indigenous mobilization against mining projects in Guatemala—are, we argue, part of a third coherent global protest cycle against economic globalization. This protest cycle has at its core grievances and opposition to the prescriptions and perceived outcomes of economic globalization—trade and financial liberalization, deregulation, privatization, tax cuts, and cuts to social spending (Harvey 2007)—and growing inequality, economic insecurity, unemployment or underemployment, and democratic decline. The targets of protest are thus more diverse and less clearly defined than in earlier cycles of contentious protest. Moreover, compared to the two previous protest cycles against economic globalization, which tended to involve protest actions more geographically concentrated in either the developing South or the developed North, today's cycle of protest is more globally dispersed, and is reflected in a myriad of multiscale processes of contention against economic globalization. Smith's recent study of what she calls the "competition between the neoliberal and democratic globalization projects" (2008, 8), captures part of this ongoing process of contentious politics. More specifically, what we would identify as the second global protest cycle, occurring largely in the post–Cold War era, Smith feels has been defined as a contest between these two visions of "how the world should be organized" (2008, 8).

In fact, we agree with Moghadam's (2013) argument that there have been two previous cycles of collective action and protest, which should encourage us to analytically link earlier phases of structural adjustment and trade liberalization to the most recent period of unrest against austerity, inequality, and corporate power. The structural adjustment policies advocated by the IMF and the World Bank—which devastated wide swaths of people across the developing South and resulted in food riots and widespread unrest in the 1980s and '90s (see Walton and Seddon 1994)—should be recognized as having contributed to a longer-term historical process of contentious political action against economic globalization (Heckscher 2002). This first protest cycle, then, which was aimed largely against structural adjustment, is connected to the second wave of mobilization against trade liberalization and financial speculation that developed in the 1990s. This is evidenced by the protests and campaigns mounted against trade agreements such as the North American Free Trade Agreement, the Maastricht Treaty of the European Union, the proposed Multilateral Agreement on Investment, the creation of the World Trade Organization after the completion of the Uruguay Round of the General Agreement on Tariffs and Trade, and the Free Trade Area of the Americas

Jeffrey Ayres and Laura Macdonald

(FTAA), which was launched in 1994 but, as discussed below, eventually defeated (Smith 2001; Smith and Smythe 1999; Shoch 2000). These protests against "free trade" clearly targeted specific instances of economic globalization, and the multilateral nature of these targets tended to foster transnational alliances among social movements. Most of the movements that emerged in this second phase failed to prevent the signing of the trade agreements they were targeting (except the FTAA), and as a result, they eventually lost steam.

In addition to reflecting on the cyclical character of protest activities, we also present a multiscalar approach to understanding transnational contentious politics drawn from critical geography. Early approaches to analyzing social movements were implicitly based on a form of methodological nationalism in which relevant processes of political mobilization were assumed to occur within discrete, territorially defined nation-states, despite evidence that social movements from an early stage often unfolded across multiple geographical sites (like temperance movements or antislavery movements). Political process models, for example, took for granted that the main targets of social movement organizing were the governmental institutions of a given country. As discussed above, early literature on transnational social movement activity tended to shift from the national to the international level of analysis. More recently, some authors have reasserted the continuing relevance of the national level (Silva 2013). All of these approaches, even if they talk about geographic scale, shifting scale, and jumping scale, tend to take for granted the analytical separation between the "national" and the "international" or "transnational," or between "inside" and "outside." As we see in the examples of protest discussed below, these analytical distinctions are increasingly irrelevant and distracting in the context of the current phase of globalization.

Transnational Contentious Politics against Economic Globalization

The latest protest cycle clearly shares a number of characteristics of what Oliver and Meyer have referred to as "waves within waves and campaigns within movements" (1998, 9). Contentious politics against economic globalization has either transcended national boundaries or played out in a multiscalar form in what Tarrow (2005; 2011) has referred to as processes of transnational contention. He has developed a rubric of three sets of contentious transnational politics, evolving from processes that are more domestic to transitional to international. This tends to maintain the separation between domestic and transnational, rather than analyzing sufficiently the complex relations between different scales (Silva 2013). However, the three types of activity he identifies provide useful insight into the multiple ways in which social forces interact across borders and in which the national and international intersect. The three sets are differentiated by their degree of cross-border permanence and connection to the potential development of genuinely transnational social movements. They are: 1) global framing and internalization/domestication; 2) diffusion and scale shift; and 3) externalization and transnational coalition formation (Tarrow 2005, 32). While these transnational processes interact and often take place simultaneously, we will present here two examples that we feel typify the more common protest mechanisms occurring within the third global protest cycle against economic globalization: global framing and transnational diffusion.

Global Framing and Contentious Claims-Making around Food Sovereignty

The spring of 2012 was a busy time for food activists in the state of Vermont, as the Vermont Right to Know GMOs coalition engaged in protest actions and rallied thousands of Vermonters against GMOs. The Vermont Right to Know GMOs coalition is a cooperative project of three major statewide advocacy groups—Rural Vermont, NOFA-VT (Northeast Organic Farming Association of Vermont), and VPIRG (Vermont Public Interest Research Group). It collaborated on a number of claims-making tactics designed to give Vermonters access to information about GMOs by requiring the labeling of genetically engineered food products sold at retail outlets in the state of Vermont.

The core messages in the Vermont Right to Know GMOs campaign— the right to know what is in one's food, the ability to make informed choices, and the ability to choose whether or not to buy genetically engineered food—echoed concerns expressed on the streets of Rio de Janeiro,

Brazil, that same spring, as peasants, small farmers, Indigenous peoples, migrants, consumer and food activists converged on the United Nations Conference on Sustainable Development. Dubbed "the third Earth Summit" following previous global meetings in Stockholm in 1972 and Rio in 1992, this massive world gathering of tens of thousands of activists mobilized to oppose the "commodification of life" and to challenge the official governmental summit to consider alternatives to the economic global agricultural model. What arguably tied these two mobilization campaigns together was a process of "global framing" through the concept of "food sovereignty," and a vision of a decentralized food system that meets the needs of local communities, supports local farmers, and sustains the working landscape.

Global framing, while considered the most domestic of transnational political processes, involves the manipulation of meanings, ideas, and interpretations at different scales, from the local and the national to the global. Specifically, global framing involves the use of internationally recognized symbols and meanings to shape local or national claims-making—when international symbols frame domestic conflicts (Tarrow 2005, 32)—as local activists consciously connect to and borrow from globally recognized messages in campaigns. Activists engage in framing processes to create simple, easy-to-understand messages or meanings, frequently highlighting the injustice of a particular context or policy, in the hopes of attracting a greater number of participants to their cause. A collective-action frame contains the meanings or messages activists use to "dignify claims, connect them to others, and help to produce a collective identity" (Tarrow 2011, 144). Frames help to "underscore and embellish the seriousness and injustice of a social condition or redefine as unjust and immoral what was previously seen as unfortunate but perhaps tolerable" (Snow and Benford 1992, 137). Global framing, then, connects local and global concerns in a process of dignifying claims as oftentimes marginalized groups find their concerns legitimized by connecting them to much more widely publicized global actions and campaigns.

Global framing around the concept of food sovereignty illustrates how local grievances about food access, safety, production, and distribution in the small state of Vermont have become increasingly intertwined with more widespread concern and global opposition to the political economy effects of market orthodoxy that have especially shaped global agricultural policies over the past two decades. Vermont has a well-recognized history as an independent-minded, countercultural, grassroots-oriented state whose citizens for centuries have emphasized direct democracy, local citizenship, and small-scale frugality (Ayres and Bosia 2011). In more recent years, Vermont's "back-to-nature" political and cultural traditions have created a social infrastructure ideal for nurturing the development of a grassroots rebellion in defense of the place of food, as it has become a state that has been in the vanguard of local actions that Starr and Adams (2003) describe as antiglobalization claims-making. Farmers' markets, urban gardening projects, farm-to-plate restaurants, community bartering, food cooperatives, and local currencies flourish in Vermont—localized actions that reflect a preference for local empowerment over how food is grown, sold, and distributed, as well as a small-scale reaction against perceived threats to Vermont's unique traditions from global economic forces. As Patel (2009) has argued, at its most basic, food sovereignty is a radical egalitarian call for social change, is concerned with a palpable inequality in power, and operates through global framing processes. Vermont food activists appropriate the food sovereignty message as a means of "challenging deep inequalities of power" at the "core of food sovereignty" (Patel 2009, 670).

Accordingly, the conceptualization of food sovereignty advanced nearly two decades ago by the international peasants' movement La Vía Campesina—created in 1993 by farmers from Latin America, North America, Asia, and Europe—underscores this concern with democratic empowerment reflected in food-related claims-making across Vermont: "Food sovereignty is the right of peoples to define their own food and agriculture ... to determine the extent to which they want to be self-reliant.... It promotes the formulation of trade policies and practices that serve the rights of peoples to safe, healthy and ecologically sustainable production" (Rosset 2003).

La Vía Campesina's origins overlap with the heyday of economic globalization in the early 1990s. During this period, many academic and political observers had become enthralled with the "end of ideology" thesis, which suggested that the collapse of the Soviet Union and the undermining of its Communist command-economy model marked the

Jeffrey Ayres and Laura Macdonald

irrefutable triumph of the United States and its capitalist market-orthodoxy model. La Vía Campesina emerged in reaction to the evolving ideological emphasis on the liberalization of trade and investment, deregulation and privatization, tax cuts, and the elimination of social programs embodied in various free trade agreements and institutions of regional or global economic governance, such as NAFTA, the IMF, and World Bank, the EU and the WTO (Desmarais 2007). La Vía Campesina evolved from its founding in 1993 in Belgium through a strong sense of unity between the challenges experienced by farmers in both the developing South and industrialized North. Reitan (2007, 152) argues that through transnational scale shift, La Vía Campesina spread globally, remaining strongly rooted in local places but networking from local to national to global, developing a strong presence amongst small-scale farmers' organizations, Indigenous peoples, and peasants from Brazil to India to France. The symbolic "glue" that connected La Vía Campesina at different scales is the concept of food sovereignty, which by the end of the 1990s had become a master collective-action frame providing groups at different scales and in different locales and national settings with an alternative to economic globalization.

To better understand how the meanings of food sovereignty have been shared through global framing, it is important to appreciate how the idea of "sovereignty" has been juxtaposed against the perceived local and national impacts of economic globalization. The conceptualization of sovereignty developed by La Vía Campesina clearly taps into the widespread concern about the implications of economic globalization for democracy. Moghadam's discussion of democratic deficits is helpful for understanding how the call for food sovereignty has become a global collective-action frame shared at different scales—and clearly appropriated by food activists in Vermont—for expressing and underscoring meanings associated with a sense of both the material injustice associated with economic globalization policies and the narrow political limitations of democracy in this era as a result of four factors:

1) displacement of decision-making from the local or national domain;

2) huge income inequalities and the concentration of wealth among an ever-smaller proportion of the population;

3) the capture of government by the business sector and other moneyed concerns; and

4) the tendency of some democratic transitions to marginalize women and minorities. (2013, 75)

Similar to activists around the world, Vermont food activists are attempting to reclaim the space for democratic action that they perceive has been eroded through the forces of globalization and the increased power of unaccountable, unelected transnational actors like multinational corporations.

The ongoing "Vermonters Feeding Vermonters" local food sovereignty campaign clearly illustrates how food sovereignty has been appropriated to shape contentious claims-making around food across the state, once again drawing upon Vermont's long tradition of embracing localism as a countervailing force against wider national or global political and economic pressures. The statewide social and economic advocacy group Rural Vermont has led the local food sovereignty campaign over the past two years, collaborating with the Vermont Coalition for Food Sovereignty as well as farmers, engaged citizens, grassroots organizations such as the Brattleboro, Vermont–area Post Oil Solutions, to encourage towns across the state to pass resolutions in support of food sovereignty (Russell 2012). During Town Meeting Day in March 2012—Vermont's still-vibrant practice of local citizen-led direct democracy in the classic New England town hall tradition—Rural Vermont successfully organized eight communities to pass local food sovereignty resolutions to support Vermont's community-based food systems. Encouraging towns across the state to embrace local food systems, the resolutions (some tailored to the particular concerns of each town) proclaimed that "these diverse communities all support the vision of a local food system that meets the needs of our community, supports our farmers, and sustains our lands" (Rural Vermont 2012).

While Rural Vermont is not formally a member of La Vía Campesina, it is a member of the National Family Farm Coalition, which is part of La

Jeffrey Ayres and Laura Macdonald

Vía Campesina. It works "through collaborative efforts locally, statewide, and nationally to ensure that policies made will strengthen family farms, sustain rural communities, and promote local food sovereignty" (Rural Vermont 2018).

Global framing is clearly at work here. Processes of transnational attribution (Reitan 2007, 19) are connecting Rural Vermont's efforts around local food sovereignty initiatives in the small state of Vermont with similar themes of local empowerment, family and community farming, and environmental sustainability on display during the mass mobilizations around food sovereignty and the People's Summit at the Rio UN+20 conference (Global Justice Ecology Project 2012). Farmer Peter Harvey, a resident of Calais, one of the Vermont towns that passed a resolution in support of food sovereignty in 2012, stated that

> Food Sovereignty is about taking back our basic rights to be able to choose what we eat in a country and state that increasingly is forcing us to eat industrially manufactured food. Food Sovereignty is about allowing people to eat food that their neighbors grow, produce, and share on a small local scale, without the threat of violence from the giant food industry and state government regulators (Rural Vermont 2012).

As farmers in Vermont identify with food sovereignty claims resonating at UN summits, "global thinking" is occurring—what Tarrow (2005, 68) identifies as the global framing process by which global symbols and meanings enter domestic political struggles. To be sure, global framing around food sovereignty in Vermont has not created formal and sustained collaborative cross-border networks between Vermont farmers and farmers in other countries. Yet, in local food sovereignty campaigns in Vermont we can see how local activists cognitively link to symbols, meanings, and ideas that resonate globally through different scales in diverse local, national, and global food sovereignty campaigns. As such, they are participating in processes of transnational contention that link, at least symbolically and ideationally, activists from remote corners of the world.

The Limits of Transnational Diffusion in North American Trade Politics

Another typical form of transnational protest identified by Tarrow (2005) takes the form of "diffusion," which involves the spread of similar claims and protest tactics across international borders. Transnational diffusion may unfold as relational diffusion, involving the transfer of claims, tactics, and information through networks of trust and preexisting social ties, or through non-relational diffusion, characterized by the spread of information through mass media and electronic communications. Transnational diffusion contrasts, then, with the previous category of "framing," which again occurs solely on domestic territory (in our previous case in Vermont) and involves the manipulation of globally recognized meanings and symbols to shape specifically domestic conflicts. Transnational diffusion can be seen in the decades of resistance to economic globalization in the form of trade agreements among North American partners. Social activists in Canada, the United States, and Mexico have collaborated and interacted dynamically over time and adopted similar claims, forms of analysis, and repertoires of contention in their opposition to these agreements. A historical overview of the evolution of North American contentious politics reveals two key points: 1) there has been some direct trinational cooperation illustrating clearly relational diffusion at different phases among activists in the three countries, although this cooperation has been limited and sporadic, and has never been sufficiently institutionalized to be termed a transnational social movement; and 2) North American contentious politics has been cyclical in character, with clear highs and lows in protest activity. Moreover, this narrative also reveals how state-level strategies and the limited form of regional integration adopted across the continent has constrained the potential for deeper and more sustained forms of transnational collaboration.

The first phase of contentious protest activity in response to international trade agreements in North America was national rather than transnational in character, but was a clear precursor to what we have described as the second cycle of transnational protest activity that focused heavily on opposition to trade agreements. The decision by the Canadian and US governments to negotiate a Canada–US Free Trade Agreement

(CUSFTA), beginning in May 1986, launched an unprecedented level of social movement organizing in Canada in opposition to the agreement. Two main coalitions emerged, one based in Quebec, the Réseau Québecois sur l'Integration Continentale, and the other based in English Canada (first called the Pro-Canada Network and later the Action Canada Network, or ACN). These coalitions brought together a diverse group of actors who had previously had only limited contact with each other—labor movements (traditional opponents of free trade), nationalist organizations (the Council of Canadians), environmentalist groups, churches, farmers' organizations, women's organizations, and a wide range of other actors representing a diverse cross section of Canadian society and cultural elites.

As well, two political parties, the centrist Liberals and the center-left New Democratic Party, opposed the agreement, which did find strong support in the big business community as well as the governing Progressive Conservative Party (Ayres 1998). Because of the unprecedented diversity of the anti-free-trade coalitions, these groups had to develop new forms of thinking about globalization (not a word in common use in this period), and the ways in which trade politics (formerly perceived as a relatively technical and apolitical topic) had broad and menacing implications for such diverse issues as women's rights, social policy, the environment, and cultural identity, as well as more traditional topics such as employment (Macdonald 2005). The Canadian activists thus pioneered new forms of analysis of the disruptive impact of economic globalization and new techniques of protest and dissent.[2] Nevertheless, the victory of the Progressive Conservative Party under Brian Mulroney in the so-called "free-trade election" of 1988 ensured the deal's passage, despite opposition from the other two political parties and a wide range of Canadian civil society.

This protest activity did not, however, "go global" or even binational in this phase because of the low level of concern among the American public about Canada and the asymmetric levels of dependence between Canada and the United States. A 1988 poll showed that 90 percent of Canadians had an opinion on the CUSFTA, while only 39 percent of Americans interviewed were aware of the agreement (Thompson and Randall 1997, 286–7). According to John Foster, a leading figure in Canadian transnational activities, Canadian activists "found it difficult to identify friends" in Washington since their concerns about issues such as cultural sovereignty, control over water and resources, and regional investment "were not an easily understood language inside the Beltway" (2005, 210).

This relative inattention to trade politics among American civil society shifted rapidly and dramatically, however, when the US, Canadian, and Mexican governments decided to negotiate a North American Free Trade Agreement in 1992. Both US and Mexican civil society mobilized rapidly in opposition to the agreement, with substantial transnational diffusion occurring in the form of shared tactics and claims-making against NAFTA. Canadian activists, who predicted that NAFTA would occur, had begun reaching out to Mexican civil-society groups in the late 1980s, and they had participated in a forum in Mexico City in 1990. A few months later, the Red Mexicana de Acción Frente al Libre Comercio (RMALC) coalition was formed. There were contacts and communications between Mexican and Canadian activists that had worked in the Action Canada Network—with RMALC activists directly crediting that group's coalition-building style as a model for their own unfolding work in Mexico. Shortly after the formation of RMALC, more contacts ensued between North American groups as Canadian activists met with their US counterparts in Washington (Foster 2005, 153).

After 1990, trinational linkages flourished among the Canadians, Mexicans, and two US-based coalitions, the Citizens' Trade Campaign (which spearheaded the legislative campaign against NAFTA and the fast track authority), and the Alliance for Responsible Trade, which had a longer-term focus and mobilized at the grassroots level throughout the United States (Macdonald 2005, 30). The important role of Congress in trade decisions and the more permeable nature of the political opportunity structure in the United States created greater openings for civil-society participation than the more centralized form of decision-making in Canada under a majority government, and certainly Mexico's still authoritarian political context. This situation created incentives for transnational alliances, since Canadian and Mexican movements could attempt to block the agreement by cooperating with their US allies in order to influence Congress. Throughout this period, civil-society participants from the three countries developed a shared analysis of the problems created by the free trade deal for the majority of the citizens of the three countries, and they adopted similar tactics accordingly.

This intense period of joint lobbying, advocacy, and protest led to the emergence of a process in the United States and Mexico that the Canadians had pioneered: the linking of trade issues to a wide range of social issues, such as the environment, women's issues, poverty, and social development, as well as the traditional concerns of trade unions and farmers' organizations. This trinational activity also had some impact on the domestic orientation of Canadian and US social movements, as groups from the North, especially trade unions, were challenged by their Mexican counterparts to reexamine their traditional nationalist and at times xenophobic attitudes. Although some important differences remained in the analyses of the three countries' anti-free-trade coalitions, movement participants developed a series of trinational statements and documents that presented critical analysis of the assumptions underlying regionalization, pushed for greater transparency in the negotiation of the deal, and developed alternative policies based on concern for equity, environment, labor rights, and social justice. Even in this phase of transnational cooperation—which illustrated significant relational diffusion between activists and groups increasingly collaborating with each other to protest NAFTA—linkages between actors in the three countries still remained relatively informal. According to Foster, the key links between the diverse civil-society actors represented by the national coalitions "were often working groups representing or reporting to larger coalitions. The working groups met quite frequently and developed intense working relationships with their counterparts in each country, while national coalitions met much less frequently and developed less collaborative and more general positions" (2005, 210). As a result, Tarrow's (2005) concept of "transnational diffusion" of protest activities is a more appropriate category for understanding trinational social movement activity in North America than notions that expect higher levels of coordination and organizational development.

The trinational coalition eventually failed to block the signing of NAFTA, although US president Bill Clinton did include novel trade and environment side accords in order to appease opposition within his own party and in civil society more broadly. This phase of trinational opposition against NAFTA marked the high tide in relations among civil-society actors in the three countries during what we have called the second phase of mobilization and protest against economic globalization. Not surprisingly, this high level of activity and cooperation across borders abated somewhat after the signing of the agreement. In particular, the sparse institutional framework established by NAFTA (in comparison with the EU or even APEC or Mercosur) created a political opportunity structure remarkably impervious to civil-society interventions (Ayres and Macdonald 2009; 2012a). In this context, the North American region was shaped more by "double bilateralism" than by strong trinational linkages (Golob 2012). The advance of the free trade agenda in the form of the FTAA initiative created new opportunities for transnational cooperation and continued diffusion of claims against free trade policies. North American civil-society actors became leading players in the construction of the Hemispheric Social Alliance (Foster 2005), a transnational alliance dedicated to derailing the agreement that would have created a free trade zone including all of the nations of the Americas excluding Cuba. This alliance continued to use tactics developed in the North American context, including demands for the release of negotiating texts and the development of alternative proposals to free trade deals. This time, civil-society actors, combined with New Left governments emerging in South America (particularly Brazil and Argentina), successfully opposed the signing of the FTAA.

At the same time, the previously supportive context for civil-society cooperation after the fights against NAFTA and the FTAA has declined in the current phase of economic globalization in the North American region. After 9/11, North American governments attempted to achieve higher levels of regulatory harmonization and security cooperation in the form of the Security and Prosperity Partnership of North America (SPP). The SPP was, if anything, less transparent and open to civil-society participation than NAFTA, since governments were explicitly attempting to bypass the popular debate and legislative review that had threatened the ratification of NAFTA by working through trinational committees of government officials (see Ayres and Macdonald 2012a). After the SPP initiative disappeared in 2010 with the election of President Obama, Canadian and US officials have pursued the same goals—but without Mexico—in the form of a security perimeter that would embrace Canada and the United States. The logic of double bilateralism has thus come to limit the political opportunity structure for joint tactics across the three countries, and the United States' customary disinterest in Canada has resulted in little transnational cooperation in response to the security perimeter (Ayres and Macdonald 2012a). Initially, in the case of the Trans Pacific Partnership (TPP), all three countries joined in talks, which led to some joint activity and diffusion of protest tactics. However, the election of US president Donald Trump, his use of populist and nationalist anti-trade and anti-Mexico rhetoric, and his January 2017 executive action formally withdrawing the United States from the TPP, has only reaffirmed double bilateralism. During the talks over the renegotiation of NAFTA, which culminated in the United States–Mexico–Canada Agreement (USMCA), civil-society groups in each country attempted to influence the process, but there were no sustained trinational linkages. In truth, the links between civil-society actors have largely faded almost twenty years after the implementation of NAFTA.

Overall, the history of transnational contentious politics against free trade highlights several key aspects of our argument. First, we see in this narrative the rise and fall of protest activity over time, with organizing peaking during the second phase of economic globalization and declining during the current, more diffuse and complex phase of economic globalization. Thus, it highlights the highly conjunctural nature of mobilization, as well as movements' tendencies to wax and wane over time unless faced with highly favorable conditions. Secondly, this contentious political behavior conforms strongly to Tarrow's (2005) concept of transnational diffusion. The protest campaigns and activist groups based in the three countries shared ideas, tactics, and knowledge over time, but the actual coordination of protests was minimal, and institutionalization was nearly nonexistent. Ultimately, the low level of institutionalization of both NAFTA and the trinational coalitions opposed to it arguably contributed to the eventual decline of trinational activism.

Conclusion

This chapter has sketched out the complex and often messy and incomplete character of transnational protest activities in the modern era. Economic globalization has resulted neither in the "politicization" or "depoliticization" of protest activities. Neither has protest inexorably spread to take on purely global characteristics or definitively retrenched to local or national terrains. Instead, as we have described, protest activities have tended to be cyclical in character, with phases of ebb and flow. During the most recent phase of the long cycle of protest against economic globalization, durable, sustained, and coordinated actions across national boundaries have been rare, despite the hopes of earlier authors writing about the transnationalization of protest. Instead, as we have described in our two case studies of advocacy around food sovereignty and against North American free trade, activists have learned to draw upon frames, discourses, and strategies developed elsewhere, and have adopted them in response to local realities. Activists thus constantly engage in "scale-jumping," making strategic use of transnational methods rather than abandoning the local and the national in the pursuit of global dreams. This tendency may in part reflect the paucity of political opportunities available at the transnational level, as we see in the case of advocacy against free trade, but it also points to the tenaciously local and place-based nature of many aspects of the contemporary struggles against economic globalization, as the case of food sovereignty politics makes clear.

Finally, this discussion clearly has relevance for the larger questions raised in this book about the relationships between democracy, protest, and globalization. Economic globalization is commonly seen as raising thorny issues for democracy because it involves the transfer of authority away from at least potentially accountable and democratic actors, such as states, to transnational bodies that are unelected, nontransparent, and that lack mechanisms for democratic participation. While optimistic accounts might suggest that the transnationalization of protest is a viable response to the transfer of political authority to these institutions of global governance in this era, our discussion highlights some of the problems with this approach. The inherently cyclical, transitory, and geographically uneven character of transnational protest described in this chapter means that the potential for these protests to make a strong contribution to global democratization is quite limited. In fact, the current global backlash against economic globalization, illustrated in the 2016 British vote to leave the European Union, the election of US president Donald Trump, and the rise of antiimmigrant and xenophobic attitudes across the United States and Europe seems to portend more broadly a spreading antidemocratic trend. While democratic struggles are inevitably multiscalar and can benefit from transnational processes of framing and diffusion, much of the work of democratic struggle remains stubbornly local and/or national in character.

Notes

1   In the interest of consistency with this volume, we use "economic globalization" throughout this chapter to refer to the economic trends, policies, and institutions we have traditionally referred to as "neoliberal."

2   Note that while Canadians and Americans were launching a free trade agreement, Mexicans were engaged in diverse and widespread forms of domestic social protest against the harsh impacts of structural adjustment policies that had been adopted by the Mexican government as part of its agreement with the International Monetary Fund following the country's 1982 debt crisis.

References

Ayres, Jeffrey. 1998. Defying Conventional Wisdom: Political Movements and Popular Contention against North American Free Trade. Toronto: University of Toronto Press.

Ayres, Jeffrey, and Michael Bosia. 2011. "Beyond Global Summitry: Food Sovereignty as Localized Resistance to Globalization." *Globalizations* 8, no 1: 47–63.

Ayres, Jeffrey, and Laura Macdonald, eds. 2009. *Contentious Politics in North America.* New York: Palgrave Macmillan.

———. 2012a. "A Community of Fate? Nonpolarity and North American Security Interdependence." *Canadian Foreign Policy* 18, no. 1: 92–105.

———, eds. 2012b. *North America in Question: Regional Integration in an Era of Economic Turbulence.* Toronto: University of Toronto Press.

Council of Canadians. 2012. "A Cross Border Action: The People's Round on the Trans-Pacific Partnership (TPP)." https://vancouvercouncilofcanadians.ca/2012/12/a-cross-border-action-the-peoples-round-on-the-trans-pacific-partnership-tpp/ (accessed 11 November 2018).

Della Porta, Donatelle, Hanspeter Kriesi, and Dieter Rucht, eds. 1999. *Social Movements in a Globalising World.* New York: Palgrave Macmillan.

Desmarais, Annette. 2007. La Vía Campesina: Globalization and the Power of Peasants. London: Pluto Press.

Foster, John W. 2005. "The Trinational Alliance against NAFTA: Sinews of Solidarity." In *Coalitions Across Borders: Transnational Protest and the Neoliberal Order*, edited by Joe Bandy and Jackie Smith, 209–30. Lanham, MD: Rowman and Littlefield.

Gitlin, Todd. 1993. *The Sixties: Years of Hope, Days of Rage*. New York: Bantam.

Global Justice Ecology Project. 2012. "Reclaiming our Future: Rio+20 and Beyond: La Vía Campesina Call to Action." https://viacampesina.org/en/reclaiming-our-future-rio-20-and-beyond/ (accessed 11 November 2018).

Golob, Stephanie R. 2012. "Plus Ça Change: Double Bilateralism and the Demise of Trilateralism." In *North America in Question: Regional Integration in an Era of Economic Turbulence*, edited by Jeffrey Ayres and Laura Macdonald, 249–76. Toronto: University of Toronto Press.

Guidry, John A., Michael D. Kennedy, and Mayer N. Zald, eds. 2000. *Globalizations and Social Movements: Culture, Power, and the Transnational Public Sphere*. Ann Arbor: University of Michigan Press.

Harvey, David. 2007. *A Brief History of Neoliberalism*. New York: Oxford University Press.

Heckscher, Zahara. 2002. "Long Before Seattle: Historical Resistance to Economic Globalization." In *Global Backlash: Citizen Initiatives for a Just World*, edited by Robin Broad, 86–91. Lanham, MD: Rowman and Littlefield.

Isserman, Maurice, and Michael Kazin. 2011. *American Divided: the Civil War of the 1960s*. New York: Oxford University Press.

Khagram, Sanjeev, James Riker, and Kathryn Sikkink, eds. 2002. *Restructuring World Politics:*

Transnational Social Movements, Networks and Norms. Minneapolis and London: University of Minnesota Press.

Macdonald, Laura. 2005. "Gendering Transnational Social Movement Analysis: Women's Groups Contest Free Trade in the America." In *Coalitions across Borders: Transnational Protest and the Neoliberal Order*, edited by Joe Bandy and Jackie Smith, 21–42. Lanham, MD: Rowman and Littlefield.

Matthews, Jessica. 1997. "Power Shift." *Foreign Affairs* 76, no. 1: 50–66.

McAdam, Doug. 1982. Political Process and the Development of Black Insurgency, 1930–1970. Chicago: University of Chicago Press.

McAdam, Doug, Sidney Tarrow, and Charles Tilly. 1996. "To Map Contentious Politics." *Mobilization* 1, no. 1: 17–34.

———. 2001. *Dynamics of Contention*. Cambridge: Cambridge University Press.

Moghadam, Valentine M. 2005. *Globalizing Women: Transnational Feminist Networks*. Baltimore, MD, and London: Johns Hopkins University Press.

———. 2013. *Globalization and Social Movements: Islamism, Feminism and the Global Justice Movement*, 2nd ed. Lanham, MD: Rowman and Littlefield.

Oliver, Pamela, and Daniel Myers. 1998. "Diffusion Models of Cycles of Protest as a Theory of Social Movements." Paper presented at the 1998 Congress of the International Sociological Association, Montreal, QC.

Piven, Frances Fox, and Richard Cloward. 2000. "Power Repertoires and Globalization." *Politics and Society* 28: 413–30.

Reitan, Ruth. 2007. *Global Activism*. New York: Routledge.

Rice, Roberta. 2012. *The New Politics of Protest: Indigenous Mobilization in Latin America's Neoliberal Era*. Tucson: University of Arizona Press.

Riggirozzi, Pía, and Diana Tussie, eds. 2012. *The Rise of Post-Hegemonic Regionalism: The Case of Latin America*. New York: Springer.

Rossett, Peter. 2003. "Food Sovereignty: Global Rallying Cry of Farmer Movements." *Backgrounder* 9, no. 4. https://foodfirst.org/wp-content/uploads/2013/12/BK9_4-Fall-2003-Vol-9-4-Food-Sovereignty.pdf (accessed 11 November 2018).

Rural Vermont. 2012. "Eight communities demonstrate broad support for Vermonters feeding Vermonters". Press release, 8 March. https://vtdigger.org/2012/03/08/eight-communities-demonstrate-broad-support-for-vermonters-feeding-vermonters/ (accessed 11 November 2018).

Russell, Carl. 2012. "Food Sovereignty, Food as Community." *Vermont's Local Banquet* 20. http://www.localbanquet.com/issues/years/2012/spring12/sovereignty_sp12.html (accessed 11 November 2018).

Shoch, James. 2000. "Contesting Globalization: Organized Labor, NAFTA, and the 1997 and 1998 Fast Track Fights." *Politics and Society* 28, no. 1: 119–50.

Silva, Eduardo, ed. 2013. *Transnational Activism and Domestic Movements in Latin America: Bridging the Divide*. New York: Routledge.

Smith, Jackie. 2001. "Globalizing Resistance: the Battle of Seattle and the Future of Social Movements." *Mobilization* 6, no. 1: 1–20.

———. 2008. *Social Movements for Global Democracy*. Baltimore, MD: Johns Hopkins University Press.

Smith, Jackie, Charles Chatfield, and Ron Pagnucco, eds. 1997. *Transnational Social Movements and Global Politics: Solidarity beyond the State*. Syracuse, NY: Syracuse University Press.

Smith, Jackie, and Hank Johnston, eds. 2002. *Globalization and Resistance: Transnational Dimensions of Social Movements*. Lanham, MD: Rowman and Littlefield.

Smith, Peter, and Elizabeth Smythe. 1999. "Globalization, Citizenship and Technology: The MAI meets the Internet." *Canadian Foreign Policy* 7, no. 2: 83–105.

Snow, David, and Robert Benford. 1992. "Master Frames and Cycles of Protest." In *Frontiers of Social Movement Theory*, edited by Morris D. Aldon and Carol M. Mueller, 133–55. New Haven, CT: Yale University Press.

Spring, Katie. 2012. "Rural Vermont GMO Protest Recap." 20 September. http://www.ruralvermont.org/agriculture-in-the-news/rural-vermont-gmo-protest-recap-by-katie-spring/ (accessed 11 November 2018).

Starr, Amory, and Jason Adams. 2003. "Anti-Globalization: the Global Fight for Local Autonomy." *New Political Science* 25, no. 1: 19–42.

Tarrow, Sidney. 2005. *New Transnational Activism*. New York: Cambridge University Press.

———. 2011. *Power in Movement: Social Movements, Collective Action, and Politics*, 3rd ed. New York: Cambridge University Press.

Thompson, John Herd, and Stephen J. Randall, eds. 1997. *Canada and the United States: Ambivalent Allies*. Montreal and Toronto: McGill-Queen's University Press.

Tilly, Charles, Louise Tilly, and Richard Tilly. 1975. *The Rebellious Century: 1830–1975*. Cambridge, MA: Harvard University Press.

Walton, John, and David Seddon. 1994. *Free Markets and Food Riots: the Politics of Global Adjustment*. Cambridge, UK: Blackwell.

4

Collective Action in the Information Age: How Social Media Shapes the Character and Success of Protests

Jennifer M. Larson

As protests unfolded worldwide in the early twenty-first century, main-stream media were abuzz with praise for the apparently crucial role of on-line social media. Protests in Iran were dubbed the "Twitter Revolution" (Hounshell 2011). Protests in Egypt were dubbed the "Facebook Revolution" (Talbot 2011). The Occupy Wall Street movement was dubbed the "Tumblr Revolution" (Graham-Felsen 2011). Headlines declared: "Tunisians Abroad: Facebook, Regular Citizens Key to Revolution" (Yan 2011); "Social Media Sparked, Accelerated Egypt's Revolutionary Fire" (Gustin 2011); "Turkey's Social Media and Smartphones Key to 'Occupy Gezi' Protests" (Dorsey 2013); "Social Media Spreads and Splinters Brazil Protests" (Stauffer 2013).

These optimistic accounts raise an important question for the study of social movements: Does access to social media cause protests to be different than they would have been without such access? And ultimately: Are they more likely to be successful?

Determining if and how modern protests would have differed in a world without social media is difficult. However, careful study of the way social media are being used by twenty-first-century protesters, combined with theory to help generalize from empirical examples, illuminate plausible effects.

Social media platforms like Twitter and Facebook are now standard protest tools, used to plan and spread the word about protests before they occur, and to report on them from the ground (Tufekci and Freelon 2013). In locations across the globe, activity on social media spikes in the area near a protest immediately prior to and during the protest (Steinert-Threlkeld et al. 2015). However, despite the widespread use of social media by protesters, and traditional media's excitement about these platforms, their precise effect on the ultimate success of protests remains an open question.

This chapter examines the use of social media in modern protests. It begins by describing these tools and reviewing their potential to change the character of protests. As I argue, the presence of social media *can* increase the size, frequency, and international visibility of protests. I then consider the set of conditions under which the presence of social media would affect the outcomes of protests, focusing on when and how they may do so. While it is too early to say whether the presence of social media has had a definitive causal effect on protest outcomes, this chapter suggests that the effect of social media should vary with context and circumstance. Understanding the potential, contingent mechanisms by which social media could affect outcomes is important not only for a theory of social movements, but also for designing empirical studies that can meaningfully detect the connection between social media and protest success.

The Nature of Social Media

The term "social media" refers to a large set of platforms that allow communication and information sharing within virtual communities. Users access these online platforms via any device with Internet capability, including mobile smartphones, and then use them to share and retrieve content, including messages, photos, and videos. These media platforms are "social" in that users can identify a set of other users as their contacts and then share content with some or all of them. Twitter, Facebook, Instagram, and Tumblr are some of the most popular platforms, though updates to these and the emergence of new platforms are common. Each offers a slightly different set of features to accomplish the sharing of various forms of content between contacts.

Three common features are relevant to understanding the role social media plays in protests. First, conditional on having access, the cost of sharing content is very low. Composing a message on Twitter (a "tweet") takes seconds. Uploading video becomes easier with every update. Snapping photos with a phone is quick and sharing them is one or two clicks away. Even easier than *creating* content is *forwarding* content that others have already created. With the click of a button, content received from a social contact can be shared with all other social contacts. One implication of this is that the bar for "newsworthiness" can be substantially lower for users of social media than for users of more traditional forms of communication or dissemination. Lots of information about any event can be easily passed along, and in real time.

Second, content can reach many people simultaneously. If users want to they can broadcast their content to their whole set of social ties. Facebook users can post content that reaches all of their contacts; Twitter users can post tweets that all of their followers can read. Since the effort required to do so is low, lots of content can reach a large number of people simultaneously.

Third, because content is shared within virtual communities, the sender and receiver often have a real interpersonal connection of some sort. Alerts about something going on or invitations to some activity are not coming from just anybody; they are often coming from personally known sources, and recipients often know many of the other recipients too. Users passing content along to their social ties are effectively vetting and personally endorsing it.

Exactly which social media applications are selected and how they are used in protests can vary (see Tufekci and Freelon 2013 for an overview), but activity throughout Turkey's 2013 protests provides a textbook example. As the BBC reported, "[participants] have used Twitter to share information about how to survive the protests; Facebook sites provide news updates on the situation in occupied Gezi Park; while photographs of the protests have been shared on Flickr and Tumblr and video on sites such as YouTube" (Hutchinson 2013).

Social media can be used at any stage of a protest. Long prior to a planned protest, they can be used to spread information about grievances or claims. This information may become the unifying motivation and goal, or "cause," of the protest. Immediately prior to a planned protest, social media can help coordinate logistics—when and where the protest will be held. During a protest, news about conditions and events can be broadcast live from the scene. As a protest is breaking up, social media can spread word of the next steps, document its success, and lament its setbacks.

Under the right conditions, these three common features—low costs, large audiences, and personal sources—could make protests larger and more frequent than they would have been without social media. The next sections of this chapter consider the conditions under which social media would and would not have this consequence in theory.

The Case for Optimism: How Social Media Can Positively Impact the Character of Protests

To identify the effect of social media on protest outcomes, we need to understand their impact on the character of protests. Social media can affect protests by changing the behavior of individuals who may turn out to the protest—"prospective participants"—as well as by changing the behavior of others who were never going to turn out (perhaps because they live too far away) but whose support could matter for the protest. Both can impact how large, frequent, or visible protests will be in theory, given certain assumptions about how people decide whether to participate in a protest or not.

How Social Media Can Increase Turnout at Protests

Suppose there is a group of people who are dissatisfied with current conditions—perhaps their country's unequal income distribution or an unpopular political leader. These people have grievances; they prefer some change to the status quo. Holding a protest is one option to try to change the status quo. We would call such a protest "successful" if it results in a change to the status quo in the direction of the preferences of those with grievances (perhaps a policy concession or a change in leadership).

The process by which a group of people with grievances coalesces into an organized protest is complicated, and the motivation underlying any person's decision to join in can vary widely. Suppose three things are true about this process: 1) the effort that any person would need to expend to join a protest decreases with the transparency of the logistical details; the easier it is to learn about a protest, and the more carefully the event is planned, the less effort it takes to join in; 2) the effort that any person would need to expend to join a protest decreases with the number of others planning to attend; if many show up, costs are expected to be more widely distributed, individuals may face fewer consequences, and there may be strong peer pressure to attend; and 3) a person's willingness to expend a certain amount of effort increases with the emotional intensity of his or her desire for change; that is, the more a person believes in the cause and finds change necessary or perhaps even a duty, the more willing he or she is to participate. If a person's likelihood of doing something is decreasing in the effort required, then these three assumptions imply that social media may make protests larger and more frequent via three mechanisms.

Mechanism 1: Social Media Allow Users to Spread News of Grievances in Rapid, Convincing, Emotionally Provocative Ways

Users of social media are not bound by professional standards of even-handedness and objectivity. Quite the contrary, these media are understood to disseminate personal viewpoints. Occupy Wall Street offers a case in point of this use of social media. The Occupy movement coalesced around the cause of equality (see chapter 8). Responding to heightened income inequality in the United States, members of the movement referred to themselves as "the 99 percent" (those in the ninety-ninth percentile of the income distribution), in contrast to "the 1 percent" (those in the right tail of the income distribution). In the early days of the movement, some users of the photo-sharing social media platform Tumblr created a blog devoted to the cause. The page was titled "We Are the 99 Percent," and on it users posted photos of themselves holding signs describing their plight (Rosen 2011). Not only were these stories personal, they included real faces with which to relate. Posts to the blog flooded in, and by the time of the

Zuccotti Park protests, nearly a hundred new posts a day were being added (Graham-Felsen 2011).

This kind of shared personal experience of hardship can influence a protest movement in two ways. First, if people are compelled by these personal accounts, more people may come to share the grievance, and people may feel more strongly aggrieved. Given the assumptions described above, this would increase the number of people willing to join a protest organized around this cause. Second, the knowledge that such convincing personal accounts are shared widely on the social media platform may generate the belief that others are also being convinced to turn out. If a belief that more people will join in the protest makes participation easier, then social media may increase participation in protests in this way as well.

Convincing accounts of hardships (perhaps even substantiated with photos and video) can be broadcast easily in real time from the ground on social media, which could boost the number of participants at moments crucial to a protest movement.[1] This reasoning led many to speculate that the Arab Spring protests were products of social media:

> No revolution in history has been recorded so comprehensively, and in such minute detail. . . . Future social historians will gorge themselves on evidence like this, the micro-detail of social responses to unrest: but for now, its importance lies in the way it enables participants to judge what kind of history is being made in real time. Banned from reporting in Iran, the mainstream media quickly began to realize the value of this user-generated content, and to run it. The momentum of the protests fed off this cycle of guerrilla news-gathering, media amplification, censorship and renewed protest. (Mason 2012, 35)

Because online social media can transmit personalized messages, even from the protest itself, these tools have the potential to motivate others to support the cause and attend the protest. A person hearing these accounts over social media knows that her social contacts, whose judgment or esteem she may value, endorse the cause. Given the three assumptions described above, the result can be an increase in protest participation. Not only can this boost the size of a protest already planned, it also can make future protests more likely to occur.

Mechanism 2: Social Media Help Users Coordinate the Protest

That social media can be used to plan events has been well documented. Castells explains the various ways that Facebook was used to organize Occupy events: "[Facebook groups] served as directories to help members stay in touch with each other, send private messages, or post on each other's walls. The groups were also used for organizing: to make announcements, post calendar items and send messages to all members of the group" (2012, 175). The Arab Spring uprisings also began with organizational details broadcast over social media (Castells 2012, 103). Examples abound of tweets communicating times and places of events. Since messages can rapidly reach a wide audience at a low cost, social media serves as a useful, flexible tool for making protest information known, thereby reducing the effort required of potential protesters.

Users are organized into virtual communities within social media applications. This not only means that a person can share news with many others; it also means that others can share that news as well. News spreads along a virtual social network, which has two implications. First, a very large number of people can be reached. Second, those who are reached know they are part of a community in which everyone was reached. When logistical details of a protest are shared in this way, lots of people know that many others have heard the details as well. In fact, many of those who heard are personal contacts, which creates pockets of common knowledge: users can infer that their social contacts know, and that their contacts know that their contacts know. Common knowledge among social cliques can substantially reduce the expected costs of protesting (Chwe 2000). Given the three assumptions described above, both implications may cause turnout in protests to be higher than it would have been without the presence of social media, and may increase the frequency of protests as well.

Mechanism 3: Social Media Can Broadcast Specific Pleas to Turn Out to a Protest

While there are examples of social media indirectly encouraging turnout by drawing more people in to the protesters' cause, there are also examples of social media being used to explicitly encourage turnout. Some users post general or targeted invitations to a protest. When protests in Egypt were brewing, Asmaa Mafhouz created videos and posted them. In her "vlog" (close-up video message), she announced that she and others were going to Tahrir Square. In a particularly charged plea, she declared: "People, have some shame! I, a girl, posted that I will go down to Tahrir Square, to stand alone, and I'll hold a banner. All that came were three guys. . . . I'm making this video to give you a simple message: we're going to Tahrir on 25 January" (quoted in Mason 2012, 11). Emotional appeals from trusted sources that can reach many people can both increase emotional attachment to the cause and convince potential participants that turnout will be high, which may in turn boost participation in protests. Moreover, given that these invitations reach social cliques, pockets of common knowledge can boost their efficacy in the way described in mechanism 2.

How Social Media May Increase Protest Visibility

The previous section established that, given the three assumptions about how a person decides whether to join a protest, the presence of social media can increase both the size and frequency of protests. Social media can also shape the character of protests by influencing the behavior of people beyond those who may show up at the protest.

The wide reach of content can help news of hardships reach audiences beyond the potential participants of a protest. One consequence is that news of protests can reach international audiences. For example, Wall and Zahed (2011) traced the trajectory of YouTube videos produced in Egypt before the 2011 protests in Tahrir Square as they were shared through social media first in Egypt, and then in Saudi Arabia. They eventually made their way to the United States and even into major US news outlets like the *New York Times* and the *Washington Post*. Accounts shared on social media are easy for major international news outlets to find and report on: the content can be made publicly available, and is centralized, searchable, and often organized (for instance by the inclusion of a hashtag). Protesters, aware of this possibility, will often tweet in English rather than the local language (Tucker et al. 2014). News reaching the outside world through social media is qualitatively different from other forms of information that reaches the outside since it can be from participants themselves and is disseminated in real time. Eltantawy and Wiest argue that this was the case in Egypt: "Once again, social media introduced a powerful mobilization resource that protesters utilized to address the world while events were unfolding. This is a significant development in social mobilization, as it was the protesters themselves who disseminated information, pictures, and videos— not just reporters and group leaders" (2011, 1215). International attention may fuel the motivation of those at the protest,[2] but may also generate extra pressure on the regime or target of the protest. The presence of social media may allow groups to forge transnational ties or compensate for the lack of existing ones (see chapter 3).

The Case for Pessimism: How Social Media Can Depress Protest Attendance

It is important to note that the boost in size and frequency discussed above is conditional on the assumptions underlying the decision to participate. If the three assumptions stipulated above do *not* reflect the way that people are motivated to protest, then the presence of social media may actually *reduce* turnout from the level it would have been had social media not been used.

While the three assumptions are plausible in general, there are also scenarios in which they are unlikely to hold. Take assumption 2, that knowledge that more people will turn out makes a person more likely to turn out to protest. This assumption is plausible in contexts in which people expect blowback to be less severe in large crowds, or expect the protest to be met with mild opposition. In other contexts, though, especially those in which the grievances are felt with less conviction, or the opposition to protesters is expected to be particularly brutal, a competing incentive to shirk may be present. In such a case, the larger the number of people willing to put themselves on the line for the cause, the *less* a person would feel compelled to join (perhaps because his marginal impact on the success of the protest is smaller, or his presence or absence is less likely to be noticed). If this were the case, the more social media helps to create the impression that many will turn out, the *less* likely a user of social media would be to turn out. Relatedly, in these contexts, assumption 1 may not hold either: if logistical details are presented so clearly that prospective protesters know that all other prospective protesters know that attending would be easy, they may guess that many will show up, obviating the need for them to show up themselves. In these contexts, the ease with which information about the cause and about logistics flows through social media compounds the incentive to shirk. Social media would then function to depress turnout.

The above describes a problem of collective action—people are not so dedicated to the protest cause that they personally desire to participate, and they are willing to free ride on the participation of others. A separate problem could depress participation as well. Even if a person is not inclined to free ride, she may be dissuaded from participating if the messages reaching her on social media make participation appear too costly. Vivid, personal accounts may credibly reveal that participation would be dangerous, unpleasant, or difficult. Consider again the YouTube video posted by Asmaa Hafhouz in Egypt, which declared: "I, a girl, posted that I will go down to Tahrir Square, to stand alone, and I'll hold a banner. All that came were three guys" (quoted in Mason 2012, 11). This is an invitation to another attempted protest. While some may find this motivating, others may learn from it that the next protest is likely to be perilous. Similarly, a blog on the *Guardian* website posted a series of distressing tweets sent by video journalist Mohamed Abdelfattah in Cairo (with lags in between): "Tear gas," "I'm suffocating," "We r trapped inside a building," "Armored vehicles outside," "Help we r suffocating," "I will be arrested," "Help !!!," "Arrested" (quoted in Siddique, Owen, and Gabbatt 2011). On the one hand, this post served as a real-time news source and could help rally others to join in. On the other hand, this line of tweets may have made joining in sound less appealing and more dangerous. Those who conclude that attending the protest would actually be harder than they thought may be dissuaded from participating.

While these forces acting to depress turnout are present in theory, whether and when the collective-action problem or the revelation-of-cost problem render the presence of social media a net negative for protests is an important open question.

An additional possibility is that the opportunity to share content on social media may force out real participation. The idea that some may retweet a tweet, comment on a blog, or join a Facebook page and then do nothing further has been dubbed "slacktivism." Morozov sums up the problem as follows: "But harmless activism wasn't very productive either: what do 100 million people invited to join the Facebook group '100 Million Facebook members for Democracy in Iran' expect to get out of their membership? Is it just a gigantic exercise in collective transcontinental wishful thinking? Do they really expect that their 'slacktivism'—a catchy new word that describes such feel-good but useless Internet activism— would have some impact?" (2009, 13).

On the one hand, "slacktivists" who share content online but are unwilling to take to the streets can help so long as their sharing encourages others to act. On the other hand, if these slacktivists *would* have participated in the physical protest but now, thanks to social media, they pass information along *instead*, then even granting the mechanisms above, the net impact on protest size and, ultimately, success, is ambiguous. The issue is that, for some, social media may serve as a substitute for real action. If they would have protested but instead opt out when presented with the easier option of sharing on social media, then the presence of social media and its accommodation of "slacktivists" has the potential to depress protest attendance. Recent research uses survey evidence to show that, among a sample of Italians who discussed the 2013 election on Twitter, participating in low-cost activities like tweeting about the election was positively associated with participating in higher-cost activities like contacting politicians and attending events (Vaccari et al. 2015). This supports the conclusion that on net, even if some tweet instead of participating in more high-cost activities, more tweet *in addition* to participating in these activities. To rule out the problem of slacktivism wholesale, future research will need to confirm that the number who tweet *instead of* participating in higher-cost activities is low in general.

Domestic Political Institutions and Social Media

The cases for optimism and pessimism outlined above explore how social media impact the character of protests. In certain circumstances, access to social media would increase the size, frequency, and visibility of protests; in others, access would decrease the size and frequency. These changes in the character of protests should affect groups' ability to change the status quo, since larger, more frequent, or more visible protests should be more likely to achieve their ends. To understand how social media impact protest success, an additional factor must be accounted for.

Protesters do not organize in a vacuum. Rather, they coordinate in a strategic environment containing those who prefer the status quo. In the recent global waves of protest, the actors most interested in thwarting change have been existing governments.

Social media are relatively new technologies, and the relationship between governments and social media is constantly evolving. Governments behave as though social media can help protesters, and some have taken steps to block its use in one way or another. When dissidents in Iran were using Twitter to voice protest, the government and the dissidents were regularly changing tactics in response to each other's actions. Dissidents would use social media, especially Twitter, while governments would block access; dissidents would find new means of access, the government would target those, and so on. As the *Washington Times* reported in the midst of this back-and-forth, "Hackers in particular were active in helping keep channels open as the regime blocked them, and they spread the word about functioning proxy portals. . . . Eventually the regime started taking down these sources, and the e-dissidents shifted to email. The only way to completely block the flow of Internet information would have been to take the entire country offline, a move the regime apparently has resisted thus far" (Washington Times 2009). Clever, technology-savvy protesters helped protect access to social media, and the government actively tried to thwart their efforts.

Egypt's government took the more drastic approach that the Iranian government was avoiding: they shut down the Internet. According to Castells, Egypt's Internet was uniquely suited for full-scale shutdown:

Jennifer M. Larson

Egypt's great disconnection was an entirely different situation from the limited Internet manipulation that took place in Tunisia, where only specific routes were blocked, or Iran, where the Internet stayed up in a rate-limited form designed to make Internet connectivity extremely slow. Disconnecting the Internet in Egypt was relatively easy, compared with what would be necessary in democratic countries. In Egypt there were only four major ISPs, each of which had relatively few routers connecting them to the outside world. (2012, 85)

Blocking access to certain websites, slowing access to certain websites, and shutting the Internet down altogether are some strategies that have been employed by governments facing serious protests. These strategies may be easier in less democratic regimes, in which access is more centralized.

Of course, whether blocking access actually thwarts protests is also an open question. One clever study made use of the Internet shutdown during the Tahrir Square protests in Egypt to measure the impact of social media access for the Egyptian protests. Because people lost access to social media during the shutdown, the study was able to compare the same protest with and without access to social media. Hassanpour found that protest activity not only did not decrease during the shutdown, it actually increased: "[the Internet shutdown] implicated many apolitical citizens unaware of or uninterested in the unrest; it forced more face-to-face communication, i.e., more physical presence in streets; and finally it effectively decentralized the rebellion on the 28th through new hybrid communication tactics, producing a quagmire much harder to control and repress than one massive gathering in Tahrir" (2014, 10). Of course, this at best tells us what happens when social media are present and then restricted, not what would have happened had social media never been present. However, this does suggest that shutting down the Internet or blocking access to specific social media websites is not necessarily the government's optimal strategy.

Making online social media difficult or illegal to use is not the only strategy available to a government. It can also allow full access, but use social media to its own ends. For another recent example in Turkey, the government has used social media to identify dissidents and gather evidence serving as grounds for their arrest: "Turkish police on Wednesday arrested 25 people they accused of using Twitter and social media to stoke anti-government sentiment during protests that have engulfed the country. . . . The authorities appear to have taken their cue from Turkey's prime minister, Recep Tayyip Erdogan, who denounced Twitter as a 'menace to society,' adding: 'The best examples of lies can be found there' " (Harding and Letsch 2013). There are reports that Israel uses social media like Facebook to identify potential pro-Palestinian protesters in order to blacklist them (Protalinski 2011). Moreover, combing social media for information about who will be gathering where can give anti-protest forces an advantage in breaking up a protest once it starts to form.

In addition to using the content of social media to its advantage, governments also have the option of generating social media content of their own. Posting from ostensibly private accounts to muddle the information environment, confuse logistical details, and argue against the cause are all options that social media make possible.

The set of strategies that governments will use in response to protests organized over social media is still in flux. Using information to target protesters, curtailing access, and adding information to manipulate a protest movement are just a few options.

These tactics suggest an interesting relationship between domestic regime type and social media function. Conditional on having access to social media, these platforms in principle narrow the gap between democratic and autocratic states—users in either can broadcast information widely, and associate online. Of course, access may not be equal; autocratic states may be more willing to intervene to prevent access or to co-opt social media use for their own ends. Generating fake news and spreading propaganda may be more feasible for or attractive to nondemocratic leaders. Governments' responses to social media use is evolving; if these platforms give nondemocratic governments greater access to the plans of prospective protesters, or richer tools to thwart or mislead protest efforts, the ultimate impact could differ by domestic institutional environment. Although apparently a useful tool for the pursuit of democracy in nondemocratic settings, social media may be less effective in exactly these settings.

Moving Forward

Though the era of social media has only recently begun, the study of the use of these tools in protest is an active research area that has already revealed a number of important insights about modern social movements. Some of these pertain to who uses social media and how when organizing protests. One recent study focuses on participants in the 2015 Charlie Hebdo demonstration in Paris. A comparison of people who sent tweets from the protest site in Paris with others who sent tweets from Paris but away from the protest site reveals that protest participants occupy different network positions within Twitter—in general they have more followers and their followers have more followers (Larson et al. forthcoming). Moreover, protesters are highly interconnected on Twitter, suggesting that pockets of shared knowledge and influence, which social media facilitate, play a role in motivating protest participation.

Relatedly, a study of Twitter activity during the Arab Spring reveals that those who occupy relatively peripheral network positions play an especially important role in turning others out to the protest (Steinert-Threlkeld 2017). Studies of messages sent on Twitter during Istanbul's Taksim Gezi Park protest in 2013 and the United for Global Change demonstration in 2012 show that those with fewer connections on Twitter have a large impact in the aggregate by passing along messages from others, resulting in a wide reach of protest-relevant messages (Barberá et al. 2015). Certain Twitter users, by nature of their ability to bridge distinct communities on the platform, are responsible for messages jumping from social group to social group, which may help to organize and influence turnout in protests (González-Bailón and Wang 2016). It is increasingly clear that social media plays an important role in spreading information about all aspects of protests widely, and our understanding of exactly how this happens improves with each new study.

Whether or not this information-sending function translates into greater protest success is a much more difficult question to answer. In a widely circulated *New Yorker* piece, Malcom Gladwell praised social media's ability to make use of weak connections between people, but doubted its use in scenarios like protests: "The Internet lets us exploit the power of these kinds of distant connections with marvelous efficiency.

It's terrific at the diffusion of innovation, interdisciplinary collaboration, seamlessly matching up buyers and sellers, and the logistical functions of the dating world. But weak ties seldom lead to high-risk activism" (2010). Whether a high-risk action like participating in a protest can be encouraged or even *caused* by social media, and whether this translates into greater protest success, are important but elusive questions.

One hurdle is the difficulty of testing the causal mechanism. In order to conclude that the use of social media *causes* protests to be more impactful, the ideal experiment would take a set of nascent protests that are as similar as possible in all aspects that could affect their level of success and randomly assign the use of social media to some but not others. Obviously, this experiment is unlikely to be conducted.[3]

Correlations have been observed between social media activity and protests (Steinert-Threlkeld et al. 2015). For instance, "In Tunisia, for example, 20 percent of blogs were evaluating Ben Ali's leadership on the day he resigned from office (January 14), up from just 5 percent the month before. Subsequently, the primary topic for Tunisian blogs was 'revolution' until a public rally of at least 100,000 people took place and eventually forced the old regime's remaining leaders to relinquish power" (Howard et al. 2011, 3). Without knowing what the protests would have looked like without the use of social media, it is difficult to conclude that social media activity caused the protests or boosted participation from what it would have been in a world without social media.

Social media's causal effect on protest success depends on how social media change the character of protest. In addition to the ways social media are connected to protest character discussed above, there are other possible channels through which these tools may alter protest outcomes from what they would have been had social media not been available. One is through altering the composition of protesters. Do the demographics of those who protest look different in a world with social media, and do these demographic differences impact protest success?

We might imagine that the composition of protesters does bear on protest success, perhaps by affecting which types of causes are found to be worthy of protest or how much pressure the group can place on the government.

Much of the real-time information about protests is shared and received on smartphones. This means that the primary demographic that may be affected by content shared over social media is a narrow one composed of technologically savvy young people. This may be a different demographic than was active in previous waves of protest (Howard et al. 2011). For instance, Castells writes that

> at the end of 2010, an estimated 80 percent of Egyptians had a cell phone, according to research from Ovum. About a quarter of households had access to the Internet as of 2009, according to the International Telecommunications Union. But the proportion was much higher among the 20- to 35-year-old demographic group of Cairo, Alexandria and other major urban centers, who, in their majority, be it from home, school or cybercafes, are able to access the Internet. (2012, 57)

Whether this demographic is particularly well suited to motivate others to join them, and whether their goals are aligned with those of other prospective protesters, remains to be seen.

Conclusion

In short, while a number of questions cannot yet be definitively answered, we know that social media are a set of tools that allow users to share content with many other users very rapidly, and that in the information age, people with Internet access do use social media throughout all stages of protest. The information that people share using social media is often personal and emotional. Before protest events, such media are used to spread word of the cause, plan the logistics of upcoming events, and recruit participants. During protests, people post and pass along news from the ground. Afterwards, people report details, assess progress, and start planning anew.

We know that social media activity spikes before protest events, and when access is abruptly cut off, people turn to the streets. Whether access to social media on net makes protests more likely, widely attended, or effective at inducing change is still ambiguous. Whatever the causal mechanism or net causal impact, governments are taking notice. Responses like shutting down the Internet, tracking down key social media features, and attempting to legislate use of the media suggest that governments are betting in favor of a net increase in protest success due to social media unless they take action.

In theory, social media can cause protests to be better attended and more likely to be successful than they would have been in a world without social media. These tools make coordinating and popularizing claims and grievances particularly easy. With them, protesters have unprecedented access to international audiences, offering a channel for global linkages. So long as authoritarian regimes are unsuccessful at blocking or co-opting social media activity, these tools can be useful in any institutional environment. Of course, under the right circumstances, these tools have the power to work against protest success as well. It is important to carefully consider the ways that social media may or may not be helpful for protest outcomes in order to design studies that answer lingering questions central to the study of social movements in the information age.

Notes

1   This mechanism can be viewed as an extension of resource mobilization theory (see McCarthy and Zald 1977). Viewed through this lens, social media is a tool that allows quick and effective mobilization of human resources. It allows easy access to existing social networks, pools of human capital, and even offers the means to quickly forge new connections between people. Groups possessing grievances and behaving according to the assumptions described in this chapter are better able to mobilize human resources if they have access to social media than if they do not.

2   The ability to quickly transmit news internationally may also serve to aid protests via a frames mechanism (see Snow et al. 1986). If coordinating on a common understanding of the need for protest is helpful, social media can not only align potential participants' views within an area of interest, but also help to export already developed frames from more mature protests abroad. One unique opportunity the era of online social media presents to researchers of frames stems from the fact that online activity leaves a trace. To the extent that posts on social media accurately represent a person's understanding of a frame, then the consistency, spread, and evolution of frames can be studied on a scale never before possible.

3   Understanding the causal mechanism by which social media helps or hinders protests is especially crucial for evaluating potential interventions in terms of their usefulness

in bringing about democratic government. Obviously, it would be useful to know the answer to certain questions, such as: If we handed everyone living under an autocratic regime a reliable smartphone, could we expect democracy to follow? Many intermediate questions stand in the way, but any knowledge we could glean of the causal mechanism brings us closer to understanding and potentially even influencing the course of protests.

References

Barberá, Pablo, Nina Wang, Richard Bonneau, John T. Jost, Jonathan Nagler, Joshua Tucker, and Sandra González-Bailón. 2015. "The Critical Periphery in the Growth of Social Protests." *PLoS one* 10, no. 11. https://doi.org/10.1371/journal. pone.0143611 (accessed 14 November 2018).

Castells, Manuel. 2012. *Networks of Outrage and Hope: Social Movements in the Internet Age*. Malden, MA: Polity Press.

Chwe, Michael Suk-Young. 2000. "Communication and Coordination in Social Networks." *The Review of Economic Studies* 67, no. 1: 1–16.

Dorsey, Steve. 2013. "Turkey's Social Media and Smartphones Key to 'Occupy Gezi' Protests." *Huffington Post*, 9 June. http://www.huffingtonpost.com/2013/06/09/ turkey-social-media-smartphones-occupy-gezi-protests_n_3411542.html (accessed 2 July 2013).

Elantawy, Nahed, and Julie B. Wiest. 2011. "Social Media in the Egyptian Revolution: Reconsidering Resource Mobilization Theory." *International Journal of Communication* 5: 1207–24.

Gladwell, Malcolm. 2010. "Small Change: Why the Revolution Will Not Be Tweeted." *New Yorker*, 4 October. http://www.newyorker.com/reporting/2010/10/04/101004fa_ fact_gladwell?currentPage=all (accessed 2 July 2013).

González-Bailón, Sandra, and Nina Wang. 2016. "Networked Discontent: The Anatomy of Protest Campaigns in Social Media." *Social Networks* 44: 95–104.

Graham-Felsen, Sam. 2011. "Is Occupy Wall Street the Tumblr Revolution?" *Good*, 17 October. http://www.good.is/posts/is-occupy-wall-street-the-tumblr-revolution (accessed 2 July 2013).

Gustin, Sam. 2011. "Social Media Sparked, Accelerated Egypt's Revolutionary Fire." *Wired*, 11 February. http://www.wired.com/business/2011/02/egypts-revolutionary-fire/ (accessed 2 July 2011).

Harding, Luke, and Constanze Letsch. 2013. "Turkish Police Arrest 25 People for Using Social Media to Call for Protest." *Guardian* (London), 5 June. http://www. guardian.co.uk/world/2013/jun/05/turkish-police-arrests-social-media-protest (accessed 2 July 2013).

Hassanpour, Navid. 2014. "Media Disruption Exacerbates Revolutionary Unrest: Evidence from Mubarak's Natural Experiment." *Journal of Political Communication* 30, no 1: 1–24.

Hounshell, Blake. 2011. "The Revolution Will Be Tweeted." *Foreign Policy* (July/August). http://www.foreignpolicy.com/articles/2011/06/20/the_revolution_will_be_tweeted (accessed 2 July 2011).

Howard, Philip N., Aiden Duffy, Deen Freelon, Muzammil Hussain, Will Mari, and Marwa Mazaid. 2011. "Opening Closed Regimes: What Was the Role of Social Media During the Arab Spring?" Project on Information Technology and Political Islam, working paper. https://papers.ssrn.com/sol3/papers.cfm?abstract_id=2595096 (accessed 14 November 2018).

Hutchinson, Sophie. 2013. "Social Media Plays Major Role in Turkish Protests." *BBC*, 4 June. http://www.bbc.co.uk/news/world-europe-22772352 (accessed 2 July 2013).

Larson, Jennifer M., Jonathan Nagler, Jonathan Ronen, and Joshua A. Tucker. Forthcoming. "Social Networks and Protest Participation: Evidence from 130 Million Twitter Users." *American Journal of Political Science*. http://goo.gl/jBH1eH (accessed 18 November 2018).

Mason, Paul. 2012. *Why It's Kicking Off Everywhere: The New Global Revolutions*. London: Verso.

McCarthy, John D., and Mayer N. Zald. 1977. "Resource Mobilization and Social Movements: A Partial Theory." *American Journal of Sociology* 82, no. 6: 1212–41.

Morozov, Evgeny. 2009. "Iran: Downside to the 'Twitter Revolution." *Dissent* 56, no. 4: 10–14.

Protalinski, Emil. 2011. "Israel Uses Facebook to Blacklist Pro-Palestinian Protesters." *ZDNet*, 10 July. http://www.zdnet.com/blog/ facebook/israel-uses-facebook-to-blacklist-pro-palestinian-protesters/2113 (accessed 2 July 2013).

Rosen, Rebecca J. 2011. "The 99 Percent Tumblr: Self-Service History." *Atlantic*, 10 October. http://www.theatlantic.com/technology/archive/2011/10/ the-99-percent-tumblr-self-service-history/246385/ (accessed 2 July 2013).

Siddique, Haroon, Paul Owen, and Adam Gabbatt. 2011. "Protests in Egypt and unrest in Middle East—as it happened." *Guardian* (London), 25 January. http://www.guardian.co.uk/global/blog/2011/jan/25/middleeast-tunisia (accessed 2 July 2013).

Snow, David A., E. Burke Rochford, Jr., Steven K. Worden, and Robert D. Benford. 1986. "Frame Alignment Processes, Micromobilization, and Movement Participation." *American Sociological Review* 51, no. 4: 464–81.

Stauffer, Caroline. 2013. "Social Media Spreads and Splinters Brazil Protests." *NBC News*, 22 June. http://www.nbcnews.com/technology/social-media-spreads-splinters-brazil-protests-6C10418084 (accessed 2 July 2013).

Steinert-Threlkeld, Zachary C. 2017. "Spontaneous Collective Action: Peripheral Mobilization during the Arab Spring." *American Political Science Review* 111, no. 2: 379–403.

Steinert-Threlkeld, Zachary C., Delia Mocanu, Alessandro Vespignani, and James Fowler. 2015. "Online Social Networks and Offline Protest." *EPJ Data Science* 4, no. 1: 1–9.

Talbot, David. 2011. "Inside Egypt's 'Facebook Revolution.' " *MIT Technology Review*, 29 April. http://www.technologyreview.com/view/423884/ inside-egypts-facebook-revolution/ (accessed 2 July 2011).

Tucker, Joshua A., Megan Metzger, Duncan Penfold-Brown, Richard Bonneau, John Jost, and Jonathan Nagler. 2014. "Protest in the Age of Social Media: Technology and Ukraine's #Euromaidan." *Carnegie Reporter* 7, no. 4: 8–20.

Tufekci, Zeynep, and Deen Freelon. 2013. "Introduction to the Special Issue on New Media and Social Unrest." *American Behavioral Scientist* 57, no. 7: 843–7.

Vaccari, Cristian, Augusto Valeriani, Pablo Barberá, Rich Bonneau, John T. Jost, Jonathan Nagler, and Joshua A. Tucker. 2015. "Political Expression and Action on Social Media: Exploring the Relationship between Lower- and Higher-Threshold Political Activities Among Twitter Users in Italy." *Journal of Computer-Mediated Communication* 20: 221–39.

Wall, Melissa, and Sahar El Zahed. 2011. "I'll Be Waiting For You Guys: A YouTube Call to Action in the Egyptian Revolution." *International Journal of Communication* 5: 1333–43.

Washington Times. 2009. "Iran's Twitter Revolution." *Washington Times*, 16 June. http://www.washingtontimes.com/news/2009/jun/16/irans-twitter-revolution/ (accessed 2 July 2013).

Yan, Holly. 2011. "Tunisians Abroad: Facebook, Regular Citizens Key to Revolution." *CNN*, 26 January. http://www.cnn.com/2011/WORLD/americas/01/18/tunisia. us.unrest/index.html (accessed 2 July 2013).

Schools for Democracy? The Role of NGOs in Protests in Democracies in the Global South

Carew E. Boulding

Protest in developing countries is sometimes characterized as potentially destabilizing or threatening to democracy, but growing evidence shows that protest can coexist with democracy even in the younger and poorer democracies of the world. In Latin America in 2005, for example, 38.7 percent of respondents reported they had taken part in protests, and 15 percent said they had protested recently in activities like authorized demonstrations, unauthorized demonstrations, riots, land occupations, and blocking traffic—all in countries that can reasonably be classified as democracies (Latinobarómetro 2005). More recently, surveys from the AmericasBarometer show between 8 and 13 percent of respondents reporting having taken part in protest within the last year.[1]

What factors drive contemporary protests in developing democracies? The literature on voter participation and social movements suggests that how people interact in their daily lives—what types of associations they join, how often they attend meetings of community organizations, how they interact with their neighbors—is an important determinant of how they choose to engage in political life. In developing democracies, nongovernmental organizations often make up an important part of associational life. This chapter explores how NGO activity influences the ways in which ordinary people associate with one another and how they participate in politics, particularly contentious politics. NGOs today make up an important part of civil society in most developing countries, where they have taken on service-delivery and advocacy roles in numbers that have grown exponentially since the 1980s. Instead of social clubs and civic groups, today much of the fabric of civil society in developing countries is comprised of NGOs. There have been, however, few systematic efforts to analyze the role these organizations play in changing political participation and collective action, especially as they relate to protest activity.

This chapter uses survey evidence to explore the relationship between NGOs and protest in Latin America and in other democracies in the developing world, demonstrating that NGOs play an important and nuanced role in facilitating protest.[2] First, across all the countries in the 2005 Latinobarómetro survey (one of the few surveys that asks a direct question about contact with NGOs), people who report contact with NGOs are significantly more likely to have participated in protest than people who have not interacted with an NGO. The World Values Survey for the same year shows a similar relationship between associational membership and protest in developing democracies outside of Latin America. People who are members of associations are more likely to protest than non-members. Although studies of political participation in wealthy democracies have long pointed to associational life as important for facilitating protest, little work on NGOs in developing democracies makes this connection. Instead, the strong conventional wisdom held by both scholars and policymakers is that NGOs strengthen democracy by training citizens to participate in the democratic process, not by training protesters.

Second, and perhaps more surprising, although NGO contact is associated with protest in every country in the study, the effect is strongest in countries where elections are flawed. Having contact with an NGO in a country where elections are marred by election fraud, low public confidence, weak and changeable political parties, or limited competition makes people more likely to protest. The effect of contact with an NGO in a country where elections are clean and competitive, and where political parties are strong and stable, is weaker, although still present. NGOs have a strong impact on protest, but that impact is shaped by the context of the quality of democratic elections in a country.

NGOs and Protest in Developing Democracies

Both NGOs and membership associations influence the decision to engage in political life through direct and indirect mechanisms. In practice, NGOs in the developing world do many of the same things that other voluntary associations do, but often with greater financial resources since they are more likely to be supported by international donors (Hulme and Edwards 1997). NGOs work in service provision (health care, sanitation, education, etc.) and they can work in advocacy (providing education, legal services, or directly lobbying the government). NGOs also often target their activities toward needy communities, bringing new resources to historically excluded populations. NGOs, by virtue of being problem-oriented organizations, also create new opportunities for association. Sometimes this happens directly, as when NGOs organize workshops and forums for communities to discuss issues, but it can also happen indirectly as people wait in line to get vaccines for their children, or obtain a driver's license, or any of the quotidian activities that occupy everyday life. Both the resources NGOs provide and the opportunities for association facilitate political participation much in the same way membership in other types of community organizations or voluntary associations is thought to: people who know each other, trust each other, and have some recognition of shared problems are more likely to decide to engage in political action.

Table 5.1 summarizes the key differences between NGOs and other membership associations, all of which can fall under the broader label of civil society. This table shows how these terms are commonly used, although in practice there is also a great deal of overlap between categories. NGOs are nonprofit organizations primarily focused on humanitarian objectives. They can be large, international organizations or small, community-based organizations, and the range of activities they engage in is vast, including service provision (such as health care, water, sanitation, housing), advocacy, research, or a combination thereof. Although some NGOs are also membership associations, the universe of associations is much larger, and includes community groups, churches, professional groups, and sports groups. These organizations together are sometimes referred to as "civil society," separate from the government and from business.

TABLE 5.1 Comparing Civil-Society Organizations: NGOs and Membership Associations

Civil-Society Organizations

	NGOs	Membership Associations
Definition	Nongovernmental, nonprofit organizations primarily focused on humanitarian objectives	Voluntary, membership-based organizations involved in a wide range of activities distinct from government and business

Examples	International NGOs
	    CARE
	    Save the Children
	    World Vision
	    Catholic Relief Services
	    Amnesty International
	
	Local service-provision NGOs
	    Health care
	    Sanitation services
	    Housing
	    Education
	
	Advocacy NGOs
	    Women's empowerment
	    Capacity-building
	    Environmental advocacy
	    Indigenous rights
	
	Research NGOs
	    Policy advice
	    Think tanks
		Community groups
		    Neighborhood associations
		    Youth groups
		
		Sports and recreation
		
		Churches
		
		Labor unions
		
		Arts or music groups
		
		Educational groups
		
		Professional associations
		
		Consumer organizations
		
		Charity and volunteer groups
		
		Advocacy groups
		
		Social movements

All of these types of organizations have grown in number and influence in the developing world over the last hundred years, but most rapidly since the 1980s. In 1909 there were fewer than 200 international NGOs in the world; in 1956 there were more than 1,000; and in 2005 there were more than 20,000 (Werker and Ahmed 2008, 75).[3] Similar growth in the number of domestic NGOs has been documented in countries across the developing world, including Nepal, Bolivia, India, Tunisia, Brazil, and Thailand (Edwards 2009, 21). This growth can be attributed in part to the growing availability of foreign aid funds for NGOs involved in development projects. Since the 1980s, there has been a shift in foreign aid spending away from governments (many of which were plagued by corruption) toward NGOs. NGOs in the developing world have become the face of civil society for foreign aid donors seeking to promote democracy through the strengthening of civil society (Ottaway and Carothers 2000).

Considerable portions of both multilateral and bilateral aid are channeled through NGOs, and many organizations have whole units devoted to strengthening ties with NGOs and building civil society. The World Bank, for example, involves civil-society organizations through policy consultations, information sharing and training, grant making, and in setting poverty-reduction strategy goals. The World Bank estimates that 5 percent of its total annual portfolio (or about $1 billion) is channeled to civil-society organizations through grassroots development programs (World Bank 2006, xv). This effort to support civil society by collaborating with and funding NGOs and other civil-society organizations is found across the major donors, including the US and European aid agencies (Howell and Pearce 2002). Understanding how these diverse organizations affect political life is a challenging task. As these organizations become more numerous across the developing world, however, it is also a critically important one for many audiences, including international donors, governments in the developing world, academics, and NGO representatives.

What role do these organizations play in shaping political participation? There is abundant evidence from wealthier countries that associational life facilitates political participation (Burns, Schlozman, and Verba 2001; Rosenstone and Hansen 1993; Verba and Nie 1987), but whether that participation takes the form of voting or the form of protest is shaped more by the larger question of how well democratic political institutions—especially elections—are functioning. People who are motivated to participate are more likely to vote when there is little fraud or corruption in the electoral process, when political parties represent meaningful choices, when there is real political competition, and when reasonable people have confidence that participating in elections might affect outcomes they deem important. These conditions are not fully met in any election, even in "advanced" democracies, but there is real variation in each of these factors that influences the likelihood that individuals see voting as a meaningful activity. And, where elections are failing on some or all of these counts, a motivated person views contentious political action favorably.

Dissatisfaction with formal mechanisms of participation is not only a function of electoral fraud or corruption; it can also be a function of electoral outcomes. More specifically, democratic governments' failures to respond to the needs or interests of constituents can channel political participation into nontraditional and contentious forms of participation. For example, widespread dissatisfaction with formal voting can occur when elections are technically working fine but people have little confidence that electoral participation will produce substantive benefits. In fact, in some cases, the formal mechanisms of democratic governance may be functioning quite well, but the government is performing poorly in terms of meeting the real needs of citizens, or offering choices on issues that concern most people.

This is not to make the case that the individual activities, political leanings, or degree of activism that NGOs engage in do not matter. They quite obviously do matter. But there is also abundant evidence that the influence organizations have is not limited to their stated goals or outright activist pursuits. On the contrary—and this is the core of many of the arguments that claim that associations are the key to understanding stable civil society—organizations shape citizens' interactions, their engagement with the state, even when their stated political aims are very limited. That is, even organizations that seek a low profile, never actively engage in politics, do not offer workshops on political engagement, etc., still bring resources into a community, and more importantly create associational space where neighbors and community members can talk (while waiting in line for a vaccine, for example, or attending a public meeting on a proposed irrigation scheme). This simple interaction—talking between neighbors in an environment with the suggestion of solving problems—facilitates political action because those neighbors who do run into each other at an NGO office are more likely to discuss shared problems, and to trust each other enough to try to do something about them, than neighbors who have had no such opportunity.

For example, if you lived in a neighborhood where many NGOs are working, your chance of knowing your neighbors, having a shared sense of the problems facing your community, and deciding to take some action is higher than it would be if you lived in a neighborhood with no NGOs, community organizations, or voluntary associations. But the choice about how you are going to proceed—Are you going to vote? Are you going to sign a petition? March to the capital? Throw rocks and break windows?—is shaped by which options seem most effective in the context in which you live. Obviously, the context in which this decision is made is a vastly complex one involving a host of impulses, weighing costs and benefits and other practical considerations, but in general, we can expect that in cases where elections are viewed as rigged, corrupt, or irrelevant to the real policy issues at stake, it is more likely that people will pursue other tactics.

Survey Evidence: NGOs, Associational Membership, and Protest

Looking at the patterns of contact with NGOs and participation in political protest by country is a useful starting point for exploring these issues more systematically. Even at the country level, a clear pattern emerges: people in countries with high rates of contact with NGOs tend to experience higher rates of political protest. Figure 5.1 shows the relationship between NGO contact and protest in Latin America. Bolivia, Mexico, and Paraguay top the graph, with protest rates around 50 percent, and contact with NGOs between 30 and 40 percent. Brazil is unusual in its very high rates of NGO contact and relatively low protest compared with Bolivia and Mexico. Overall, the pattern is clear and fairly consistent: countries in which people are more likely to contact an NGO also witness higher rates of participation in nonvoting political action. Figure 5.1 also includes developing democracies from outside of Latin America, for which World

FIGURE 5.1 Contact with NGOs or Membership Associations and Protest Rates by Country

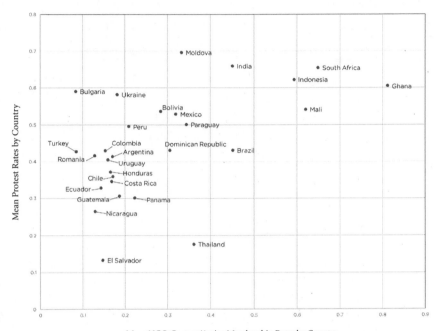

Mean NGO Contact/Active Membership Rates by Country

Values Survey data are available on membership rates and protest rates. Although the World Values Survey does not ask a direct question about NGOs, membership in associations serves as a useful proxy. A similar pattern is visible for the countries outside Latin America: countries with higher rates of involvement with voluntary organizations also tend to have higher rates of participation in protest activities. The pattern is similar if the measure for protest that only counts respondents who claim to have participated in demonstrations is used.

To test the effect of NGO activity and civil-society membership on political participation more systematically, I estimate models of protest participation using both individual-level variables from the survey responses and country-level factors, first for Latin America and second for a sample of developing-world democracies outside of Latin America. Because both individual- and country-level factors are important for understanding the effect of NGOs, I estimate multilevel mixed-effects logistic regression.[4] The individual-level variables are drawn from responses to the 2005 Latinobarómetro survey and the 2005 World Values Survey. Country-level variables come from a variety of sources, detailed below.

Data and Models

Individual-Level Variables

For the Latinobarómetro survey, the measure of protest is coded as "1" if the respondent participated in any of the contentious political actions listed in the survey (participating in demonstrations of any sort, riots, land or building occupations, or blocking traffic). *Protest* is coded as "0" if the respondent did not participate at all. It is also coded as "0" for those who voted or signed a petition but did not participate in the more contentious forms of participation. In the World Values Survey, *protest* is coded as "1" for respondents who have or "might" have participated in peaceful demonstrations. Similar variables capture the response to questions about signing petitions and joining in boycotts

The best measure of NGO contact comes from the Latinobarómetro in 2005, which asks a direct question about contact with NGOs in the past three years. This measure captures individuals who have sought out direct contact with NGOs, not just passive encounters with NGO activity. In this sense, it measures a direct individual effect, not the broader, more diffuse effects of having NGOs in a community. On average across all countries in the sample, 22.48 percent of respondents have contacted NGOs, ranging from a low of 13 percent in Nicaragua to a high of 45.18 percent in Brazil. This high rate of NGO contact is consistent across recent surveys. In 2001, the only other year this question was asked, 22.82 percent of respondents contacted an NGO. Both surveys include questions on associational activity, including membership in a variety of organizations. Since the World Values Survey does not ask a direct NGO question, associational membership is used as the main independent variable for the non–Latin American countries.

To control for other individual-level factors that affect political participation, I include variables for demographic factors (gender, age, education, personal income), and political attitudes (trust in government, interpersonal trust, life satisfaction, political ideology, political interest, personal experience with corruption, and political knowledge). To control for the possibility that some people are more active in all political participation, I control for having voted in the last election.

Country-Level Factors

Quality of democratic elections is the main country-level variable of interest. Since elections can fail to perform well in a number of ways (both procedurally and in terms of outcomes), measuring this concept requires some careful thought. First, if political parties are not organized around the issues that are important to people, or are not stable enough to offer meaningful cues from one election to another, elections fall short. Second, fraud, corruption, voter intimidation, vote buying, or any number of other directly fraudulent actions, can tarnish elections, which would impinge on an election being considered "free and fair." Finally, even if there are not obvious indications of fraud, elections can be considered less than effective if there is widespread dissatisfaction with the process of voting, or the choices available in an election. That is, even if elections appear to be running fairly regularly without blatant fraud, people are still likely to look for other venues for participation if they have little confidence that voting can accomplish their aims.

In order to capture this conception of variation in the effectiveness of elections as a tool for participation, I use the index of party institutionalization compiled by the Inter-American Development Bank (Berkman et al. 2008). This index captures all the important election criteria described here, including the strength and issue-orientation of political parties, the degree to which the election is free and fair, and how much confidence voters have in the process. I chose the party institutionalization index as the most complete measure of the extent to which ordinary people perceive elections to be working, both procedurally and in terms of outcomes, but using other indications of the quality of democratic elections yields similar results. Specifically, the World Bank's good governance indicators produce very similar interactive effects as the party institutionalization index.[5]

Specifically, the index is composed of five measures. First is a measure of the extent to which there is a "stable, moderate and socially rooted party system to articulate and aggregate societal interests," which is taken from the Bertelsmann Transformation Index (Berkman et al. 2008, 14). Second is an indicator of confidence in political parties and elections based on the World Values Survey. Third is a measure of vote volatility as an indicator of political competition.[6] Fourth is a measure of the extent to which the elections are considered free and fair based on elite surveys conducted by Berkman et al. (2008, 14). And fifth is the age of the political party system according to the Database of Political Institutions, which is included as a measure of how well political parties are able to provide continuity between elections. Together, these five factors give a complete summary of how well electoral institutions are functioning in the eyes of ordinary people. This index is correlated at 0.70 with the Freedom House measure of democracy, so they are obviously related to other indicators or measures of quality of democracy, without merely measuring the same things.

Since there are only eighteen countries covered in the Latinobarómetro survey, including too many country-level variables poses a problem for estimation. However, there are several other country-level factors aside from party institutionalization that might influence the individual-level relationships we observe in the data. To address this concern, the full multilevel model is estimated with each of the following country-level variables separately, to check for the robustness of the individual-level relationships. The main result—that individuals who have contact with NGOs are more likely to participate in protest—is robust to the inclusion or exclusion of each of the following country-level variables: Freedom House democracy score, the Human Development Index, and civil-society density (measured a country's average membership from the survey).

Findings: NGOs and Protest

Using the data described above, I first explore the hypothesis that people who have contact with NGOs are more likely to protest. The results are presented in Table 5.2. The models estimate protest participation using

TABLE 5.2 Protest in Latin America

INDIVIDUAL-LEVEL FACTORS		
NGO contact	0.769***	1.877***
	(0.04)	(0.35)
Membership in associations	0.405***	0.384***
	(0.03)	(0.04)
Female	-0.299***	-0.274***
	(0.03)	(0.03)
Age	-0.012***	-0.013***
	(0.00)	(0.00)
Education	0.027***	0.026***
	(0.00)	(0.00)
Personal income	0.000	-0.004
	(0.02)	(0.02)
Trust in government	0.039*	0.011
	(0.02)	(0.02)
Interpersonal trust	0.029	0.059
	(0.04)	(0.04)
Life satisfaction	-0.109***	-0.092***
	(0.02)	(0.02)
Left-right ideology	-0.002***	-0.002***
	(0.00)	(0.00)
Political interest	0.299***	0.321***
	(0.02)	(0.02)
Experience with corruption	0.346***	0.311***
	(0.04)	(0.05)
Political knowledge	0.150***	0.136***
	(0.02)	(0.02)
Voted	0.050	0.078
	(0.04)	(0.04)
Constant	-1.508*	
	(0.62)	

TABLE 5.2 Protest in Latin America con't

INTERACTIONS		
NGO contact X party institutionalization		-0.659**
		(0.20)
COUNTRY-LEVEL FACTORS		
Party institutionalization	0.312	1.656*
	(0.34)	(0.72)
Observations	18887	18887
No. of countries	18	18

NOTE: Table entries are maximum likelihood estimates with estimated standard errors in parentheses generated using the command xtmelogit in Stata 10. ***p<0.01, **p<0.05, *p<0.1.
SOURCE: Latinobarómetro (2005).

multilevel mixed-effects logistic regression models based on maximum likelihood. Model 1 estimates the effect of contact with NGOs on protest, controlling for the country-level measure of party institutionalization. Model 2 models the cross-level interaction between NGO contact and party institutionalization to test whether the relationship between NGO contact and protesting is constant across countries with different quality democratic elections (or, as I suspect, whether NGOs have a stronger relationship to protest in countries where elections are not working well).

Contact with an NGO is positively associated with participating in protest activity at a statistically significant level in all three specifications. The individual variables in the model illustrate tendencies of participation in Latin America. Women and older people are less likely to protest. More educated people protest more on average, which is consistent with findings from studies of protests in Europe and North America, but runs counter to the characterization of protest in Latin America as a pro-poor movement made up largely of the uneducated. Interpersonal trust and trust in government have no significant effect on protest. Less-satisfied, left-leaning people who are both interested in and knowledgeable about politics are much more likely to protest than their satisfied, right-leaning counterparts with little interest in politics.

These individual-level factors are stable in the interaction model, where the party institutionalization index is included in the estimation (Model 2). The index overall is a very poor predictor of protest: none of the variables are significant and only between 4 and 5 percent of the variance is explained by country-level factor, but the significance of the individual-level variables hold.[7] The individual results are also robust to the inclusion of the country-level variables discussed above, although only compulsory voting laws are statistically significant: countries with compulsory voting laws not surprisingly have higher voting rates as well (results not shown here). The weak predictive power of the country-level variables can be partly attributed to the relatively small number of countries in the sample. With only eighteen countries, and over twenty thousand individual-level observations, only very strong cross-country relationships would likely be significant.

One concern with these models is that politically active people might be more likely to contact NGOs *and* more likely to participate in political actions, without any causal relationship between the two. If this were the case, we might still observe a positive and significant relationship between contact with NGOs and protest and voting, but not because NGOs influence protest directly. To the extent that this relationship still represents a serious departure from conventional characterizations of the type of effects that NGOs have, the finding is still of interest. More importantly, the measure of contact with an NGO is only correlated at 0.16 with political interest. That is, although people with high levels of interest in politics are slightly more likely to contact NGOs than those that are not at all interested in politics, the difference is relatively minor.

Similar models using questions from the World Values Survey in developing-world democracies outside of Latin America yield very similar results. Using the measure of membership in associations instead of NGO contact, I estimate similar models of protest in developing democracies outside of Latin America. The Latin American countries where the World Values Survey was conducted are not included in these models in order to allow for a clear comparison between Latin America and other regions.[8] Several patterns stand out. First, membership in associations is a positive and significant predictor of participation in all the nonvoting types of participation (signing a petition, joining a peaceful demonstration, or joining

TABLE 5.3 Protest in Non–Latin American Developing Democracies

	PROTEST
Active membership in association	2.499***
	(0.374)
Female	-0.339***
	(0.042)
Age	-0.015***
	(0.001)
Education	0.406***
	(0.048)
Income	0.020*
	(0.010)
Life satisfaction	-0.045***
	(0.010)
Life Confidence in government	0.070**
	(0.024)
Trust in people	-0.04
	(0.052)
Ideology	-0.023**
	(0.009)
Political interest	0.353***
	(0.023)
Political Voted	0.154**
	(0.056)
INTERACTION	
Active member X party institutionalization	-1.117***
	(0.200)
COUNTRY-LEVEL FACTORS	
Party institutionalization	0.519
	(0.696)

TABLE 5.3 Protest in Non–Latin American Developing Democracies con't

VARIANCE COMPONENTS	
Country level	0.010
	(0.004)
Observations	11015
No. of Countries	11
-2 X Log likelihood	13593.5738

NOTE: Table entries are maximum likelihood estimates with estimated standard errors in parentheses generated using the command xtmelogit in Stata 10 ***p<0.01, **p<0.05, *p<0.1 Countries are included in the sample if they are nominally democratic (score higher than a 6 on the combined Freedom House score), and have an income below $12,000 per capita. The countries included are: Bulgaria, Ghana, India, Indonesia, Mali, Moldova, Romania, South Africa, Thailand, Turkey, and Ukraine.

a boycott). Just as we see in Latin America, involvement with civil-society organizations has a larger and more consistent effect on protest behavior than it does on voter turnout in developing democracies. Table 5.3 presents the results of three models using a different measure of non-voting political activity as the dependent variable. The coefficient for membership in associations is positive and significant in each model, showing that people who are connected with civil-society organizations are more likely to participate in demonstrations, more likely to sign petitions, and more likely to join boycotts than similar nonmember individuals. These models yield similar results: membership is significantly associated with protest.

Since the multilevel regression estimates include individual responses from multiple countries, and since the interaction term suggests the effect of NGOs may be quite different under different quality-of-democracy conditions, it is helpful to look at the relationship between NGO contact (or membership in associations) and protest for each country as well as the aggregate patterns. Table 5.4 summarizes the results of the full logistic regression by country for the key variables of interest. A few patterns stand out. First, the effect of NGO contact or associational membership on protest is strong and consistent across Latin America. In all eighteen countries in the sample, NGO contact has a positive and significant relationship with protest. Second, the effect of NGOs appears to be stronger and more consistent than other types of associational membership activities. Although NGO contact is positively associated with protest in *every* country, membership is a significant predictor of protest in most, with the exception of Argentina, Costa Rica, El Salvador, Guatemala, and Honduras. Similar results are evident outside of Latin America. Although membership has no effect on voting or protests in two countries (Bulgaria and South Africa), in every other country in the sample, membership in associations is a good predictor of participation in political protest. Despite the small number of countries represented here, the pattern is remarkably similar to what we observe in Latin America—in almost every case, membership in associations increases the likelihood of political protest, while the effect on voting is much less consistent.

People who are involved with NGOs and civil-society organizations are more likely to engage in a wide range of political actions, including voting, peaceful protest, and contentious protest. However, it would be misleading to claim that the relationship between civil society and participation is constant across different contexts. In fact, there is a great deal of variation in the strength of the relationship between individual involvement with civil society and protest. Although in most cases, contact with NGOs makes protest participation more likely, in some countries the effect is fairly weak. In others, it is very strong.

What explains the variation in the strength of the relationship between civil society and political participation across countries? What explains the relative impact on voting versus participation in contentious politics? Here, I return to the idea that how well the democratic political system is working is critical for understanding the effect of NGOs on protest. This section explores the role that civil society plays in mobilizing political participation under conditions that are common in democracies in the developing world: democratic institutions, including regular elections, but also problems with corruption, rule of law, and poor government performance. Does civil society have the same effect on political participation under conditions of crises of the democratic process? Does civil society influence political participation differently when the government is failing in terms of providing material benefits?

TABLE 5.4 Relationship between NGOs, Associational Membership, and Protest

COUNTRY	EFFECT ON PROTEST		NO. OF RESPONDENTS
	NGO Contact	Membership	
Argentina	+	.	1,200
Bolivia	+	+	1,200
Brazil	+	+	1,204
Bulgaria		.	530
Chile	+	+	1,200
Colombia	+	+	1,200
Costa Rica	+	.	1,200
Dom. Rep.	+	+	1,000
Ecuador	+	+	1,200
El Salvador	+	.	1,010
Ghana		+	706
Guatemala	+	.	1,000
Honduras	+	.	1,000
India		+	725
Indonesia		+	1,185
Mali		.	572
Mexico	+	+	1,200
Moldova		+	765
Nicaragua	+	+	1,000
Panama	+	+	1,008
Paraguay	+	+	1,200
Peru	+	+	1,200
Romania		+	735
South Africa		.	2,286
Thailand		+	1,475
Turkey		+	1,081
Ukraine		+	476
Uruguay	+	+	1,200
Venezuela	+	+	1,200

NOTE: "+" indicates a positive and significant coefficient ($p<0.01$) in the country-specific, fully specified logistic regression with robust standard errors. "." indicates no statistically significant relationship. Data for Latin American countries from Latinobarómetro (2005) and data for all others from the World Values Survey (2005).

Carew E. Boulding

Civil-society activity can be thought of as a stimulant for participation, but how that participation is channeled depends on how well democratic processes are perceived to be working. When the context is one of unresponsiveness—because of either problems with the democratic process, such as electoral fraud, or problems with government performance, such as a chronic inability to address serious poverty—individuals involved with NGOs and associations are more likely to direct their organized energies toward contentious politics than standard institutional participation like voting. Even at the extremes, civil society is only one small part of why people decide to engage politically and make the effort to participate, which is even more reason to expect that the form of participation will be shaped by the larger political context. In cases where the government is failing to perform well, in terms of either the democratic process or overall government performance, NGOs are more likely to have a stronger impact on promoting protest and less of an impact on voting.

These patterns raise some interesting questions about the importance of the political context in shaping the relationships between NGOs, associations, and political participation. To illustrate the conditional effect of how well institutions are functioning, I look more closely at the interaction between party institutionalization and contact with NGOs. In other words, I explore how the relationship between contact with NGOs and voting and political protest change under different conditions of party institutionalization. It is my contention that NGOs do more to stimulate political protest when party institutionalization is weakest. That is, where political parties are unstable, extreme, or disconnected from the needs of average citizens, where confidence in the ability of political parties to represent interests is low, where the fairness of elections is reasonably questioned, people involved with NGOs are more likely to take to the streets than to form orderly lines at voting booths.

To test for this conditional relationship, I estimate the models of protest and voting with a cross-level interaction term for the party institutionalization index and membership, and present the marginal effect of NGO contact at varying levels of party institutionalization. I do this first for the Latin American countries and then for the World Values Survey countries (see Figure 5.2). As party institutionalization increases, contact with NGOs has a declining effect on political protest. At low scores on the

FIGURE 5.2 Marginal Effect of NGO Contact and Active Membership on Protest

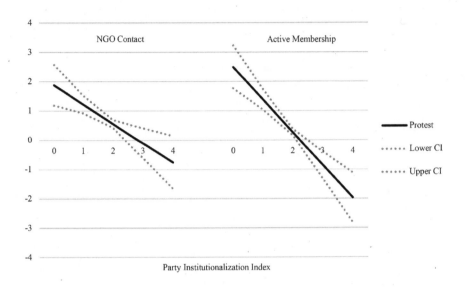

NOTE: NGO contact data from Latinobarómetro (2005) and active membership data from World Values Survey (2005).

party institutionalization index, NGO contact has a significant effect on protest, but the effect diminishes as elections and political parties work better. At a score of 3 or 4, NGOs no longer have a statistically significant effect on protest.

The graph for developing democracies outside of Latin America also shows a clear negative trend—at low levels of the party institutionalization index (where confidence in elections is low, political parties are young and unstable and claim only tenuous ties to real interests in society) membership in associations has the strongest effect on protest. As the party institutionalization index increases, the effect of membership weakens, until it becomes insignificant at an index score of 4. In other words, when elections and political parties seem to be working well as mechanisms for communicating to the state, membership in civil-society organizations does not predict protest behavior. The marginal effect of membership on voting is not significant at any value of the party institutionalization index, which is not surprising given the weak significance of the relationship between membership and voting in most of the models estimated in this chapter.

Conclusion

This chapter presents surprising evidence that NGOs and other associations serve as an important mechanism for protests, even at the individual level. That is, people who are actively involved in civic life are more likely to participate in all forms of political action—including contentious political behavior along the lines of protests and demonstrations.

Despite the very robust finding that associational membership and contact with NGOs increases protest, there is real variation in the strength of this effect, as well as the relative influence of civil society on different types of participation. I have made the case that the form participatory action takes is largely determined by the context of how well the democratic institutions of elections and political parties are functioning. Where political parties are weak and unstable and people have little confidence in them, and where elections are viewed as fraudulent or unfair, membership in civil-society organizations does more to boost protest than it does to boost voting. What this finding suggests is that civil-society activity makes it easier for people to engage politically, and more likely that they will choose to participate. More interesting, NGOs play a crucial role in facilitating political protest—especially where democratic institutions are not working well. When voting is most likely to be ineffective, NGOs encourage other types of mobilization that may be more effective, including political protest.

Notes

1   13 percent in 2008, 8 percent in 2010 and 2012, across a pooled sample of all countries. Thanks to the Latin American Public Opinion Project (LAPOP) and its major supporters (the United States Agency for International Development, the Inter-American Development Bank, and Vanderbilt University) for making the data available. The LAPOP data is available at https://www.vanderbilt.edu/lapop/.

2   For a more detailed exploration of how NGOs affect political participation in different contexts, including voter turnout, see Boulding (2010; 2014).

3   The statistics cited by Werker and Ahmed and referenced here come from the Union of International Associations.

4   For a discussion of the advantages of multilevel modeling, see Steenbergen and Jones (2002).

5   The World Bank's (2010) good governance score averages scores on indices of rule of law, control of corruption, and government effectiveness.

6   Vote volatility is calculated by taking the absolute value of the difference between votes or seats won in the current election and votes or seats won in the last election, summing the results for all parties, and dividing this total by two (Berkman et al. 2008, 14). The data used in these calculations are taken from Mainwaring and Zoco (2007).

7   For the model of protest, rho=0.040.

8   Estimating the models for the Latin American countries using the World Values Survey data yields very similar results to those using Latinobarómetro data—membership is a significant predictor of protest activity in Brazil, Chile, Colombia, Mexico, and Peru when estimated using either logistic regression by country, or using multilevel, mixed-effects logistic regression, with the same control variables as the main models.

References

Boulding, Carew. 2010. "NGOs and Political Participation in Weak Democracies: Sub-national Evidence on Protest and Voter Turnout from Bolivia." *Journal of Politics* 72, no. 2: 456–68.

———. 2014. *NGOs, Political Protest, and Civil Society.* New York: Cambridge University Press.

Burns, Nancy, Kay Lehman Schlozman, and Sidney Verba. 2001. *The Private Roots of Public Action: Gender, Equality, and Political Participation.* Cambridge, MA: Harvard University Press.

Edwards, Michael. 2009. *Civil Society.* Cambridge, UK: Polity Press.

Howell, Jude, and Jenny Pearce. 2002. *Civil Society and Development: A Critical Exploration.* Boulder, CO: Lynne Rienner Publishers.

Hulme, David, and Michael Edwards. 1997. *NGOs, States and Donors: Too Close for Comfort.* New York: Palgrave Macmillan.

Latinobarómetro. 2005. "Opinión Pública Latinoamericana Dataset." http://www. latinobarometro.org/latContents.jsp (accessed 9 July 2017).

Mainwaring, Scott, and Edurne Zoco. 2007. "Political Sequences and the Stabilization of Interparty Competition." *Party Politics* 13, no. 2: 155–78.

Ottaway, Marina, and Thomas Carothers. 2000. *Funding Virtue: Civil Society and Democracy Promotion*. Washington, DC: Carnegie Endowment for International Peace.

Rosenstone, Steven J., and John Mark Hansen. 1993. *Mobilization, Participation, and Democracy in America*. New York: Macmillan.

Silva, Eduardo. 2009. *Challenging Neoliberalism in Latin America*. New York: Cambridge University Press.

Scartascini, Carlos, and Maria Franco. 2015. "Political Institutions, State Capabilities, and Public Policy: An International Dataset (2014 Update)." *Database of Political Institutions*. https://publications.iadb.org/handle/11319/8351 (accessed 3 December 2018).

Steenbergen, Marco R., and Bradford S. Jones. 2002. "Modeling Multilevel Data Structures." *American Journal of Political Science* 46, no. 1: 218–37.

Verba, Sidney, and Norman H. Nie. 1987. *Participation in America*. Chicago: University of Chicago Pres.

Werker, Eric, and Faisal Z. Ahmed. 2008. "What do Nongovernmental Organizations Do?" *Journal of Economic Perspectives* 22: 73–92.

World Bank. 2006. "World Bank—Civil Society Engagement: A Review of Years 2005 and 2006." http://www.worldbank.org/en/about/partners/civil-society (accessed 9 July 2017).

———. 2010. "Governance and Anti-Corruption, WGI 1996–2009." http://info.worldbank. org/governance/wgi/#home (accessed 9 July 2017).

World Values Survey. 2005. "WVS Dataset." http://www.worldvaluessurvey.org/ WVSDocumentationWV5.jsp (accessed 9 July 2017).

PART III:
CASES AND CONSEQUENCES

The Ebbing and Flowing of Political Opportunity Structures: Revolution, Counterrevolution, and the Arab Uprisings

Paul Kingston

The concept of political opportunity structures has come under signifi-cant fire in recent years by social movement theorists. Defined most gen-erally as "the opening and closing of political space" (Wiktorowicz 2004, 14), the political opportunity structure has been described as being too broad—soaking up almost every contextual aspect of the social movement environment like a "sponge" (Robinson 2004). It has also been criticized for being too focused on objective conditions rather than perceptions, emotions, and cultural norms—ignoring in particular the possibility that political and normative threats (as opposed to political opportunities) could be of equal importance in motivating contestation and collective action. Finally, it has been critiqued for being too static—focusing for the most part on a snapshot analysis of political structures rather than on the dynamic and contingent ways that openings come and go as a result of the iterative interaction of structures and social movement agents.

These critiques can be usefully analyzed in the context of the Arab world prior to the outbreak of the Arab Spring in 2011. The Arab Spring was an unprecedented wave of popular mobilization across the Arab world, particularly within the region's republican regimes, that toppled dictators in four countries, led to political reform in several more, and precipitated the outbreak of civil conflict in others, especially in Syria, whose brutal civil conflict is still ongoing. These developments caught observers and experts of the contemporary Arab world off guard—mainly because the overwhelming focus of most scholars had been on the remarkable resilience of authoritarian systems of governance in the region (see Gause 2011). Even a recent volume on social movements in the Middle East—an excellent collection of articles published just before the Arab Spring broke out—worked from the premise that the resilient authoritarian conditions that characterized the region provided little in the way of objective conditions, let alone movement resources, for popular mobilizations and revolt (Beinin and Vairel 2011).[1] In short, scholars of social movements, political scientists, and/or the whole array of policy experts assumed that the resiliently limited political opportunity structures in the Arab world were the decisive factors militating against the possibility of widespread social and political mobilization in the region.

Given the apparent strength of authoritarianism in the region, why did political opportunities suddenly open up in January of 2011? Why were those openings so transitory? In short, how can one explain the sudden ebbing and flowing of political opportunity structures during the Arab Spring and its aftermath? To that end, this chapter examines various components of the social movement framework—namely grievances, resource mobilization, and political opportunity structures—in the context of the pre– and post–Arab Spring Middle East. A wealth of scholarship has documented the widespread and intensifying grievances in the region fueled by deteriorating socioeconomic conditions, growing poverty rates, unaccountable repression, corruption, and the narrowing of networks of power and privilege. Scholars have also identified important facilitating conditions in the decade prior to the outbreak of the Arab Spring—ones driven by such factors as the spread of regional satellite television networks, the increased use of new social media, and the rise of a new generation of activists eager to experiment with new, informal forms of networking. Lynch (2012, 67) described these as contributing to a structural transformation in the Arab public sphere(s), increasing the possibilities of translating the simmering grievances in the region into collective action.

Yet, scholars of social movements tell us that grievances and facilitating conditions do not necessarily translate into popular mobilization, especially in the face of what seemed to be a highly unfavorable set of political opportunity structures in the region. Hence, the third component of this chapter will investigate the dynamics that led to sudden openings in the political opportunity structures in many states of the region. In part, these can be explained by the cumulative effects of years of state repression—eventually surpassing "threshold levels" as a result of particularly arbitrary and lethal acts of state violence against ordinary citizens. The waves of popular mobilization that ensued, in turn, rebounded into the political arena, activating a parallel politics of contestation within many of the regimes that transformed minor cracks in their internal institutional alliances into genuine political opportunities for sustained social mobilization and, in some cases, regime change. In short, through a dynamic, if contingent, process, political opportunity structures that had at best been hidden and latent in the pre–Arab Spring era, were transformed and opened up overnight by the recursive dynamics unleashed by the process of social mobilization itself. In the concluding remarks, we will investigate briefly why it has been so difficult to sustain these dynamics, leading in most cases to the counterrevolutionary reconsolidation of previous authoritarian regime structures.

On the Eve of the Arab Spring(s): Widespread Socioeconomic and Political Grievances

On the eve of the Arab Spring, objective socioeconomic and political conditions in the region were ripe for oppositional mobilization. Initially, in the early postcolonial Arab world, many of the regimes had formulated "nationalist-populist social pacts" with their populations—a series of implicit, informal, but collective agreements specifying the norms and institutions that would underpin relations between these regimes and their societies. Heydemann (2007) has outlined several features of these postcolonial pacts that include: a preference for redistribution over growth; a preference for states over markets; a preference for protecting local markets from global trade; and an emphasis on the organic unity of the polity. The key to these informal agreements was both their reciprocal nature—bringing state and society together into a series of mutually binding obligations—and their relative success. Early on, the Arab world was able to boast some impressive results. These included high rates of economic growth and significant steps, such as land reform, toward redressing some of the huge imbalances of wealth and power in the region that had grown up during the colonial period. Such redistributive successes were financed by the influx of significant amounts of both strategic and financial rent from investment and/or bilateral aid flowing from oil revenues.

Recent decades, however, have seen the substance of these "pacts" whittled away as the regime's informal redistributive commitments have given way to increasing economic and political concentrations of power. While the regimes have shown remarkable "adaptive capacities," keeping some of the normative and institutional elements of the founding pacts while creating new, more narrowly based and hegemonic governing arrangements, the substance of these informal pacts have gradually been emptied by a variety of processes (Heydemann 2007; Heydemann and Leenders 2013). I will touch on three such processes, which I argue have been particularly important in laying fertile soil for the Arab Spring revolt. They include: 1) the turn towards neoliberal economic policies in the region and the resulting increase in poverty levels, unemployment, and concentrations of wealth; 2) the narrowing of political networks of power in the region—as symbolized by the increasingly prevalent move toward family rule, if not dynastic succession, among the republics as well as the monarchies; and 3) the increasing reliance of all regimes on the coercive and surveillance power of their police and security forces.

Theoretically, the neoliberal turn in the Middle East was designed to raise productivity and improve living standards, especially in rural areas where many countries in the region were felt to have a comparative advantage. The reality, however, was quite the opposite. Despite the rigorous and "exemplary" implementation of market-oriented reforms in Tunisia, for example, conditions for the majority living in the rural and semi-urban peripheries were described as a "nightmare," featuring as they did increased levels of poverty, rising levels of land concentration, and decreasing levels of employment. As noted by one analyst, "the workers have become beggars" (Droz-Vincent 2011a, 130). In Egypt, Lesch (2012) wrote of similar effects on rural society, including increasing rents for tenant farmers and decreasing delivery of state support in crucial areas such as subsidies for pesticides and fertilizers, the provision of electricity, water, and phone service, along with a more general drop in state investment in rural infrastructure. Indeed, on the eve of Egypt's uprising, it was estimated that close to 50 percent of the population was living in poverty (Kandil 2012, 216).[2] In Syria, where a tentative program of market-oriented reform accelerated in the mid-2000s after the consolidation of power by Bashar al-Assad, the Ba'ath Party's policy of promoting a "social market economy" similarly led to increasing rates of poverty, unemployment, and falling living standards, especially in the more peripheral areas of the country outside of central Aleppo and Damascus. Indeed, while aggregate poverty rates in Syria have risen dramatically, reaching 33 percent in the years leading up to the uprising, these rates have been particular high in the provinces where the revolts have been waged. The northeast, in the central areas around Homs and Hama, and in the south around Deraa, where the Syrian uprising first began, experienced the highest poverty rates (International Crisis Group 2011).

Socioeconomic conditions in the region's urban areas have also become increasingly precarious for the majority of the population. Unemployment levels have been among the highest in the world on a regional basis, reaching 25 percent as compared to the global average of around 14 percent (Filiu 2011, 32; Shehata 2012, 107), with unemployment rates in countries like Yemen reaching levels as high as 40 percent (Fattah 2011, 80). The intensification of privatization in the last two decades has had a particularly pernicious effect on the region's working classes. Veltmeyer has estimated that the number of workers in privatized corporations in Egypt fell precipitously, while the working conditions for those remaining have undergone "a massive downgrading" typified by wage reductions, the absence of medical and social insurance, and greater job insecurity (2011, 612). The employment prospects for the region's burgeoning youth population have also suffered a steep decline, with estimates of youth unemployment in Egypt as high as 50 percent. Indeed, Shehata (2012) reveals that 75 percent of new job entrants into the Egyptian labor market must wait at least five years for their first job. The situation is even worse for the educated youth of the country, over 95 percent of who were unemployed in the mid-2000s. This has severely disrupted the life path of many of the region's youth and contributed to high levels of social frustration, symbolized perhaps most poignantly by the fact that "the Middle

East has the highest rate of delayed marriages in the developing world" (Shehata 2012, 108).

In addition to growing rates of poverty and resiliently high rates of unemployment, a powerful engine of social frustration has been the perception and reality of rising inequality, a clear violation of the equity-oriented normative foundations of the social pacts of the early postcolonial Arab world. Scholars of Egypt's political economy, for example, write of an "ever-widening gap between a few rich and the poor masses of society" (Holger 2012, 254), with neoliberal policies having effectively transferred wealth from the middle classes to "a tiny layer of the country's elite" (Veltmeyer 2011, 612). According to some estimates, 15 percent of Egypt's population controls virtually all of the country's wealth (Lesch 2012, 28). A similarly regressive trend in the distribution of wealth has been reported in Ba'athist Syria, with 20 percent of the population consuming almost half of the country's GNP, leaving the bottom 20 percent of the population to consume only 8 percent of the country's GNP (Haddad 2012). Driving the increasing concentrations of wealth across the region has been the dual tendency within neoliberal policies to raise revenues through regressive taxation while decreasing levels of state social expenditure. Soliman, for example, writes of the shift from a rentier state to a "predatory tax state" in Egypt that has featured the implementation of an "inflation tax" (the printing of money) and a sales tax, both of which hit workers and lower-level civil servants with fixed salaries the hardest (2012, 54). At the same time, the new system of income tax has reduced tax burdens for corporate and professional elites. These changes have been coupled with broad-based reductions in state social expenditures, especially with respect to the subsidization of fuel and basic foodstuffs. Asya al-Meehy (2011), for example, has written of the deterioration in both the amount and quality of traditional *baladi* bread in Egypt; similar processes have been underway for years throughout the Arab world. When combined with the effects of the 2008 global financial downturn, consequent reductions in the flow of remittance income, and increases in food prices, the effect of this regional turn towards neoliberalism has led to "systematic economic pressures" being placed on the region's popular and salaried middle classes, eventually driving them, as Soliman writes, into "the ranks of the opposition" (2012, 61).

Contributing further to the deepening popular resentment towards the political status quo has been the narrowing of networks of power and privilege in the region. This was symbolized by the growing hegemony of presidential families and their corrupt entourages, such as the Mubaraks in Egypt and the Ben Alis in Tunisia—especially the latter's wife and her family, who was sometimes referred to as the "Marie Antoinette of Tunisia" (Gelvin 2012, 40). Also fanning the flames was the increasing power of the "sons of the regime" in Syria, which revolved around the president's cousin Rami Makhlouf, whose businesses (especially SyriaTel) in the early days of the Syrian uprising were targeted and destroyed by protesters (Haddad 2012). With respect to the "networks of privilege" around the Saleh family in Yemen, Carapico similarly writes of popular disgust at "the grotesque enrichment of the regime cronies at the expense of the many" (2013, 124). Meanwhile, the majority of Yemen's citizens had to contend with "deteriorating standards of living; obscenely bad hospitals, and roads; skyrocketing price of meat, staples, and even clean water; the lack of jobs for college and high-school graduates . . . [and] grandiose pageants of presidential power." According to Carapico, "these and other daily insults fed popular alienation, despair, and frustration, most notably among the youth" (2013, 124). Compounding and eventually igniting these frustrations was the move toward institutionalizing the power of these networks through dynastic succession—the transfer of political power within the family (as had already taken place in Syria in 2000). In Egypt, for example, scholars described the possibility of Mubarak passing power onto his son Gamal as "one of the most sensitive issues for the 'Egyptian street' " (Holger 2012). This served to "galvanize unusual levels of popular outrage," as was demonstrated during the 2010 assembly elections by the systematic destruction of election posters depicting Gamal (Filiu 2011, 87).[3]

The major underlying source of political frustration in the region has been the myriad legal, institutional, and coercive obstacles to any kind of civic or political life. Citizens of most of the region's republics have lived within legal environments underpinned by longstanding emergency decrees that have resulted in numerous restrictions when trying to participate in civic life. Kienle has noted that, "authoritarian regimes in more or less subtle ways controlled almost all major [societal] organizations" (2012, 532). It has also rendered virtually meaningless their participation in political life—with already highly restricted systems of "liberalized" autocracies experiencing processes of "deliberalization" in the years prior to the outbreak of the Arab Spring, notably in Egypt in the late 2000s (Lesch 2012), with elections being increasingly restricted across the region if not cancelled altogether.[4] Finally, citizens in all countries have faced increasingly unaccountable and violent police and security forces. Gelvin, for example, noted in Tunisia an "all-pervasive security apparatus [designed] to monitor, frighten, and repress the population" (2012, 39).[5] Kienle (2012) pointed to the complete unwillingness of any of the region's regimes to respect universal standards of human and political rights. It was not surprising, therefore, that particularly brutal forms of state violence inflicted by police and security officials against ordinary citizens generated intense sociopolitical anger—referred to in the Algerian context as *hogra*, defined as "something worse than scorn and disdain, a mixture of vilification and humiliation" (Filiu 2011, 31). In trying to explain the salience of such anger, Filiu remarked that "it is impossible to categorize and measure the intensity of the disillusion of those Arab youngsters when confronting such an impasse blocking his/her legitimate desire to contribute to collective activity," and that, "for many, there just seems to be 'no future' " (2011, 35).

Hence, the Arab world prior to the outbreak of the Arab Spring was ripe with objective conditions conducive to widespread popular dissent. Rising levels of poverty and inequality, narrowing networks of power and privilege, and the consolidation of increasingly repressive and unaccountable systems of state violence across the region presented citizens of most countries in the Arab world with great cause to seek fundamental changes in their social, economic, and political circumstances. Yet, such widespread grievances do not translate by themselves into collection action—this depends on the existence of two crucial factors: the cultivation of mobilizational resources by agents of collective action; and the emergence of political opportunities through which agents of mobilization can push their collective agendas. It is to how these two crucial factors manifested themselves in the period leading up to the outbreak of the Arab Spring in the Middle East that we now turn.

Resource Mobilization Dynamics Prior to the Outbreak of the Arab Spring(s)

Despite the resilience of authoritarian systems of governance in the Arab world, the decade prior to the outbreak of the Arab Spring also witnessed a relatively hidden build-up of new forms of oppositional "social capital" that would become crucial in determining the impact and scope of the uprisings. Underlying this development of mobilizational resources in the Arab world was what Lynch has described as "deep structural changes in the Arab public sphere," brought about, in particular, by the growth of new media in the region symbolized by the emergence of Al Jazeera (2012, 67). For many years, what existed of an Arab public sphere had been dominated by the sum total of the region's massive security apparatus, which sought to control the flow of information both within as well as across borders. The Al Jazeera phenomenon not only technologically challenged these authoritarian instincts, making such rigid control "increasingly impossible," it also began a process of constructing "a radically new Arab public sphere" that opened up space for trenchant critiques of politics in the region (Lynch 2012, 75).

Two particular impacts of the emergence of this new Arab public sphere were crucial to the dynamics unleashed by the Arab Spring protests: 1) the use of a common set of discourses and repertoires, and 2) the emergence of a cascading dynamic across much of the Arab world. Lynch, for example, argues that the Arab Spring uprisings "unfolded as a single, unified narrative of protest," featuring common slogans such as "the people want the end of the regime," the call for dignity (*karama*), bread (*aish*), and nonviolence (*silmiyya*), and the declaration of Fridays as "days of rage" (2012, 8). This new, more open, critical, and bold Arab public sphere also contributed to the cascading effects of the Tunisian and Egyptian uprisings across the Arab world. "The televised Tunisian miracle," wrote Lynch, "is what galvanized the Egyptians and convinced them that they too could hope for real change" (2012, 88). This success, in turn, had a similar effect in more distant countries, such as Bahrain and Yemen, despite the latter's very limited Internet penetration rates. As one protester in Yemen declared, "Thank you Tunisia for your inspiration" (Lynch 2012, 83). Even in Syria, a country that many felt would be immune from the dynamics of the Arab Spring, commentators remarked on the existence of "a feverish atmosphere of anticipation . . . as people sensed that events in Tunisia and Egypt had changed political opportunity structures in their country as well" (Leenders and Heydemann 2012, 141).

The development of a more participatory regional Arab public sphere also reverberated back into the various national arenas in the decade prior to the Arab uprisings. The locus of this activism was less in the realm of the region's formal oppositional representatives—be they political parties or civil-society representatives—which remained, to varying degrees, contained and controlled by existing authoritarian systems of "liberalized authoritarianism." Rather, this participatory dynamic emerged, by and large, from within the ranks of extra-institutional oppositional movements. Although political analysts may have missed the political significance of these developments, they were not unknown, and did not come about completely unexpectedly. As Abdelrahman argued when writing of Egypt's "decade of protest" prior to the outbreak of its Arab Spring, "social and political change . . . [did] not arise from a vacuum [but rather was] . . . the result of a long process of accumulation, mobilization, networking, and the evolution of a different, more inclusive political culture. Movements and groups almost always build upon experiences of previous groups and can, in the process, be absorbed into larger and newer projects" (2011, 423).

Throughout the region, these mobilizational experiences were numerous and took several forms. These ranged from huge foreign-policy-oriented demonstrations in a variety of Arab countries in the early to mid-2000s (in support of Palestine in 2000; Iraq in 2003; the rival mass mobilizations that surrounded the Lebanese Independence Intifada in 2005), to percolating activism by professional syndicates in many Arab countries. They also included dramatic increases in the protest activities of labor, especially in Egypt after 2004, where there emerged what was described as "the longest and strongest wave of worker protests since the end of World War Two" (Bishara 2012, 85). The rising extra-institutional activism of increasingly politicized youth networks throughout the region also contributed to the experience. This steady, if scattered, flow of protest activity in many Arab countries helped to explain the surprising scope of Arab Spring protests in at least three significant ways. The first revolves around the cumulative, horizontal expansion of extra-institutionalized protest networks, a process that Abdelrahman (2011) argued facilitated diffusion and brokerage across a variety of protest constituencies—helping to spread new ideas, new strategic calculations, and new repertoires and modes of political activism, not only within particular national arenas but also between global and local ones.

The second important impact was the nascent development of cross-cutting ties within previously highly fragmented and localized political opposition movements. Youth activists across the region were particularly deliberate in trying to foster the development of cross-ideological and cross-class linkages—symbolized by the efforts of the April 6 Movement in Egypt to support that country's budding grassroots labor movement in 2008. These networking processes helped to foster the development of "a new dynamic and inclusive political culture" among oppositional activists (Abdelrahman 2011, 408) that, during the heat of the Arab Spring protests, would complicate the efforts of incumbent regimes to employ successfully their long-standing practice of divide and rule (Goldstone 2011).

The third cumulative effect of this array of protest activity and networking was the nibbling away at the wall of fear that all regimes carefully cultivated. The propensity of pre–Arab Spring protest activity to target increasingly political issues of national (not local) importance is illustrative of this process. This included the signing of the Damascus Declaration by Syrian opposition activists in 2005 despite the post–Damascus Spring repression of oppositional activity, as well as the campaign against dynastic succession by the *Kefaya* movement in Egypt, whose activities were described as having "breathed new life into Egyptian politics" (Lesch 2012, 33). It also includes the rising militancy of labor in the region, particularly in Egypt and Tunisia, the scope of whose protests expanded to target national, rather than localized, leaders and institutions (corporatist trade union federations, parliaments, councils of ministers, etc.) (see Shehata 2012). Abdelrahman argues forcefully, for example, that all of these mobilizational developments were cumulative, with the success of each initiative contributing "to the creation of something bigger" (2011, 423).[6]

The final facilitating condition that emerged in the immediate pre–Arab Spring era was the learning processes that surrounded the skillful instrumentalization of new social media by youth activists. By the time of its uprising, for example, Tunisia was reputed to have one of the highest rates of connectivity in the Arab world (Murphy 2011, 300). This is evidenced by the fact that over 2 million Tunisians changed their Facebook profiles to a revolutionary icon in one day (Lynch 2012, 77). A similar expansion of online access emerged in pre–Arab Spring Egypt, with over 160,000 blog sites being recorded by 2008—many of which were openly critical of Egypt's political conditions (Filiu 2011, 46; Shehata 2012, 117). This increasing public access to cyberspace was further exemplified by the burgeoning number of Internet cafes throughout the region—even in tightly controlled Syria. Paralleling this expansion of the online world in many parts of the region was the dramatic increase in the use of mobile phones, with Lynch (2012) arguing that in some locales, rates of use were on par with those in Europe. This expanding world of online access offered several advantages to would-be revolutionary activists—facilitating new forms of oppositional organization that ultimately forged shifts, if not openings, in political opportunity structures, mainly because it was difficult for state security forces to completely shut down their more hidden networking and mobilizational activities. Online opposition activists, for example, developed networks that tended to be loose, lacking in centralized and hierarchical leadership, and characterized by political orientations described as ideologically flexible, hybrid, and cosmopolitan—features that came to define the Arab Spring protests themselves. This is aptly described by Abdelrahman as "orderly without an organization, inspired without a leader, and single-minded without a genuine political ideology" (2011, 423). In turn, these new styles of networking and mobilization fostered significantly reconfigured structures of political opportunities in the region. They reduced the "transaction costs" of promoting oppositional information flows across a wider audience and increased the costs of regime repression as a result of their ability to transmit information about regime abuse to external actors—all of which weakened the ability of regimes to maintain their hegemonic "walls of fear" (Lynch 2011, 304).

Yet, all of these potentially significant developments in resource mobilization on the part of a nascent opposition within many Arab countries prior to the outbreak of the Arab Spring(s) did not necessarily translate into a revolutionary situation. They cannot be used as an analytical tool through which history can be read backwards as there was no inevitability as to their impact or result—especially given the reality of authoritarian resilience in the region. As scholars have well documented, civil society in all Arab countries remained weak and politically ineffectual. In the case of Syria, it was utterly crushed. Furthermore, political society remained tightly controlled. Despite the efforts of a new generation of extra-institutional activists to forge inclusive, crosscutting oppositional networks, most analysts agree that these efforts remained a work in progress, unable to overcome their predominantly localized and atomized nature. Facebook, for instance, did not by itself "kill Mubarak," in contrast to some popular claims (Barber and Youniss 2013). Indeed, as a testament to the surprising nature of the various mobilizations that transpired during the season of the Arab Spring(s), most activists did not expect their efforts to have been so richly rewarded. In order to come to a fuller understanding of the complex dynamics that led to the unfolding of the various Arab protests, we need to turn our analytical attention to the final prong in the social movement framework—political opportunity structures—and address the overarching questions posed in this chapter: Why did political opportunities suddenly open during the early phases of the Arab Spring(s)? Why were these openings seemingly so fleeting?

Forging Political Opportunities: Social Mobilization, Intra-Regime Contestation, and the Role of Contingency

According to Alimi and Meyer (2011, 477), the unity of the ruling elite coalition is "the critical variable" in determining the nature of political opportunities for those wanting to promote transformative social mobilization. In a variation on this theme in the context of the Middle East, Heydemann and Leenders (2013, 5) suggest that the key to the resilience of authoritarian systems of governance in the region has been not so much their willingness to use coercive force, but rather their ability to adapt to changing circumstances and stay connected. In short, over the longer term, authoritarian resilience is the result of a regime's "relational qualities," both inside the state itself as well as between the regime/state and its society. As we will see, it was the weakening nature of state-society relations in certain countries, combined with the emergence of visible cracks in intra-regime relations—sparked by the mobilizational process itself—that opened up opportunities, not only for social mobilization, but also in some cases for political transformation.

First, there were signs that political institutions created in the early stages of many of the nationalist-populist authoritarian regimes of the region—namely ruling parties—were experiencing declines in capacity and legitimacy in the years leading up to the Arab Spring(s). Soliman (2012), for example, has written about the increasing weakness of the regime-dominated National Democratic Party in Egypt in the years before the uprising. This is symbolized by the decreasing representation of labor within the party, the increasing dominance of neoliberal elites whose social and political roots within Egypt were described as being "very shallow," and the more general increase in the number of independent parliamentarians that, Soliman has argued, pointed to a more general fragmentation of Mubarak's political apparatus. These dynamics were paralleled in Syria by the declining representativeness and influence of the Ba'ath Party, a principle pillar of Ba'athist legitimacy in the regime's early years. Initially a channel for the transfer of power to Syria's marginalized classes in both rural and peripheral urban areas—giving them both a greater voice and a share of the regime's resources—the Ba'ath Party gradually abandoned its social roots in favor of the interests of Syria's urban elites. This increasingly left Syria's more marginalized constituencies "to their own devices" (International Crisis Group 2011, 16). Indeed, the role of the Ba'ath Party itself in managing state-society relations in Syria gradually gave way to the more dominant influence of Syria's security apparatus, transforming the initial redistributive logic of Ba'ath Party governance into one characterized by its more extractive and predatory qualities. The result, as Caroline Donati has so poignantly argued, was "the diminishing relevance of the Ba'ath Party as a mechanism for the neo-patrimonial mediation between state and society" (2009, 347). Not only did this weaken regimes' ability to manage state-society relations, it also pointed to the more general weakening of the political apparatus vis-à-vis the parallel centers of power within these regimes revolving around the military and/or security apparatuses. This was made visible in both Egypt and Syria by the targeting of ruling-party buildings during the initial stages of their respective uprisings. In the post-uprising period in Egypt, the narrowly based neoliberal political class seemed to utterly collapse in the face of challenges weighed against them.[7]

The changing dynamics of relations between the various power centers of the regimes affected by the Arab spring(s) proved decisive in determining the extent of political opportunities for politically transformative social mobilization. These dynamics were symbolized by the unwillingness of the military in several countries (as in Tunisia and Egypt)—or at least sections of the military (as in Libya, Yemen, and to a much lesser extent in Syria)—to fire on protesters and/or support the existing regime. To some, this was a surprising development. Regimes had spent significant resources trying to "coup-proof" their regimes. They had either channeled significant resources in support of their corporate interests (large budgets, significant modernization programs, access to opportunities in the private and/or black market sectors, etc.). Or, they had guaranteed the compliance of the military through extensive mechanisms of political control (intensive oversight of security services, creation of privileged and loyal military units, use of foreign mercenaries, etc.) (see Bellin 2004). The result was a seemingly cooperative and, in some cases, co-opted relationship between political and military elites, allowing the former to call upon the latter for support in particularly dire circumstances—such as the repression of the Islamist insurgency in Egypt in the 1980s and early 1990s (Droz-Vincent 2011b).

Yet, behind the surface of this seeming regime unity were seeds of dissent. In short, certain regimes were more "coup-proofed" than others. In some, latent fault lines formed around the insufficient satisfaction of the military's corporate interests (such as in Tunisia, Egypt, and Libya); in others, these grievances aligned with primordial fault lines inside the military itself (as was the case in Yemen and to a much lesser extent Syria). Kandil (2012) has extensively documented the growing sense of grievance within the Egyptian military. Challenging the perceived wisdom that it had enjoyed extensive privileges within the Egyptian ruling coalition, he described the military's socioeconomic privileges as being "humble" in relation to the luxurious living standards enjoyed by the country's upper-middle and elite classes. He also described its "reputed economic empire" as being "considerably more modest" than what was commonly believed. The military's financial power within the regime itself had also suffered a consistent, if not precipitous, decline, symbolized by the fall of military expenditure as a percentage of GNP, from its peak of 33 percent in the 1970s to its nadir of 2.2 percent in 2010 (Kandil 2012, 182–3). On the strategic side, Kandil (2012, 187–90) has argued that latent corporate resentment within Egyptian military circles cut even deeper—fueled by the constraining and depoliticizing influence of Egypt's geostrategic alliance with the United States, which ensured that its military capacity would remain subordinate to that of Israel. All of this contributed to a significant decline in the military's relative influence within the Egyptian ruling coalition. It was left trailing behind the rising influence of Gamal Mubarak and his coterie of neoliberal elites, as well as that of Egypt's police and security forces, which benefited greatly from the decisive evolution of the Egyptian regime "from a military to a police state" during the Mubarak era (Kandil 2012, 199).[8] In short, on the eve of its uprising in 2011, the cohesion and unity of Egypt's ruling coalition was by no means secured, brought into question by the various grievances flowing beneath the surface within the Egyptian military sector.

Latent grievances of an entirely different nature permeated the military sectors in the Arab Spring countries of Yemen and Syria. These were caused by ethnic, religious, and/or tribal factionalism within these regimes as a whole, which cut across the various weakly institutionalized power centers. In Syria, divisions of a sectarian nature have been kept in check by the coercive hegemony of, for the most part, Alawite-dominated security networks that have managed to sustain the compliance and subordination of the predominantly Sunni military rank and file. In Yemen, whose modern state is the result of an informal power-sharing agreement among the country's dominant tribal elements, the coherence and unity of the state—and of the military institutions inside that state—depended upon vigilant attention to a balanced distribution of resources and power across the various dominant tribal groupings (Knights 2013). In the years leading up to Yemen's uprising, that balancing act was replaced by President Saleh's attempt to increase the power of his own family networks within the state, including its military apparatus. This upset the balance of power within Yemen's "complex, overlapping and competitive network of families, clans, and tribes" (Fattah 2011, 82). According to Michael Knights, this represented "a breach of the contract" upon which the Yemeni state—and

Saleh's leadership of that state—was based (2013, 276). Given the degree to which this Yemeni power-sharing tribal contract permeated all formal institutions of the state, including the military, the preconditions existed for its partial defection.

The question remains, however, as to what transforms grievances—be they percolating throughout society or within the state apparatus itself—into the type of collective action that can challenge existing political equations. Moreover, what is the relationship between these two processes? What happens when the two sets of grievances—societal and intra-regime—interactively collide? It is within this recursive and iterative analytical space that a more complex understanding of the political opportunities—and political limitations—of the Arab Spring uprisings can be found. The most important point to be made here is that there is really no way of predicting in advance how these iterative processes will unfold and what factors will prove decisive, despite the existence of numerous facilitating preconditions that have been documented above. Goodwin (2011) rightly stresses the importance of contingency and unpredictability in transforming seemingly small and insignificant events into catalysts for major social and political upheavals.

Nonetheless, there were a series of crucial factors in both launching the cascading Arab Spring protests and igniting processes of contestation within several Arab regimes themselves. I will highlight three such factors that helped to translate objective conditions for effective social mobilization into significant political action on the ground: 1) inopportune episodes of arbitrary state violence; 2) the initial use of nonviolent strategies of popular mobilization; and 3) the ambivalent reactions of regional and global actors. Much intellectual effort has been expended by social movement theorists to unpack the relationship between state violence and social mobilization. Schneider has suggested that this work has produced some of social movement theory's "most robust findings" (2011, 481). It is argued, for example, that arbitrary state violence can produce moral outrage, increase the solidarity of core activists, sensitize normally passive members of a population to the need for change, and bring external actors in as allies—all the while weakening the legitimacy of the regime in question. In the various national contexts within which Arab Spring mobilizations occurred, one can point to numerous examples of arbitrary state violence that seemed to activate these dynamics. These include the administrative abuse of Mohammad Bouazizi, which resulted in his self-immolation in Tunisia, and the murder in police custody of Khaled Said and Ahmad Shaaba in Egypt, which laid the groundwork for significant mobilizations among youth activists. Also critical were the torture of several high school students and the subsequent torture and murder of the thirteen-year-old Hamza al-Khattib in southern Syria, which sparked the ongoing uprising there, as well as the firing on crowds of peaceful protesters in Sanaa's Change Square and Manama's Pearl Roundabout, in Yemen and Bahrain respectively. All sparked feelings of moral outrage among the general public above what might be called "threshold levels," therefore facilitating the efforts of social activists to promote mass demonstrations. There is no objective understanding of what these threshold levels might in fact be, with Goodwin arguing that they "are not simply a given, but may shift radically in the space of a few days or even hours" (2011, 454). It is nonetheless clear that these particular episodes of arbitrary state violence proved crucial in sparking the mobilization processes that gave birth to the various Arab Springs.

The second crucial factor in translating mass social contestation into genuine political opportunities was their predominantly nonviolent nature. As Nepstad (2011) argues, nonviolent strategies of social mobilization under certain conditions complicate the calculations, if not immobilizing the decision-making process, of state actors when it comes to the use of repression, especially those within the military. In particular, she argues that when the military shares a common identity with the protesters (as in Tunisia and Egypt), when protests reach the kind of mass levels that make repression costly (as in many of the Arab Spring contexts), and when the military itself can perceive benefits arising from defection (certainly the case in Tunisia and Egypt, to a partial extent in Libya and Yemen, and to a very limited extent in Syria), the possibility of a temporary but politically transformative alliance between the military (or portions of the military) and the protesters emerges. It should be stressed that this equation linking nonviolent protests to military defections is a contingent one—note the inability of three plus months of heroic nonviolent demonstrations in the early stages of the uprising in Syria to effect significant degrees of defections from the regime's armed forces. But, where regime control over the military apparatus was not hegemonic, the possibility existed that non-violent mass demonstrations could change the incentive structure within the military's decision-making processes, activating latent but real opportunities for them to redress their own grievances by joining forces with protesters in seeking political change.

The third factor influencing the possibility, timing, and outcome of processes of social mobilization is the influence and post-mobilization reactions of external actors. Alimi and Meyer, for example, stress that political opportunities are "nested" within a larger international structure of political alliances, adding that, "dissidents routinely look beyond their governments to make judgements about the likelihood of support from outside the state" (2011, 477). In the unfolding of the various Arab Springs, these factors, in conjunction with the internal dynamics of the regimes themselves, seem to have been crucial in determining the degree to which political opportunities remained opened or suddenly closed once social-mobilization processes were unleashed. In short, they had a decisive impact on the degree to which the ensuing iterative processes between protesters and aggrieved power centers within the state were synergetic or not. Clearly, the emergence of robust international support for the uprising in Libya proved crucial in the eventual ousting of the Gaddafi regime in Libya—providing tangible and powerful incentives and resources for Libyan protesters to sustain their antiregime campaign. In Tunisia and Egypt, the nonviolent nature of oppositional mobilization handcuffed the external allies of the Ben Ali and Mubarak regimes in the West, removing the possibility that they might sanction a repressive regime response and, hence, gave crucial time and space for the iterative dynamics between protesters and the military to play out. Moreover, the tightness of regional alliances among the various monarchies of the region—backed by the strategic, if tacit, support of the United States and benefitting from a "learning process" with respect to the perceived consequences of the weakness of coercive regime responses in the Arab states of the Mashreq—ensured that oppositional social mobilization, even in Bahrain, where protests became widespread, would face resiliently limited and, ultimately, closed, political opportunity structures, removing the possibility of a synergetic iterative process emerging. Finally, where external involvement has been robust but in competition—as became the case with Syria—political opportunity structures remain in flux. Their further opening or subsequent closing has become increasingly dependent on the ways in which this external competition ultimately unfolds.

Conclusion

It is clear from the analytical narrative outlined above that the opening up of political opportunity structures in the Arab world in 2010–11 cannot be explained solely with reference to the existence of "objective conditions" in the region—be they related to the existence of widespread socioeconomic and/or political grievances among the population or latent grievances within the regimes themselves. These were certainly significant—forming the landscape without which there would have been no Arab Spring(s)—but by themselves, they were insufficient to explain the timing, let alone the amazing scope, of the various uprisings. Grievances may have been plentiful among the region's populace and the resources and experience needed to promote widespread forms of social mobilization may have accumulated in the period before the uprisings. The political divisions within the various political structures in the region may also have been festering—creating latent political opportunity structures that social movement entrepreneurs might have been able to take advantage of given favorable circumstances. Yet, in the absence of factors that unleash new iterative and dynamic processes—ones that force changes in the calculations of actors at a variety of political levels—be it within society, the state, or the regional/global arena, it is unlikely that any of these grievances, mobilizational resources, or political opportunities will be translated into significant political transformation. In the case of the Arab Spring(s), the most important factors seem to have been the timing of particularly brutal acts of state violence, the predominantly nonviolent and mass nature of the protests, and the ways in which the various national political arenas were integrated into regional and global alliance networks. Such factors provided greater or lesser space for iterative processes to build up.

What do these analytical narratives of the various Arab Springs contribute to the debates surrounding the concept of political opportunity structures? It certainly suggests, first and foremost, that political opportunity structures cannot be analyzed in a static manner. Rather, they ebb and flow as a result of a dynamic process of interaction with processes of social mobilization themselves; in short, the existence and salience of political opportunity structures are highly contingent. Second, it is also clear that political opportunity structures can emerge due to threats emanating from the political system—threats that can transform a fatalist reluctance to resist into an activist moral outrage—as much as from the apparent weaknesses within regime structures themselves, weaknesses which in authoritarian political systems can be extremely difficult to detect. In turn, this suggests that attempts to define the concept of political opportunity structures in a narrow manner ignore the inherently important element of uncertainty and unpredictability in determining what kinds of political opportunity structures are relevant to any historical situation of social contestation and in what manner they unfold. In sum, it appears that the "sponge-like" nature of the concept of political opportunity structures may retain analytical, though perhaps not "scientific," utility.

The highly contingent nature of political opportunity structures is plain to see in the post–Arab Spring(s) Middle East. As processes of social contestation and mobilization have diminished and fragmented (though certainly not disappeared) in the region, political opportunity structures have also diminished. In some countries—such as Tunisia, where democratic regime change has been achieved—there remains the challenging task of cleansing pre-uprising political structures of the resilient presence of political elements from the past regime. In other countries, however, regime change has been extremely limited—characterized at best by a change in the personnel at the top (Yemen), by the coexistence of a widespread revolt with a powerfully resilient regime structure (Syria), by the complete reversal of initially promising democratic change and the retrenchment of military power (Egypt), or in the case of all the monarchies, by no political change at all (Bahrain et al.). In short, as the dynamics of social mobilization diminished (or have been repressed), the iterative processes and pressures that were able to forge political opportunities within many (but not all) regimes in the region have also diminished, giving back space to actors within the political realm to reconstruct or reassert their political hegemony. Yet, given the continued existence of objectively unfavorable socioeconomic conditions in the region and the now empowered nature of popular forces, it will be much more difficult for networks of power to protect this re-found space. Hence, rather than returning to the previous status quo of resilient authoritarian systems of governance, it is more likely that the Arab world is about to enter into a period of increased and overt political contestation. This new era will be characterized by continued, if fluctuating and cyclical, efforts on the part of political activists in the region to reignite the kind of iterative processes that temporarily pried open political opportunity structures during the Arab Spring(s).

NOTES

1   Indeed, one of the overarching purposes of that volume is to focus, both empirically and theoretically, on issues of social movement demobilization and fatigue.

2   According to Kandil, the effects were plain to see in the suburbs of Cairo, where 10 million rural migrants "lived in slums with no schools, hospitals, clubs, sewage systems, public transportation, or even police stations [and] which had become a Hobbesian world of violence and vice" (2012, 208).

3   In describing the sum total of these popular frustrations, Holger argued that "people were antagonized by the degree of patronizing arrogance and pretension with which the ruling class, which made politics itself a 'gated community,' communicated to them that they were tedious subjects of the state rather than its citizens" (2012).

4   Lesch (2012) notes the increasing control of elections in the late 2000s by the Egyptian Ministry of the Interior. This started with the municipal council elections of 2008, in which Egypt's ruling party, the National Democratic Party (NDP), won 99 percent of all municipal seats. It is also evident in the blatantly rigged 2010 National Assembly elections, in which the NDP won 94.7 percent of the seats. Holger (2012, 259) has described this as a "tipping point" in terms of social frustration with the ruling elite, especially given the fact that it was popularly believed that the result was engineered by the Ministry of the Interior in order to ensure a smooth process of succession from Hosni Mubarak to his son Gamal. In other republics, national assembly elections were cancelled (Yemen in 2008, Tunisia in 2009) in order to prevent voices of political discontent with the ruling status quo from being electorally expressed.

5   According to Gelvin, "the Tunisian government expanded and intensified repression to such an extent that Human Rights Watch declared Tunisia to be one of the most repressive states in the world" (2012, 58).

6   This increasingly bold dynamic also emerged within Arab cultural circles. Lynch uses the example of Tunisia rapper El General, whose songs became directly critical of the corruption and paternalism of Ben Ali, remarking that "previously, most songs had been indirect, avoiding a frontal denunciation of the political situation. By breaking the taboo, El General became a symbol of the Tunisian Revolution, and his songs became known across almost the entire Arab world" (2012, 239).

Paul Kingston

7   In Syria, by contrast, although the Ba'athist regime clearly lost control of the countryside and the peripheral urban areas of the country, it has still managed to maintain its elite-oriented core political networks, both within its own Alawite community, as well as between these and Syria's other urban-based communal business and religious elites.

8   Indicative of the rising influence of the security forces is the dramatic increase in expenditures on security matters—higher than the military by 2002 at 6 percent of GDP—and the equally significant increase in the number of people employed in the sector, surpassing 2 million by 2002.

REFERENCES

Abdelrahman, Maha. 2011. "The Transnational and the Local: Egyptian Activists and Transnational Protest Networks." *British Journal of Middle East Studies* 38, no. 3: 407–24.

Alimi, Eitan, and David Meyer. 2011. "Seasons of Change: Arab Spring and Political Opportunities." *Swiss Political Science Review* 17, no. 4: 475–9.

Al-Meehy, Asya. 2011. "Meta-Narratives: Unpacking the Revolutions in Egypt and Tunisia." *e-International Relations*, 8 May. http://www.e-ir.info/2011/05/08/transcending-meta-narratives-unpacking-the-revolutions-in-egypt-and-tunisia.

Barber, Brian K., and James Youniss. 2013. "Egyptian Youth Make History: Forging Revolutionary Identity amid Brutality." *Harvard International Review* 34, no. 4: 68–75.

Beinin, Joel, and Frederic Vairel, eds. 2011. *Social Movements, Mobilization, and Contestation in the Middle East and North Africa*. Stanford, CA: Stanford University Press.

Bellin, Eva, 2004. "The Robustness of Authoritarianism in the Middle East: Exceptionalism in Comparative Perspective." *Comparative Politics* 36, no. 2: 139–57.

Bishara, Dina. 2012. "The Power of Workers in Egypt's 2011 Uprising." In *Arab Spring in Egypt: Revolution and Beyond*, edited by Bahgat Korany and Rabab El-Mahdi, 83–104. Cairo: American University of Cairo Press.

Carapico, Sheila. 2013. "No Exit: Yemen's Existential Crisis." In *The Arab Revolts: Dispatches on Militant Democracy in the Middle East*, edited by David McMurray and Amanda Ufheil-Somers, 120–7. Bloomington: Indiana University Press and MERIP.

Donati, Caroline. 2009. *L'Exception Syrienne: Entre Modernization et Resistance*. Paris: Cahiers Libres.

Droz-Vincent, Philippe. 2011a. "A Return of Armies to the Forefront of Arab Politics?" Istituto Affari Internazionali, Working Paper 11/21. http://www.iai.it/pdf/DocIAI/iaiwp1121.pdf.

———. 2011b. "Authoritarianism, Revolutions, Armies and Arab Regime Transitions." *International Spectator* 46, no. 2: 5–21.

Fattah, Khaled. 2011. "Yemen: A Social Intifada in a Republic of Sheikhs." *Middle East Policy* 18, no. 3: 79–85.

Filiu, Jean-Pierre. 2011. *The Arab Revolution: Ten Lessons from the Democratic Uprising.* London: Hurst and Company.

Gause, F. Gregory, III. 2011. "Why Middle East Studies Missed the Arab Spring: the Myth of Authoritarian Stability." *Foreign Affairs* 90, no. 4: 81.

Gelvin, James. 2012. *The Arab Uprisings.* New York: Oxford University Press.

Goldstone, Jack A. 2011. "Cross-Class Coalitions and the Making of the Arab Revolts of 2011." *Swiss Political Science Review* 17, no. 4: 457–62.

Goodwin, Jeff. 2011. "Why We Were Surprised (Again) by the Arab Spring." *Swiss Political Science Review* 17, no. 4: 452–6.

Haddad, Bassam. 2012. *Business Networks in Syria: The Political Economy of Authoritarian Resilience.* Stanford, CA: Stanford University Press.

Heydemann, Steven. 2007. "Social Pacts and the Persistence of Authoritarianism in the Middle East." *In Debating Arab Authoritarianism: Dynamics and Durability in Nondemocratic Regimes,* edited by Oliver Schlumberger, 21–38. Stanford, CA: Stanford University Press.

Heydemann, Steven, and Reinoud Leenders, eds. 2013. Middle East Authoritarianism: Governance, Contestation, and Regime Resilience in Syria and Iran. Stanford, CA: Stanford University Press.

Holger, Albrecht. 2012. "Authoritarian Transformation or Transition from Authoritarianism? Insights on Regime Change in Egypt." In *Arab Spring in Egypt: Revolution and Beyond,* edited by Bahgat Korany and Rabab El-Mahdi, 251–70. Cairo: American University of Cairo Press.

International Crisis Group. 2011. "Popular Protest in North Africa and the Middle East: The Syrian People's Slow-Motion Revolution." Report No. 108, 6 July. http://www.crisisgroup.org/en/regions/middle-east-north-africa/egypt-syria-lebanon/syria/108-popular-protest-in-north-africa-and-the-middle-east-vi-the-syrian-peoples-slow-motion-revolution.aspx.

Kandil, Hazem. 2012. *Soldiers, Spies, and Statesmen: Egypt's Road to Revolt.* London: Verso.

Kienle, Eberhardt. 2012. "Egypt after Mubarak, Tunisia after Ben Ali: Theory, History, and 'the Arab Spring.'" *Economy and Society* 41, no. 4: 532–57.

Knights, Michael. 2013. "The Military Role in Yemen's Protests: Civil-Military Relations in the Tribal Republic." *Journal of Strategic Studies* 36, no. 2: 261–88.

Leenders, Reinoud, and Steven Heydemann. 2012. "Popular Mobilization in Syria: Opportunity and Threat and the Social Networks of Early Risers." *Mediterranean Politics* 17, no. 2: 139–59.

Lesch, Ann. 2012. "Concentrated Power Breeds Corruption, Repression, and Resistance." In *Arab Spring in Egypt: Revolution and Beyond*, edited by Bahgat Korany and Rabab El-   Mahdi, 17–42. Cairo: American University of Cairo Press.

Lynch, Marc, 2011. "After Egypt: The Limits and Promise of Online Challenges to the Authoritarian State." *Perspective on Politics* 9, no. 2: 301–10.

———. 2012. *The Arab Uprisings: The Unfinished Revolutions in the Middle East*. New York: Public Affairs.

Murphy, Emma C. 2011. "The Tunisian Uprising and the Precarious Path to Democracy." *Mediterranean Politics* 16, no. 2: 299–305.

Nepstad, Sharon Erickson. 2011. "Nonviolent Resistance in the Arab Spring: The Critical Role of Military-Opposition Alliances." *Swiss Political Science Review* 17, no. 4: 485–91.

Robinson, Glen E. 2004. "Hamas as a Social Movement." In *Islamic Activism: A Social Movement Theory Approach*, edited by Quintan Wiktorowicz, 112–41. Bloomington: Indiana University Press.

Schneider, Cathy Lisa. 2011. "Violence and State Repression." *Swiss Political Science Review* 17, no. 4: 480–4.

Shehata, Dina. 2012. "Youth Movements and the 25 January Revolution." In *Arab Spring in Egypt: Revolution and Beyond*, edited by Bahgat Korany and Rabab El-Mahdi, 105–24. Cairo: American University of Cairo Press.

Soliman, Samer. 2012. "The Political Economy of Mubarak's Fall." In *Arab Spring in Egypt: Revolution and Beyond*, edited by Bahgat Korany and Rabab El-Mahdi, 43–62. Cairo: American University of Cairo Press.

Veltmeyer, Henry. 2011. "Unrest and Change: Dispatches from the Frontline of a Class War in Egypt." *Globalizations* 8, no. 5: 609–16.

Wiktorowicz, Quintin, ed. 2004. *Islamic Activism: A Social Movement Theory Approach*. Bloomington: Indiana University Press.

"You Taught us to Give an Opinion, Now Learn How to Listen":[1] The Manifold Political Consequences of Chile's Student Movement

Sofia Donoso and Nicolás M. Somma[2]

William Gamson's (1975) path-breaking study conceptualized the political impact of social movements in terms of new advantages (new policies) and/or acceptance by the authority that the movement is challenging. In the last two decades, however, there has been an upsurge of literature that seeks to explain the outcomes of social movements beyond these two dimensions (Amenta et al. 2010; Bosi and Uba 2009; Bosi, Giugni, and Uba 2016). Movements can shape public policies and institutions (Amenta and Caren 2004; Giugni 2004; Uba 2005); the public agenda (Baumgartner and Mahoney 2005; Burstein and Linton 2002; Burstein and Sausner 2003); elections (McAdam and Tarrow 2010); and political parties (Glenn 2005; Heaney and Rojas 2015; LeBas 2011; Piccio 2016; Schwartz 2006; Schlozman 2015). In this way, over the past ten or so years, we have gained purchase on the question of how social movements impact politics in a broader sense. Despite these significant advances, however, extant research often focuses on one of these different outcomes. The links between the different types of social movement impacts thus remain unspecified. This overlooks how various outcomes relate to each other, and above all, how they often are part of processes of scale shift that we commonly observe when examining the development of social movements.

This chapter analyzes the interactive relationships between social movements, policies, and political opportunity structures throughout successive protest waves, and how these relationships, in turn, shape social movements' political impact. We do so by focusing on the student movement in Chile. Since the mid-2000s, protest waves spearheaded by high school and university students have put education at the top of the policy agenda. After massive protests in 2006, the first administration of President Michelle Bachelet (2006–10) reformed the Constitutional Law of Education, bequeathed by the military regime, and introduced new institutions to improve the quality of education. The pressure exerted by students in the 2011 nationwide protests then broadened the scope of the student movement's demands. After regaining power in 2014, part of President Bachelet's policy agenda, which was backed by a broad coalition of center-left political parties, included an overhaul of the education system, a tax reform to make the proposed education reforms financially sustainable, and a new constitution to replace the one left by the military regime.

The student movement in Chile sheds light on the processes of scale shift, which McAdam, Tarrow, and Tilly define as the "change in the number and level of coordinated contentious actions to a different focal point, involving a new range of actors, different objects, and broadened claims" (2001, 331). For example, a scale shift has occurred when an issue, tactic, or frame that had its origins at the local level is adopted at the national level (Soule 2013, 2). The case study analyzed in this chapter also invites us to think dialogically about the impact of social movements. Movements influence policies, and policy changes alter the conditions under which activists mobilize. As Schattschneider famously argued, "new policies create a new politics" (quoted in Pierson 1993, 595).

Yet, as we show in this chapter, the political impact of the Chilean student movement goes beyond its policy outcomes. In line with recent literature that seeks to bridge the relationship between social movements and political parties (Goldstone 2003; Heaney and Rojas 2015; McAdam and Tarrow 2010), we argue that the protest waves led by the student movement have also polarized the dominant center-left coalition internally, and motivated the creation of new political parties and coalitions. In doing so,

Sofia Donoso and Nicolás M. Somma

student protests in Chile have shifted both the content and the terms of the political game.

This chapter draws on interviews with student activists, organizational documents, newspaper accounts, secondary literature, and an original database on protest events for the 2000–12 period. We structure our account as follows. In the first section, we briefly review the literature on the political impacts of social movements. We then analyze the interactive relationship between education policies, shifts in the political opportunity structures, and student protests in Chile since the reinstatement of democracy in 1990. Depicting the growth of Chile's student mobilizations into a nationwide social movement with demands that go beyond the field of education, we analyze the impact of education polices on the student movement and vice versa. At the high school level, successive reforms produced patent inequalities among school types in terms of educational achievements. In higher education, education policies introduced by the military regime and continued by democratic governments increased enrolment rates in higher education, but also produced high levels of indebtedness and discontent. Since the mid-2000s, the articulation of this disgruntlement by student organizations, in turn, put pressure on the political system, gaining important allies within the center-left, who then introduced new education policies.

The last section examines the political impact of the student movement after the 2011 protest wave, and especially beyond its policy outcomes. The center-left coalition, in power between 1990 and 2010, moved to the left when it regained power in 2014 by integrating the Communist Party. We suggest that student mobilizations during 2011 and afterwards were one reason for this move, which ended up polarizing the newly created coalition and contributing to its defeat in the 2017 national elections. Furthermore, student leaders took on the challenge of disputing the center-left coalition's policy agenda from within the political system by competing for parliamentary positions and creating their own political parties. In 2017 a leftist coalition of social movement organizations and political parties, the Frente Amplio (Broad Front), participated in parliamentary and presidential elections. The coalition enjoyed a resounding success for such a novel force: it earned twenty deputies, one senator, and 20.3 percent of the vote for their presidential candidate, Beatriz Sánchez, who was very close to making it to the second round of the elections.

The Political Impact of Social Movements beyond Policies

Social movements can have different types of impacts. These can range from both cultural (e.g., changes in practices or in public opinion) and biographical outcomes (e.g., a lifelong political engagement in the personal life trajectories of activists) to longer-term effects on politics—for example, by creating new values and personal predispositions to participate in collective action throughout life trajectories (Giugni and Grasso 2016). Yet, in this chapter, we focus on the political impact that social movements have on policy and institutional change.

In Gamson's (1975) influential work, this type of outcome is assessed according to two dimensions. First is the acceptance of the social movement by its antagonist, which involves "a change from hostility or indifference to a more positive relationship" (Gamson 1975, 31). Second, Gamson proposes to assess the impact of social movements by identifying the existence of "new advantages"—that is, the reception of the challenging group's claims by the authorities.

While Gamson's proposal paved the way for a comprehensive research agenda on social movements' interaction with the political arena and the resulting political outcomes, several shortcomings have been highlighted. To begin, the idea of acceptance overlooks the fact that social movements might be listened to and then ignored again as the negotiations with state institutions unfold. The proposed notion of new advantage is also problematic. There may be a time lag before a social movement's impact is apparent, and a movement could be considered successful due to a policy change, which then is reversed (Kolb 2007, 22). Conversely, one might reach the conclusion that the movement has not obtained a new advantage, overlooking the long-term impact that an analysis close in time to the movement's emergence could not identify. Moreover, by categorizing the adoption of a particular policy as a new advantage gained by a social movement, there is less attention on the *processes* that led to that outcome. As Soule and King cogently argue, "the final passage of a bill is not the entire story and . . . a more nuanced approach to the study of state policy change necessitates an understanding of the 'prepolicy' period" (2006, 1,872).

Accordingly, recent research has stressed the importance of studying the impact of social movements on various stages of the policymaking process. Differentiating between setting the agenda, shaping public policies, and obtaining access to government is important because social movements' capacity to influence each of these stages varies. Focusing on the legislative process, King, Cornwall, and Dahlin (2005) noted that each succeeding stage has increasingly stringent rules that make it more difficult for social movements to pass petitions. In their study of state-level women's suffrage legislation, they find that while women's organizations might be successful in introducing the issue into the legislative debate, this does not necessarily entail a favorable vote. Similarly, Soule and King (2006) examine the legislative process of state ratification of the Equal Rights Amendment in the United States and show that the civil rights movement's impact was greater in earlier phases of the legislative debate. Again, the reason is that while social movements might convince a single or a group of legislators to introduce a bill, to have it passed requires a far greater commitment on the part of parliamentarians.

Consequently, understanding social movements' political impact also requires analyzing how they are able to forge alliances and build political force by creating their own political parties. Both of these processes will impact later stages of the legislative process that ultimately will define the fate of their agenda.

Electoral campaigns are particularly fruitful for both setting the agenda and building alliances. As noted by McAdam and Tarrow (2010), during electoral periods social movements might introduce new forms of collective action that influence election campaigns. These involve both specific repertoires and frames. Social movements might also engage in proactive or reactive electoral mobilization. In the former case, social movement organizations actively participate in favor of a political party or coalition during the electoral campaign. In the latter case, instead, social movements escalate protests in the context of an election in order to avoid the coming into power of routine political actors that oppose their demands.

Additionally, movements can affect the political process by joining political coalitions beyond electoral periods (McAdam and Tarrow 2010). Schlozman (2015) shows that both the Christian right and organized labor in the United States have forged long-lasting alliances with the Republicans and the Democrats, respectively, which influenced the parties' basic priorities. Heaney and Rojas (2015) argue that movement activity is a vital part of party politics. Their study, centered on how the antiwar movement in the United States influenced the Democratic Party, shows that while the Democrats were in opposition, intersecting movement and party identities helped fuel the growth of the antiwar movement. Once the Democrats regained power under President Obama, however, the party identity was stronger than the movement identity, which partly explains the movement's decline.

Furthermore, movements may turn into parties themselves—or give rise to new parties that join the movement's cause. Party families such as labor parties and ecological parties are deeply rooted in, respectively, national trade union movements and ecological movements. Schwartz's (2006) study, focused on the United States and Canada, shows that what he names "party movements" persist over time either through the political party that is created, or by the tenacity of principles that continue to undergird political actors. More recently, in countries such as Spain, Greece, and Chile itself, the failures of traditional socialist or social democratic parties to address the concerns of their constituencies left a vacuum on the left of the political spectrum that allowed the formation of new parties such as Podemos, Syriza, and the Frente Amplio, respectively.

In addition, movements might affect party dynamics by introducing new issues into the public debate that polarize political parties internally (McAdam and Tarrow 2010). This can happen during as well as between electoral periods. In the 1960s, European and Latin American social movements engaged in debates on issues such as agrarian reform, or the discussion about undertaking a reformist or a revolutionary path to social justice, which created wedges among factions of the principal socialist parties. As we will show in this chapter, political parties and coalitions can incubate internal tensions as a result of the stands taken on the issues that social movements have put forward.

Sofia Donoso and Nicolás M. Somma

In sum, then, scholarship on movements' political impact shows that the boundaries between social movements and institutional actors are not as clear-cut as earlier assumed. As Giugni (2004) and Giugni and Yamasaki (2009) assert, the impact of social movements is often indirect, first influencing external dimensions, which then allows for the impact on the policymaking process, or obtained by the joint effect of political alliances and public support. As we show in the case of Chile, these alliances and public support are constructed over time through an interactive process in which the student movement and political authorities respond to each other.

The Interactive Relationship between Education Policies, Shifts in the Political Opportunity Structures, and Student Protests

Return of Democracy and the Education System Bequeathed by the Military Regime

Fighting alongside the political parties of the center-left, student politics were deeply intertwined with party politics during the dictatorship of General Augusto Pinochet (1973–89) (Carolina Tohá, interview with author, 2 January 2012; Yerko Ljubetic, interview with author, 16 November 2011). As democratic rule was reestablished in 1990, there were high expectations about the influence that the student movement would have on the country's development in general, and the education agenda in particular. Indeed, many members of the student cadre joined the government led by the Coalition of Parties for Democracy (Concertación de Partidos por la Democracia, henceforth Concertación) (Roco 2013, 2). Yet, this did not entail a structural reform of the education model bequeathed by the military regime in the decades to follow.

The reasons for this are multifold. Although democratic rule undoubtedly involved more opportunities to mobilize and open a policy debate, the Concertación adopted a wary approach to policymaking, and a cautious relationship to social movements. Too much mobilization on the streets was in general considered to be a threat to democratic stability (Drake and Jaksic 1999, 34). This belief was deeply rooted in the experience of political polarization that preceded the military coup. During much of the 1960s and early 1970s, political parties on the center-left actively fostered social mobilization to extend their constituencies and attain power on their own (Roberts 1998, 89). After the traumatic experience of the democratic breakdown in 1973, many political leaders reached the conclusion that social mobilization, and the ensuing political polarization, had paved the way for the military takeover. This motivated the Concertación to prioritize a moderate route to policy change, and the construction of a stable center-left coalition that could guarantee governability (Roberts 1994).

The institutional setting also motivated this governance formula. For one, after seventeen years of dictatorship, General Pinochet left power in a strong position. He not only kept a seat in the Senate until the early 2000s, when he resigned due to health reasons, but he also enjoyed wide public support: 44 percent of Chileans voted for the continuation of the authoritarian regime in the 1988 plebiscite that allowed for the reinstatement of democracy. In addition, the Concertación was left with a constitution enacted by the military in 1980. Besides defining the rules of the political game, the constitution "locked in" the majority of the sweeping reforms introduced during the 1970s and '80s, all of which were based on neoliberal principles. The Concertación also inherited a binomial electoral system, especially designed by the military to favor the construction of broad political coalitions to the detriment of smaller parties such as the Communist Party, which had a close relationship with social movements (Pastor 2004, 39). Together, these institutional constraints reinforced the Concertación leaders' belief in the need to build consensus with the right-wing opposition on all important legislation (Huber, Pribble, and Stephens 2010, 78).

Despite its historical strength, the student movement emerged from the throes of authoritarian rule in a markedly weakened position. This was the result of long years of military rule, during which student leaders were persecuted, and universities were "purified" by the dismissal of left-leaning academic and administrative staff (Garretón 1985, 105). Moreover, while expectations for the return to democracy were high, and the university system faced significant challenges in relation to both its finances and internal democratization, student leaders disagreed about the agenda for change. The blurry boundaries between movement and party identities often meant that the goals of the political parties were echoed

Sofia Donoso and Nicolás M. Somma

by social movements (Hipsher 1996, 274). Consequently, many student leaders accepted the gradual approach to policymaking undertaken by the Concertación governments.

As a result of the aforementioned constraints, structural reform was a seemingly unsurmountable task. As Pribble notes, "while important changes were enacted, there was never an attempt to alter the general structure of the education sector" (2013, 97). Instead, during its first three consecutive governments the Concertación undertook gradual reforms to the education system left by the military regime. These reforms allowed for significant progress at the primary, secondary, and tertiary levels of education, especially in terms of enrolment rates (Cox 2005). Yet, they were not enough to counteract the vast inequalities that were reproduced by the education system bequeathed by the military regime.

At the level of primary and high school education, this education model was the first in the world to adopt the voucher system at the national level (Cox 2005, 25). Drawing on Milton Friedman's neoliberal thinking, the military regime's introduction of the voucher, paid by the Ministry of Education, sought to increase consumer choice over education alternatives. Hence, in practice, the voucher is a form of subsidy subject to demand. Driven by the "Chicago boys," the military regime's civilian arm, the aim of the education reform was to augment competition between private and public schools, and thereby drive down the costs of education (Carnoy 1998, 309). The value of the voucher is based on average monthly student attendance, and it can be paid to both public and privately administrated schools.

This introduced strong incentives for the expansion of a private education market (Cox 1997, 3). During the first five years of its implementation, more than a thousand new privately administrated schools were created (Kubal 2003, 6). These state-subsidized private schools, concentrated in the urban areas, attracted middle-income families that could not afford private schools without the voucher (Torche 2005, 322). Moreover, the education system was decentralized and the municipalities, which had neither the organizational nor the financial capacity to run the schools, were given a key role in the administration of schools. As a result, public education suffered. While student enrolment in state-subsidized private schools increased from 15.1 to 32.4 percent between 1981 and 1990—a boost of approximately 50 percent—enrolment in public schools dropped from 78 to 57.8 percent in the same period (MINEDUC 2003–2004, 35).

Moreover, the three-tiered education system created by the military junta, with private schools without the voucher, state-subsidized private schools, and public schools, produced significantly different educational outcomes. About 55 percent of state-subsidized private schools applied some process for selecting students among their applicants (García-Huidobro 2007, 74). Accordingly, the worst students were left at the public schools, which could not deny them access. In turn, this produced a "de-creaming" effect: the most talented students and those with highly motivated parents went to state-subsidized private schools to the detriment of the more academically weak students, who stayed in the public schools and were left without the positive incentive of the good students (Arenas 2004, 382). This peer effect, in turn, influenced public schools' test scores, which fell in both math and Spanish between 1982 and 1988 (Carnoy 1998, 320). As the student movement would repeat throughout various protest waves, conditioning access to higher education, the education system thus produced a mechanism for the reproduction of inequality.

The reforms undertaken by the Concertación from 1990 onwards focused on improving existing financing and management schemes. In addition, a comprehensive curricular reform was undertaken and the number of hours at school was extended through the "full school day" reform. Public schools with the most vulnerable student populations were also supported through various programs. These reforms involved an increase of public expenditure on education. Between 1990 and 2012, it rose from 2.4 percent (Mineduc 2006, 39) to 4 percent of GDP (OECD 2015, 260). However, the Concertación also introduced new policies that ended up deepening the gaps produced by the education system. A notable example is the 1993 cofinancing scheme of private state-subsidized schools, which aimed at increasing private contributions to the education system.

Educational inequalities were soon apparent both in terms of funding patterns and in educational outcomes. While the working classes have increased significantly their access to upper-level education, they do not arrive on the same footing as the more advantaged students. There are important differences in academic performance (measured by the Test of University Selection, or PSU) within the three-tiered Chilean high school system. Fully private high school students achieve higher average scores in academic tests than the rest. This is especially the case compared to (poorer) municipal-school students, whose average scores are about 25 percent lower—and with the gap growing over time between 2004 and 2016.[3] Additionally, students from state-subsidized private schools score higher than students from municipal schools, and the average score of the latter has declined slightly across time. Since tertiary institutions select students based on these scores, working-class students tend to attend lower-quality institutions, while their upper-class counterparts attend the more prestigious ones, which provide further access to better jobs.

These differences do not go unnoticed among the student population. The Chilean mass media recurrently reports rankings about the "best" and the "worst" high school institutions in the country according to their average standardized score tests. Analysis of these results often emphasized the gaps between the three high school types, and the fact that students from municipal schools barely reached the most prestigious universities, which were populated by better-off students from fully private high schools. Such contrasting comparisons in the media and public debate, alongside students' everyday experience of educational inequalities, created grievances that nurtured the student movement.

The 2006 Protest Wave

While both university and high school students staged sporadic student protests during the 1990s and early 2000s, it was not until 2006 that social mobilization shifted the policy agenda in significant ways. What became known as the *Pingüino* movement—due to the students' black-and-white school uniforms—spearheaded protests and school sit-ins across the country for several weeks, something unheard of at the time (Donoso 2013). Spurred by specific demands, such as the improvement of school infrastructure and ending the authoritarian style of many school directors, the students also set in motion a national debate on educational inequalities and the neoliberal education model that sustained them.

The timing of the protests was not a coincidence. Just a couple of months before the movement took off, the Concertación began its fourth consecutive government under the presidency of Michelle Bachelet. Not a member of the party elites, and an untipped presidential candidate, Bachelet had gained popularity as minister of health and minister of defense. She campaigned on a discourse that underscored the importance of citizen participation. In doing so, she was implicitly acknowledging the need to revise the top-down approach to policymaking that had characterized the previous three governments of the center-left. As her slogan—"I am with you"—signaled, her government would be different, with a closer relationship to civil-society actors in an effort to address their concerns.

After fifteen years of democratic rule, in 2006, the year the *Pingüino* movement arose, democracy had become consolidated, and the fears of an authoritarian reversal were more a memory than anything else. In this way, there was arguably a more favorable political opportunity structure for educational reform than the country had seen in the previous decades.

"Bachelet, are you with me?" could be read on the banners at protest events, making direct reference to the pledge made by the president during her campaign. Other recurrent rallying cries, expressing the students' discontent with the education model, read: "education is not for sale," "we are students, not clients," and "no LOCE [Constitutional Law of Education]; a ghost from the dictatorship." Student grievances were thus rooted in discourses linking the current state of the educational system with Pinochet's dictatorship, a "dark age" for most Chilean youngsters.

After several weeks of street rallies, followed by school takeovers across the country, which virtually paralyzed the school system, President Bachelet announced, through a televised speech, that she was going to institute a presidential commission tasked with proposing educational reforms. Specifically, her aim was to replace the Constitutional Law of Education, which was passed by the military right before leaving power as a way of "locking in" the numerous education reforms of the 1970s and '80s.

The Presidential Commission on Education gathered eighty-one experts and civil-society actors, including several high school and university student leaders. On the one hand, the commission's weekly meetings and national discussion on the education model was a way for the Bachelet administration to demobilize the *Pingüinos*. On the other hand, the commission allowed the students to impact the public agenda. After six months of work, a final report outlining a set of proposals was submitted. Drawing on these proposals, the government sent four bills to parliament,

Sofia Donoso and Nicolás M. Somma

one of which constituted a replacement to the Constitutional Law of Education. During the next four years this bill was promulgated along with bills that created the Agency of the Quality of Education (which addressed the lack of oversight over public and state-subsidized private schools) and the School Inspectorate, and the bill on the increment of subsidy for more vulnerable students.

Each of these bills, however, had to be negotiated with the political right after the Bachelet government realized that it could not count on the necessary votes from among the Concertación parties. The bills were particularly criticized by the Christian Democrats, one of the coalition partners who feared that removing school authorities' right to select students among applicants would threaten religious schools. Christian Democrats also disagreed on the elimination of profit-making among state-subsidized private schools. In addition to the opposition among the Christian Democrats, Concertación parties such as the Party for Democracy had vested interests since some of the party members were managers of state-subsidized private schools (Burton 2012, 38).

High school students and other social actors that had mobilized alongside the *Pingüinos* were not satisfied with the resulting policy reforms, which they considered insufficient to eliminate market mechanisms from the education model. Crucially, both the massive protests in 2006 and their aftermath marked a turning point. The protests created a wedge between the Concertación and student organizations, boosted the consolidation of a broader movement for educational reform, and helped frame this movement's demands in new ways.

For one, distrust with the Concertación grew, and the student movement started to highlight the collusion between advocates of the present education model and the Concertación. The distance between Bachelet's promises of substantial reforms (or the way students interpreted her discourse), and the reality of the changes made, added a new layer of grievance to those that had already been levelled at the educational system inherited by the dictatorship. Secondly, high school and university students started to mobilize together. Before 2006, as one university student leader expressed, "there had never been a platform that was not sectorial. They [high school students] fought for their school passes, for scholarships, and we [university students] mobilized for our equivalent; our pass and our scholarships" (Giorgio Boccardo, interview with author, 17 August 2009).

Finally, as Francisco Figueroa, former vice-president of the student federation of the Universidad de Chile, states: "the secondary school demonstrations were already the precedent of what was about to happen in 2011. It was the student protests in 2006 that managed to call the attention of society on pending and broken promises from the period of democratic transition" (quoted in Hernández 2016, 62). The 2006 protests thus constituted the base for the massive protests of 2011, which became known as the Chilean Winter of Discontent.

The 2011 Protest Wave

The 2011 student protests erupted as a reaction not only to the educational model but also to the first right-wing government since the reestablishment of democratic rule in 1990. Many things had changed since 2006. By any means, the coming into power of President Piñera involved having less political allies in government. Also, it was clear that the new government of President Piñera was not going to be too responsive to any student demands that addressed the education model as a whole. The country had elected as a president a multimillionaire who thought that "education is a consumer good just like anything else" (Radio Cooperativa 2011a). At the same time, student organizations were more consolidated as a result of the sedimentation of lessons that previous protests waves had left (Donoso 2017). Moreover, the main student federations had decided to make 2011 the year of student uprising (interviews with Miguel Crispi, 1 March 2014; Camila Cea, 4 March 2014; and Joaquín Walker, 28 January 2014).[4]

Spearheaded by university students this time, the system of higher education and its financing mechanisms became the focal point of the 2011 protests. The military regime had built a system along neoliberal lines. Strong incentives for the expansion of a private market of education were created and state funding to higher education was slashed, which translated into a sharp increase in university fees (Austin 1997, 39) that tightened the budgets of those working-class students enrolling in universities. The number of private universities and technical professional institutions mushroomed. This resulted from the reduction in the requirements to create new education institutions, as well as from access to indirect state funding (competitive research funds and subsidies based on demand) (Bellei, Cabalín, and Orellana 2014, 428).

While the Concertación governments increased the amount of funding to higher education, they kept its structure, including its coordination and finance mechanisms. By decreasing state funding to the "traditional" universities, which combine public and private universities that receive state funding, the Concertación not only maintained the system created by the military but also deepened it by forcing institutions to compete for subsidies on the basis of demand. Between 1990 and 2011, state subsidies to universities increased from 44 to 74 percent of the total public expenditure on higher education (Bellei, Cabalín, and Orellana 2014, 428).

At the same time, although private universities increased in number, their students could not access private loans to finance their education. For this reason, in 2005, with strong opposition from university students, President Ricardo Lagos introduced a state-guaranteed credit. While this amplified access to higher education, it did so by relying heavily on household resources as households had to pay the loans. About 52 percent of tertiary education expenditures in Chile come from households, the highest figure for OECD countries—whose average is 21 percent (OECD 2015, 220). As Chile also has very high educational fees, households need to rely on loans provided by the banking system through state arrangements. Between 2010 and 2015, the number of young people with educational loans almost quadrupled, and the total value of such loans tripled (Kremerman and Páez 2016). Of such loans, 85 percent come from the state-guaranteed student loan program, the Crédito con Aval del Estado (CAE) introduced by President Lagos (Kremerman and Páez 2016, 21–2).

Yet the burden of this system fell on the shoulders of the less advantaged students and their families, creating deep resentment and anxiety towards the authorities that sustained it. According to the 2013 National Socioeconomic Characterization Survey, 70 percent of postsecondary students coming from the two lowest-income quintiles have educational loans, most of which are CAE loans (Kremerman and Páez 2016). However, the CAE plays a minor role in providing financing for members of the upper quintile, most of whom pay for their education out of their own pockets (Kremerman and Páez 2016, 24). Additionally, CAE students face more pressures for producing economic returns on their educational investments in the future. This is because the households of CAE students are more likely to have unemployed or inactive members than other households, and their average income is lower. Among students currently working, CAE students earn about half of the earnings of students paying for their education from their own pockets (Kremerman and Páez 2016, 27). It is no wonder, then, that demands for reforming the education system resonated more heavily among working- and lower-class students (Disi 2018). Without a doubt, the extension of the CAE and the grievances associated with it signified that there was a large student population to mobilize.

The 2011 protests started out in April and continued throughout the year. Rallies, takeovers of both schools and universities, and other repertoires of action such as flash mobs and social media campaigns, were complemented by the strong leadership of the presidents of the main university student federations.

As an indicator of the exceptionality of the 2011 protest wave, our protest event data[5] shows that during this year, 44 percent of the estimated number of participants in all protest events participated in protests with educational demands. The collective action frame diffused by the student movement centered on existing inequalities in access to higher education, the strengthening of public education institutions, and a more active role for the state in regulating and directing higher education. Our data further indicates that, in comparison to prior student protests, demands related to a structural change in the education model expanded in 2011. For example, 44 percent of the demands in 2011 were related to the education model in general, in comparison to 22 percent for the 2000–12 period. Free public education concentrated 12 percent of the demands in 2000–12, and 23 percent in 2011. By contrast, demands related to specific benefits such as the public transportation pass and free lunches, decreased in 2011 compared to the rest of the 2000–12 period.

The 2011 student protest wave quite likely contributed to a further increase in public acceptance of protest and educational reform. According to the Latin American Public Opinion Project, between 2010 and 2012, the percentage of the population that supported that people express their points of view through protest participation increased from 58 to 71 percent.[6] This figure increased from 60 percent in 2006 to 71 percent right after the 2011 protest wave. Finally, the percentage of Chileans that considered education to be the country's principal problem increased from 2.6 percent in 2010 to 5 percent in 2012.

Despite the student movement's capacity to sustain protests throughout the year, and the considerable sympathy it garnered from the public, the Piñera administration refused to respond to its petitions. Many times, the riot police cracked down on the protests instead (Washington Post 2011). While frustration was growing among student leaders, the government's lack of responsiveness raised questions about the institutional frame that guides the political game. Many student leaders were convinced that in order to achieve a new education model, political reforms were needed first. Thus, a demand for constitutional change became a recurrent rallying cry in the demonstrations. In addition, the absence of any substantial response on the part of the Piñera administration inspired many movement leaders to continue their struggle from within the political arena by competing in the 2013 parliamentary elections. This strategy proved successful as several former student leaders currently (as of 2019) occupy a parliamentary seat.

The Impact of Chile's Student Movement beyond Education Policies

Internal Polarization in the Government Coalition

As in any multiparty coalition, the Concertación was forced to accommodate different stances on education. As stated by Ernesto Águila, education expert and director of research at the Ministry of the General Secretariat of the Presidency during the Bachelet administration, "the Concertación always had at least two souls in relation to education" (interview with author, 16 November 2011). While some figures of the coalition supported a more state-led form of education, others favored further promotion of market mechanisms in the field of education (Burton 2012, 38). Moreover, the most liberal sectors within the coalition favored the voucher system and did not want to push for a more centralized education system that privileged public education (Pribble 2013, 99). At the same time, many

Concertación leaders argued that the voucher scheme would introduce incentives for parents to control the quality of the education provided to their children and allow for the collection of fees from those who can afford to pay, which would then be redistributed to people that need them more (García-Huidobro 2007, 73). These differences in opinion were not the direct result of party affiliation. In the Christian Democratic Party, for example, there were prominent figures, such as former minister of education Yasna Provoste, who openly supported student demands both in 2006 and 2011. Conversely, in the Socialist Party, which historically had been a close ally to social movements, a former party secretary famously noted, in reference to the students' demands, that they "seemed to have smoked opium." (La Tercera 2012).

During the four consecutive governments of the Concertación, these divergent positions were evident in many policy fields. Yet, what has been called the Concertación's "transversal political party"—referring to the moderates in each of the coalition parties—tended to prevail in the debates. As one student leader expressed, "the Concertación has two souls but one always loses" (Víctor Orellana, interview with author, 6 May 2011). In the field of education, two examples of the more moderate route, in which fiscal concerns were prioritized over a focus on equity, are the aforementioned copayment scheme in primary and high school education, and the CAE reform in higher education.

The student movement in 2011 shifted the power balance between the center and the left within the Concertación, resulting in a strengthened position for the latter. The protest wave spearheaded by students developed in the midst of the internal debate that the center-left coalition was undertaking after the electoral defeat of 2010. The Concertación was dispirited and in disarray. Naturally, after twenty years in government, there was a need for renewal and for a substantial discussion that could inspire a revised political agenda. In this debate, the Concertación acknowledged the need to reconnect to its social bases. In the words of Senator Fulvio Rossi, former president of the Socialist Party, "we are all responsible for not having been capable of reading the profound transformations that we as the Concertación fostered during the last 20 years. We departed from the people . . . and we forgot the citizen movements" (La Tercera 2010). In many ways, Sebastián Piñera's electoral victory in 2010 can be related to

Sofia Donoso and Nicolás M. Somma

the Concertación's growing problems, particularly the difficulty it faced renovating not only its policy proposals but also its leadership structures in order to be able to represent the ideas and interests of contemporary Chilean society (Luna and Mardones 2010).

In this context, the massive student protests in 2011 were regarded by many in the Concertación as an opportunity to redirect its policy agenda. The protests were therefore met with a lot of enthusiasm by the coalition's more left-leaning members. Crucially, in early 2013, former president Bachelet decided to run for president again in that year's presidential elections. The remarkably high approval ratings that she had enjoyed when leaving power four years earlier made her a very competitive candidate. Aware of the privileged bargaining position that this entailed, she promised to compete subject to a policy program that embraced many of the student demands. In her own words: "I understood the message of the youth very clearly" (La Tercera 2013). And: "thanks to this movement, which has been a serious movement that has a proposal, the country has better conditions to advance in what needs to be done" (Radio Cooperativa 2011b). Furthermore, Bachelet proposed to construct a broad sociopolitical alliance that could guarantee the implementation of her program. The Communist Party joined the former Concertación parties and founded the New Majority coalition, which defeated the rightist coalition by a wide margin (62 percent versus 34 percent) in the second round of the 2013 elections.

The electoral success of the New Majority meant that an ambitious reform agenda had to be implemented. Very soon, the different stances within the broad government coalition started to emerge. The proposed tax reform, which would be necessary to finance education reform, encountered opposition from both the Christian Democrats and the Socialists. The education reform, which aimed at eliminating profit-making from the education model, also met strong resistance both from within the coalition and from outside. The former became especially outspoken when President Bachelet's approval ratings plummeted in 2015 as a consequence of a corruption scandal involving her son and daughter-in-law. From this moment onwards, the more moderate factions within the New Majority no longer feared openly criticizing the government's course. In particular, Communists and Christian Democrats, both members of the

New Majority, clashed increasingly often in the debate on education, labor relations, tax reform, pension reform, and health.

The New Majority paid a high price for its internal polarization. In April 2017, the Christian Democratic Party announced that it would not compete in the primaries of the New Majority. Instead, it ratified its party president, Carolina Goic, as its presidential candidate—an unfortunate choice since Goic only obtained 5.9 percent of the vote in the elections. The remaining parties of the New Majority supported Alejandro Guillier. He lost by a considerable margin the presidential race that led the rightist leader Sebastián Piñera to La Moneda (seat of the president of the Republic of Chile) for the second time.

Creating New Political Parties and a New Coalition of Sociopolitical Forces

The student movement also impacted the political scenario in a second way—by fostering new, independent political forces. Although many Concertación leaders openly supported the student demands, there was a deeply rooted distrust against them among students. In the few occasions that Concertación leaders attended a protest event in 2011, participants signaled their discontent. For many, the continuation of the military regime's education policies under the democratic governments constituted a betrayal. Moreover, the experience of the 2006 *Pingüino* protests and its aftermath was fresh in their memory.

If anything, the 2011 protest wave convinced many student leaders that disputing power in elections was a central way to push for their agenda, and that this action complemented protests on the streets. Four former student leaders became members of parliament in 2013. Two of them (Camila Vallejo and Karol Cariola) were members of the Communist Party and thus supported the government coalition. The other two (Giorgio Jackson and Gabriel Boric) ran under their own political organizations.

From their first day in parliament, these former student leaders openly stated that although they now formed part of institutional politics, they would always have one foot on the streets. Since 2013, it has been common to see many of these members of parliament in rallies organized by the student federations.

The visibility of these former student leaders has been key in the creation of new political parties and organizations. In May 2016, Revolución Democrática, the political movement led by Giorgio Jackson, presented more than ten thousand signatures to the Electoral Service and officially became a political party. The Movimiento Autonomista, the political movement of another former student leader (Gabriel Boric), followed a somewhat different path. Although it has not founded a political party, the members of this movement have built a wide web across the country and organized thousands of people.

Preparing for the 2016 municipal elections, Revolución Democrática and the Movimiento Autonomista, together with the Izquierda Libertaria, Convergencia de Izquierda, Nueva Democracia, and the Humanist Party—all left-wing forces with a strong presence in the student movement—joined an electoral alliance. The most emblematic result of this joint effort was the electoral success of Jorge Sharp, member of the Movimiento Autonomista, and currently mayor of Valparaíso, Chile's second-largest city. This coalition-building expanded to include the fourteen organizations, which in January 2017 founded the Frente Amplio and organized programmatic meetings across the country.

The electoral success of former student leaders, both in parliamentary and municipal elections, certainly inspired other members of the Frente Amplio. For the 2017 general elections, the Frente Amplio competed for more seats in parliament across the country. In April 2017, it also announced that it would compete in the presidential elections, with the impressive results noted at the outset of the chapter. Currently, the Frente Amplio is the third largest political force in Chile. Through its many representatives it not only took the lead on some policy issues (educational reform, women's rights, the pension system, the creation of a new political constitution, and euthanasia, among others), but also became an important partner for the traditional leftist parties.

The considerable gains over a relatively short time period on the part of the political forces that have emerged from the student movement illustrate how social movements can contribute to realigning the political game. While it is too early to assess the longer-term impact of current developments, few would take exception with the claim that the student movement has paved the way for the emergence of a new political force that has joined routine political actors to shape policy issues in important ways.

Conclusions

As argued in the introduction to this volume, social movements play an important role in democracies. Through an analysis of the Chilean student movement since the democratic restoration, we have illustrated some of the ways in which social movements can affect the political process by introducing new demands into the policy agenda, and how these movements in turn are shaped by the policies and politics they helped to promote.

We concur with Goldstone's (2003) criticism of the notion of social movements as "challengers" as opposed to "members" of a given polity. Rather than "insiders" versus "outsiders," there is indeed a continuum between different forms of contention (Goldstone 2003, 1–2). Social movements should, in other words, not be considered extra-institutional actors, as "there is only a fuzzy and permeable boundary between institutionalized and noninstitutionalized politics" (Goldstone 2003, 2). In keeping with this perspective, social movements should be conceived of as a vital element of normal politics in modern societies.

The emergence of a powerful student movement since the mid-2000s—deployed first in the *Pingüino* campaign of 2006 and by university students in 2011—is rooted in the reshaping of the educational system that took place during Pinochet's dictatorship and its consolidation under democracy. A secondary-school system of unequal academic quality, segregated by class and neighborhood, plus a postsecondary system with a booming enrolment based on heavy loans, incubated a growing mass of aggrieved students. These conditions may not engender grievances among every student population (see Simmons's approach to grievances in chapter 2 of this book). In the Chilean context, however, they activated meanings—such as the similarities between the current educational establishment and Pinochet's dictatorship, or the injustice of educational institutions profiting at the expense of the working classes—that fueled student discontent and motivated collective action. By taking to the streets and seizing educational buildings, students shook a civil society that had remained quiescent since the time of the democratic transition.

While policy shaped the student movement, the opposite happened too. The 2006 campaign was one of the main drivers behind the approval of four bills that introduced some changes to the system, and the 2011 campaign forced President Piñera to correct the more abusive aspects, such as interest rates, of the educational loans policy. Perhaps more importantly, the three major reforms (education, tax, and the constitution) announced by President Bachelet during her second term (2014–18) stemmed, either directly or indirectly, from students' demands.

Yet the student movement also contributed to a major realignment of political forces. Its demands helped to push the Concertación coalition to the left through the incorporation of the Communist Party—thus giving birth to the New Majority coalition that ruled Chile between 2014 and 2018. Ranging from the centrist Christian Democrats to the Communists, the New Majority experienced internal polarization, and it formally disappeared by the 2017 elections, which were won by the political right. Perhaps more importantly, the entry of former student leaders into Congress after the 2013 election signaled the beginnings of a new political force, the Frente Amplio, which combines several small leftist parties and movements that oppose the neoliberal model, and which, as of 2019, stands as the third largest political force in Chile. Their ambition is far-reaching. In the words of Giorgio Jackson, former student leader and currently a member of Parliament: "for a long time, we were told that discontent should be expressed in the demonstrations, and that we could go home then . . . that they would undertake the changes that Chile needs. . . . But if they have not been able to address existing corruption and injustice, we have to take politics in our own hands" (El Mostrador 2017).

Notes

1   This was the slogan of the 2006 student mobilization.

2   We wish to acknowledge the support of a FONDECYT grant (CONICYT FONDECYT Regular 1160308) and the support of the Centre for Social Conflict and Cohesion Studies (CONICYT FONDAP 15130009).

3   The evidence for this paragraph comes from Tele 13 (2015).

4   The original idea was, in fact, to mobilize in 2010, but an earthquake put a full stop to that plan.

5   This is a data set covering about 2,300 protest events that took place across Chile between 2000 and 2012. It is based on the Chronologies of the Protest of CLACSO (Centro Latinoamericano de Ciencias Sociales), which gathers protest news from multiple sources. See Somma and Medel (2018) for details.

6   See the Latin American Public Opinion Project, available at http://www.vanderbilt.edu/lapop/.

References

Amenta, Edwin, and Neal Caren. 2004. "The Legislative, Organizational, and Beneficiary Consequences of State-Oriented challengers." In *The Blackwell companion to social movements*, edited by David A. Snow and Sarah A. Soule, 461–88. Malden, MA: Blackwell.

Amenta, Edwin, Neal Caren, Elizabeth Chiarello, and Yang Su. 2010. "The Political Consequences of Social Movements." *Annual Review of Sociology* 36: 287–307.

Arenas, Alberto. 2004. "Privatization and Vouchers in Colombia and Chile." *International Review of Education* 50: 379–95.

Austin, Robert. 1997. "Armed Forces, Market Forces: Intellectuals and Higher Education in Chile, 1973–1993." *Latin American Perspectives* 24, no. 5: 26–58.

Baumgartner, Frank R., and Christine Mahoney. 2005. "Social Movements, the Rise of New Issues, and the Public Agenda." In *Routing the Opposition: Social Movements, Public Policy, and Democracy*, edited by David S. Meyer, Valerie Jenness, and Helen Ingram, 65–86. Minneapolis: University of Minnesota Press.

Bellei, Cristián, Cristian Cabalín, and Victor Orellana. 2014. "The 2011 Chilean Student Movement against Neoliberal Educational Policies." *Studies in Higher Education* 39, no. 3: 426–40.

Bosi, Lorenzo, Marco Giugni, and Katrin Uba, eds. 2016. *The Consequences of Social Movements*. New York: Cambridge University Press.

Bosi, Lorenzo, and Katrin Uba. 2009. "Introduction: The Outcomes of Social Movements." *Mobilization: An International Journal* 1, no. 4: 409–15.

Burstein, Paul, and April Linton. 2002. "The impact of Political Parties, Interest Groups, and Social Movement Organization on Public Policy: Some Recent Evidence and Theoretical Concerns." *Social Forces* 81, no. 2: 381–408.

Burstein, Paul, and Sarah Sausner. 2005. "The Incidence and Impact of Policy-Oriented Collective Action: Competing Views." *Sociological Forum* 20, no. 3: 403–19.

Burton, Guy. 2012. "Hegemony and Frustration: Education Policy Making in Chile under the Concertación, 1990–2010." *Latin American Perspectives* 39, no. 4: 34–52.

Carnoy, Martin. 1998. "National Voucher Plans in Chile and Sweden: Did Privatization Reforms Make for Better Education?" *Comparative Education Review* 42, no. 3: 309–37.

Cox, Cristian. 1996. "Higher Education Policies in Chile in the 90s." *Higher Education Policy* 9, no. 1: 29–43.

———. 1997. "Education Reform in Chile: Context, Content and Implementation." Programa de Promoción de la Reforma Educativa en América Latina, Occasional Paper Series No. 8. http://archive.thedialogue.org/PublicationFiles/PREAL%20 8-English.pdf (accessed 5 November 2018).

———. 2005. "Las Políticas Educacionales de Chile en las Últimas dos Décadas del Siglo XX." In *Políticas educacionales en el cambio de siglo. La reforma del sistema escolar de Chile*, edited by Cristian Cox, 19–113. Santiago de Chile: Editoral Universitaria.

Disi, Rodolfo. 2018. "Sentenced to Debt: Explaining Student Mobilization in Chile." *Latin American Research Review* 53, no. 3: 448–65.

Donoso, Sofia. 2013. "Dynamics of Change in Chile: Explaining the Emergence of the 2006 Pingüino Movement." *Journal of Latin American Studies* 45: 1–29.

———. 2017. " 'Outsider' and 'Insider' Strategies: Chile's Student Movement, 1990–2014." In *Social Movements in Chile: Organization, Trajectories, and Political Consequences*, edited by Sofia Donoso and Marisa von Bülow, 65–97. New York: Palgrave Macmillan.

Drake, Paul W., and Iván Jaksic. 1999. *El Modelo Chileno: Democracia y Desarrollo*. Santiago de Chile: LOM Ediciones.

El Mostrador. 2017. "Fuego Cruzado: Navarrete (PPD) Ningunea Al FA Y Jackson Responde Que 'si Otros No Han Podido Encargarse de Arreglar La Corrupción Y La Injusticia, Tenemos Que Tomar La Política Con Nuestras Propias Manos.' " *El Mostrador*, 3 May 2017. http://www.elmostrador.cl/noticias/pais/2017/05/03/ presidente-del-ppd-ningunea-al-frente-amplio-y-diputado-jackson-le-responde-van-a-tratar-de-aportillarnos/ (accessed 5 November 2018).

Gamson, William. 1975. *The Strategy of Social Protest*. Belmont, CA: Wadsworth Press.

García-Huidobro, Juan Eduardo. 2007. "Desigualdad Educativa y Segmentación del Sistema Escolar." *Revista Pensamiento Educativo* 40, no. 1: 65–85.

Garretón, Manuel Antonio. 1985. "La Intervención Militar en Las Universidades." In *Universidades Chilenas: Historia, Reforma e Intervención. Tomo I*, edited by

Manuel Antonio Garretón and Javier Martínez, 101–19. Santiago de Chile: Ediciones Sur.

———. 1989. *The Chilean Political Process*. Boston: Unwun Hyman.

Giugni, Marco. 2004. *Social Protest and Policy Change: Ecology, Antinuclear, and Peace Movements in Comparative Perspective*. Lanham, MD: Rowman and Littlefield.

Giugni, Marco, and Maria T. Grasso. 2016. *Austerity and Protest: Popular Contention in Times of Economic Crisis*. New York: Routledge.

Giugni, Marcio, and Sakura Yamasaki. 2009. "The Policy Impact of Social Movements: A Replication through Qualitative Comparative Analysis." *Mobilization: An International Quarterly* 14, no. 4: 467–84.

Glenn, John K. 2003. "Parties out of Movements: Party Emergence in Postcommunist Eastern Europe." In *States, Parties, and Social Movements*, edited by Jack A. Goldstone, 147–69. New York: Cambridge University Press.

Goldstone, Jack A., ed. 2003. *States, Parties, and Social Movements*. New York: Cambridge University Press.

Heaney, Michael T., and Fabio Rojas. 2015. *Party in the Street: The Antiwar Movement and the Democratic Party after 9/11*. New York: Cambridge University Press.

Hernandez, Ivette. 2013. "Interview with Francisco Figueroa: Continuing the Conversation on the Chilean Student Movement." *Journal of Social Science Education* 12, no. 3. http://www.academia.edu/5549542/Interview_with_Francisco_Figueroa_Continuing_the_Conversation_on_the_Chilean_Student_Movement (accessed 8 November 2018).

Hipsher, Patricia L. 1996. "Democratization and the Decline of Urban Social Movements in Chile and Spain." *Comparative Politics* 28, no. 3: 273–97.

Huber, Evelyne, Jennifer Pribble, and John D. Stephens. 2010. "The Chilean Left in Power: Achievements, Failures and Omissions." In *Leftist Governments in Latin America: Successes and Shortcomings*, edited by Kurt Weyland, Raúl L. Madrid, and Wendy Hunter, 77–97. New York: Cambridge University Press.

King, Brayden G., Marie Cornwall, and Eric C. Dahlin. 2005. "Winning Woman Suffrage One Step at a Time." *Social Forces* 83, no. 3: 287–310.

Kolb, Felix. 2007. *Protest and Opportunities: The Political Outcomes of Social Movements*. Frankfurt: Campus Verlag.

Kremerman, Marco, and Alexander Páez. 2016. "Endeudar para Gobernar y Mercantilizar: el Caso del CAE" (Working Paper). Fundación Sol, Santiago de Chile. http://www.fundacionsol.cl/estudios/endeudar-gobernar-mercantilizar-caso-del-cae/ (accessed 8 November 2018).

Kubal, Mary Rose. 2003. "The Politics of Education Decentralization in Latin America: Rhetoric and Reality in Chile, Mexico, Argentina, and Nicaragua." Paper presented at the 2003 Meeting of the Latin American Studies Association, Dallas, Texas.

La Tercera. 2010. "Concertación hace autocrítica por derrota en las elecciones: 'Fuimos soberbios.' " *La Tercera*, 19 April 2010. http://www.latercera.com/noticia/

concertacion-hace-autocritica-por-derrota-en-las-elecciones-fuimos-soberbios/ (accessed 25 June 2017).

———. 2012. "No nos pongamos a fumar opio." *La Tercera*, 1 July 2012. http://diario. latercera.com/edicionimpresa/escalona-y-la-constituyente-no-nos-pongamos-a-fumar-opio/ (accessed 9 November 2018).

———. 2013. "Bachelet anuncia propuestas de gratuidad en educación: 'Entendí muy claro el mensaje de los jóvenes.' " *La Tercera*, 26 August 2013. http://www.latercera.com/ noticia/bachelet-anuncia-propuestas-de-gratuidad-en-educacion-entendi-muy-claro-el-mensaje-de-los-jovenes/ (accessed 25 June 2017).

LeBas, Adrienne. 2011. *From Protest to Parties: Party-Building and Democratization in Africa*. New York: Oxford University Press.

Luna, Juan Pablo, and Rodrigo Mardones. 2010. "Chile: Are the Parties Over?" *Journal of Democracy* 21, no. 3: 107–21.

McAdam, Doug, and Sidney Tarrow. 2010. "Ballots and Barricades: On the Reciprocal Relationship between Elections and Social Movements." *Perspectives on Politics* 8, no. 2: 529–42.

McAdam, Doug, Sidney G. Tarrow, and Charles Tilly. 2001. *Dynamics of Contention*. New York: Cambridge University Press.

MINEDUC. 2004. *Indicadores de la Educación en Chile 2003–2004*. Santiago de Chile: Ministerio de Educación de Chile.

———. 2006. *Indicadores de educación en Chile 2006*. Santiago de Chile: Ministerio de Educación de Chile.

OECD. 2015. *Education at a Glance 2016: OECD Indicators*. Paris: Organisation for Economic Co-operation and Development.

Pastor, Daniel. 2004. "Origins of the Chilean Binominal Election System." *Revista de Ciencia Política* 24, no. 1: 38–57.

Piccio, Daniela R. 2016. "The Impact of Social Movements on Political Parties." In *The Consequences of Social Movements*, edited by Lorenzo Bosi, Marco Giugni, and Katrin Uba, 263–85. New York: Cambridge University Press.

Pierson, Paul. 1993. "Review: When Effect becomes Cause: Policy Feedback and Political Change." *World Politics* 45, no. 4: 595–628.

Pribble, Jennifer. 2013. *Welfare and Party Politics in Latin America*. New York: Cambridge University Press.

Cooperativa.cl. 2011a. "Presidente Piñera: La Educación Es Un Bien de Consumo." *Radio Cooperativa*, 19 July 2011. http://www.cooperativa.cl/noticias/pais/ educacion/proyectos/presidente-pinera-la-educacion-es-un-bien-de-consumo/2011-07-19/134829.html (accessed 30 April 2017).

———. 2011b. "Bachelet: No contamos con apoyo de todos los sectores para avanzar en el fin de lucro." *Radio Cooperativa*, 7 October 2011. https://www.cooperativa.cl/ noticias/pais/educacion/movimiento-estudiantil/bachelet-no-contamos-con-apoyo-de-todos-los-sectores-para-avanzar-en-el-fin-de-lucro/2011-10-07/144017. html (accessed 30 April 2017).

Roberts, Kenneth M. 1994. "Renovation in the Revolution? Dictatorship, Democracy, and Political Change in the Chilean Left." Kellogg Working Paper 203. https://kellogg. nd.edu/sites/default/files/old_files/documents/203_0.pdf (accessed 8 November 2018).

———. 1998. *Deepening Democracy? The Modern Left and Social Movements in Chile and Peru*. Stanford, CA: Stanford University Press.

Roco, Rodrigo. 2013. "La resurrección de la FECh en Democracia." Unpublished manuscript.

Schlozman, Daniel. 2015. *When Movements Anchor Parties: Electoral Alignments in American History*. Princeton, NJ: Princeton University Press.

Schwartz, Mildred. 2006. *Party Movements in the United States and Canada: Strategies of Persistence*. New York: Rowman and Littlefield.

Somma, Nicolás M., and Rodrigo M. Medel. 2018. "What makes a big demonstration? Exploring the impact of mobilization strategies on the size of demonstrations." *Social Movement Studies*. DOI: 10.1080/14742837.2018.1532285 (accessed 5 November 2018).

Soule, Sarah A. 2013. "Diffusion and Scale Shift." *The Wiley-Blackwell Encyclopedia of Social and Political Movements* (Published Online). DOI: 10.1002/9780470674871. wbespm430 (accessed 5 November 2018).

Soule, Sarah A., and Brayden G. King. 2006. "The Stages of the Policy Process and the Equal Rights Amendment, 1972–1982." *American Journal of Sociology* 111, no. 6: 871–909.

Tele 13. 2015. "Resultados históricos PSU: Así han variado los puntajes en los últimos 12 años." *Tele 13*, 29 December 2015. http://www.t13.cl/noticia/nacional/resultados-historicos-psu-asi-han-variado-puntajes-ultimos-12-anos (accessed 1 May 2017).

Torche, Florencia. 2005. "Privatization and Inequality of Educational Opportunity: The case of Chile." *Sociology of Education* 78: 316–43.

Uba, Katrin. 2005. "Political Protest and Policy Change: The Direct Impacts of Indian Anti-Privatization Mobilizations, 1990–2003." *Mobilization: An International Journal* 10, no. 3: 383–96.

United Nations Development Programme. 2005. *Expansión de la Educación Superior en Chile: Hacia un Nuevo Enfoque de la Equidad y Calidad*. Santiago de Chile: United Nations Development Programme.

Washington Post. 2011. "Chilean riot police crackdown on student protests over education funding." *Washington Post*, 4 August 2011. Retrieved from https://ontd-political. livejournal.com/8526598.html (accessed 8 November 2018).

8

Protest Cycles in the United States: From the Tea Party and Occupy Wall Street to Sanders and Trump

Ted Goertzel

Protest movements had a major impact on political life in the United States during the protest cycle that was triggered by the economic crisis of 2007–08, peaked in 2011, and shaped the presidencies of Barack Obama and Donald Trump. The Occupy Wall Street and Tea Party movements framed the grievances of the key groups, and both had a significant impact on electoral politics. Both movements had an antiestablishment, populist cast—one coming from the left and the other from the right. This populism defeated the presidential ambitions of two well-established candidates for the presidency in 2016: Jeb Bush and Hillary Clinton.

Had the Republican Party establishment and its wealthy supporters been able to control the nomination process, Jeb Bush would have been the party's nominee in 2016, and perhaps the Bush dynasty would have had a third instatement. Hillary Clinton was primed to be the country's first woman president. But her feminist credentials, rooted in a protest cycle that peaked in the 1970s, were not enough to defeat Barack Obama in the Democratic Party primary in 2008. After serving as senator from New York and secretary of state, Hillary Clinton almost lost the party's nomination in 2016 to Bernie Sanders, an eccentric senator from Vermont who labeled himself a democratic socialist. Meanwhile, Donald Trump, a celebrity real estate developer and television personality, defeated a number of very well-funded Republican politicians to win the Republican nomination before defeating Hillary Clinton in the Electoral College, although not in the popular vote.

It was an era of declining confidence in the American political, economic, and journalistic establishments, engendered in part by the innovative use of social media by social movements and Internet innovators, including some in the Russian government (Weisburd, Watts, and Berger 2017). It was an era in which charisma trumped competence and nationalism trumped globalization. In 2016, the right emerged triumphant, at least in electoral politics, although leftist populism remains ascendant among the generations that will shape political life in the future.

The Economic Crisis of 2007–08

After a long period of improving economic conditions, the American people's expectations were suddenly dashed by the economic crisis of 2007–08. The triggering event was the collapse of a bubble in housing prices that had been stimulated by irresponsible banking practices and government policies. Investment bankers and mortgage brokers had bundled large numbers of questionable mortgages into financial packages and sold them to investors on the theory that they could not all go bad at once. But that is exactly what happens when a bubble bursts, and major investment banks and insurance companies were suddenly insolvent. Millions of people had borrowed too much money to invest in homes they really could not afford on the theory that housing prices would keep going up indefinitely. Their expectations were dashed and the economy went into a tailspin.

The financial crisis of 2007–08 was an example of what political scientist James Davies (1962; 1969) called the "J-curve of rising and declining satisfactions" (see chapter 1 in this volume). Davies's theory suggests that protest will break out when conditions suddenly worsen because people become angry and seek someone to blame for the disturbing course of events. They also seek a solution. But to do this, they need a theoretical "frame" to articulate their grievances and tell them who is at fault and what should be done about it (also discussed in chapter 2 in this volume).

Social movements compete to frame the events for their potential followers so they can mobilize them to pressure for change.

People's first reaction is usually to blame the president when the economy goes bad. As former president Harry Truman famously said, "the buck stops here." This is true even though the American Constitution severely limits the president's ability to regulate the economy. President George W. Bush was a conservative Republican whose inclination was to let the private sector take care of itself. When the crisis struck in 2007, he went so far as to allow one huge investment bank, Lehman Brothers, to go bankrupt. But his advisors persuaded him he could not let the whole financial structure collapse, so he authorized the government to buy up bad investments from several other huge investment banks and insurance companies. They were considered "too big to fail," because their failure would bring down the rest of the economy.

Protest from progressive activists was largely muted during this period, partly because President Bush was being forced by events to take many of the actions progressives would normally advocate, such as intervening in major financial institutions. In addition, President Bush's term was close to its end and many progressives put their energy into the campaign that elected Barack Obama in November 2008. President Obama, elected on a vague program of "a future you can believe in," continued many of the policies Bush had established to stabilize the financial system, and he added spending programs to stimulate economic revival. One of the most controversial was to have the government purchase shares in the General Motors and Chrysler corporations to keep them from going bankrupt. Many conservatives, including Mitt Romney, the former Massachusetts governor and likely presidential candidate, opposed this.

The J-curve hypothesis explains the upsurge in discontent following the economic crisis, but framing theory is needed to explain how the discontent was articulated into grievances that engendered a protest cycle. Unlike other protest cycles where one frame became predominant, this protest cycle was characterized by polarization between two competing frames. These were most clearly exemplified by two social movements: the Tea Party and the Occupy movement.

The Tea Party Movement

The first major social movement to emerge in this period was not a response to the crisis from the left, but a protest from the right against President Obama's anticrisis policies. This became known as the Tea Party movement (Wikipedia 2013a), in reference to the Boston Tea Party of 1773 that helped to spark the American Revolution. The movement's collective action frame was that the government, not bankers or mortgage brokers, had caused the problem, and that the less the government did about it the better. The spark that touched off the mass movement was a speech or "rant" on the floor of the Chicago Mercantile Exchange on 19 February 2009 by Rick Santelli, a former hedge fund manager who was working as a reporter for a cable network. He protested President Obama's plan to help homeowners who were unable to keep up payments on their mortgages, exclaiming: "This is America! How many of you people want to pay for your neighbor's mortgage that has an extra bathroom and can't pay their bills? . . . President Obama, are you listening?" He called for a "Chicago Tea Party" to overthrow Obama's policy (Berg 2012; Skocpol and Williamson 2012).

Santelli's rant, which went viral on the Internet, touched a nerve with many conservative Americans who felt they were losing control of the country they loved. The phrase "Tea Party" became a "meme," a unit of cultural symbolism that takes on a life of its own (Canning and Reinsborough 2010). The meme concept was introduced by evolutionary biologist Richard Dawkins (1976) as a sociological parallel to the concept of the gene in biology, a small kernel of information that shapes how an organism develops. A meme can be a slogan, a phrase, or a symbol; it becomes a meme when it spreads through a susceptible population like a virus "infecting" one person after another. Political consultants and specialists in public relations and advertising often work hard trying to invent memes that will catch on with their target populations. So do social movement leaders.

Social movement memes work best when they express a general feeling or mood or philosophy, not a specific policy proposal, although policies can be crafted to fit memes (Barnett 2011). The Tea Party meme symbolized the belief that too many of the American people have become soft and lazy and irresponsible, expecting the government to solve their problems for them. It symbolized the idea that we should cut social programs and taxes, let failed businesses go bankrupt, and wait for the private sector to revive the economy.

Many progressives thought that the Tea Party meme was a tool used by wealthy foundations and corporate interests to manipulate the public. And it is true that the Tea Party meme was promoted by right-wing organizations and mass media, especially Fox News. But it is also true that grassroots activism based on the Tea Party meme was impressive (Skocpol and Williamson 2012). Approximately a thousand chapters were organized around the country to protest President Obama's stimulus plan and especially his proposal to provide subsidized health insurance for low-income workers. Tea Party supporters tended to be Republican, white, male, married, and over forty-five. Many of them were small-business owners, few were public employees. A large number were senior citizens who were receiving Social Security and free single-payer medical care from the federal government. But their zeal for cutting government did not extend to ending these programs; they believed that they had earned them. They opposed extending medical and unemployment benefits to younger people.

The Tea Party meme was successful in mobilizing conservative Americans, but a majority of the population never adopted it. A *New York Times/CBS News* poll in April 2010 found that 18 percent of the population identified as Tea Party supporters. Tea Party activists realized that they were a minority and decided to adopt many of the tactics pioneered by progressive social movements during the protests of the 1960s and '70s. In their interviews with Tea Party activists, Skocpol and Williamson (2012) found that a surprising number cited the work of community organizer Saul Alinsky as a model for their organizational tactics, although their goals were largely the opposite of Alinsky's, who worked to improve the living conditions of the poor. The Tea Party followed Alinsky's lead in directing anger against programs that were unpopular with their constituency, rather than focusing on alternative proposals of their own.

Several Tea Party protests attracted large numbers of participants. Roughly 250,000 people participated in approximately 200 "Tax Day" rallies around the country in April 2009 (Berg 2012). A "Taxpayer March on Washington" on 12 September 2009 drew tens of thousands of participants.

These protests hammered away against government meddling in the economy in the interests of "undeserving" people. They argued that the Community Reinvestment Act, which had encouraged lenders to give mortgages to low-income people, was responsible for the wave of defaults that triggered the crisis. The solution, in their view, was to cut funds for government bureaucrats and "lazy" people dependent on handouts.

Because of its timing, the Tea Party acted as a backlash against the election of Barack Obama, although Tea Party leaders adamantly denied that Obama's race had anything to do with it. Tea Party spokespersons conceded that many of the policies they opposed—including heavy deficit spending—actually began under Republican administrations, and that they had not organized to oppose them then. But they thought they should have, and they were critical of both Republican and Democratic legislators. Instead of forming a third party, however, they thought it more effective to focus their efforts on the Republican primary elections in 2010. In so doing, they drove the Republican Party further to the right, nominating candidates who promised to end "Obamacare," President Obama's health-care reform, and cut federal spending without increasing taxes. Their efforts were rewarded in the 2010 midterm elections when there was a shift toward conservative Republicans in Congress and in state elections.

A cycle of contention often develops when heightened activism by a social movement generates intensified activism by social movements with opposing views. In this case, politicians elected with Tea Party support passed legislation in several states that provoked a militant response from activists with progressive, pro-labor views. These activists responded with demonstrations, marches, rallies, and other actions drawn from much the same repertoire of contention as that used by the Tea Party activists. This process was especially acute in several Midwestern states that had been strongly affected by the economic crisis.

Progressives Strike Back: Labor Rights in Wisconsin and Ohio

Conservative Republicans won several important state elections in 2010, including the governorship in the states of Wisconsin and Ohio. These newly elected leaders moved quickly to implement one of their key goals—weakening the role of organized labor, especially for state employees. Democratic state legislators fought these measures as best they could, sometimes using parliamentary maneuvers such as traveling out of state to deny Republicans a quorum. But they were outnumbered and were unable to stop the Republican majorities in the state legislatures.

In Wisconsin, the Republicans succeeded in passing a bill severely restricting the rights of public employee unions (Berg 2012; Kersten 2011; Nichols 2012). Protests were organized primarily by the labor movement in the state, with strong support from students at the University of Wisconsin in Madison and other progressive groups. Appeals were sent to the Wisconsin Supreme Court, which had a 4–3 majority of conservative judges. But one of the conservatives was up for reelection, which provided a political opportunity for protesters to organize to support his progressive opponent. They also organized a petition campaign to recall several newly elected Republican legislators and newly elected Republican governor Scott Walker.

Activism was most intense in the state capitol, which is located in Madison, next to the University of Wisconsin campus. On several occasions, the capitol mall filled up with protesters estimated to number 100,000 or more. Supporters came in from as far as New York City. Some of the protesters physically occupied the capitol building, setting up a sleeping area and information center and distributing food contributed by local businesses. Later, some protesters began living in tents around the capitol.

The Wisconsin protests were impressive, making it clear that there was strong opposition to antilabor policies. Their stated goal was not to make a statement, but to reverse the antilabor legislation. They could not persuade the governor or the Republican majority in the legislature to do that. They had only two practical options: to file lawsuits to reverse the legislation in court, or to file recall petitions to have the governor and recalcitrant legislators replaced. They tried both options, and won some legal victories over technicalities. The legislature reacted by correcting the technicalities and passing the legislation again. So the only definitive way to win was to file petitions for recall elections.

Under Wisconsin law a recall petition leads to a new election with candidates chosen by the political parties that had participated in the original election. The protesters succeeded in gathering more than enough signatures for recall elections against Walker and several state legislators. The other side responded by filing recall petitions against several Democratic legislators, on the grounds that they had abandoned their posts by leaving the state to avoid voting. But when it came to the actual recall elections, most of the legislators won reelection. A few Republican legislators were replaced, but not enough to change the balance in the legislature. In the most important election, Governor Walker won 53.1 percent of the 2011 recall election vote, slightly higher than the 52.3 percent that he had received when he won the office in 2010 (Wikipedia 2013a). Many Wisconsin voters felt that Walker had won his office fairly and that opponents should wait until the next regularly scheduled election to challenge him.

The political outcome was different in the state of Ohio, where newly elected Republican governor John Kasich and a Republican-dominated state legislature had passed similar legislation cutting the rights of state employee unions (Burstein 2012). Ohio provided a better political opportunity than Wisconsin, since it had a law that allowed opponents to file a petition to repeal the new laws without recalling the governor or legislators from office. This meant that the movement did not have to directly confront Governor Kasich, who was quite popular in the state. The protest organization We Are Ohio succeeded in framing the legislation as an attack on Ohio's schoolteachers, fire fighters, nurses, and police officers. The labor unions financed much of the campaign and mobilized many of the activists, but the campaign literature and advertisements did not emphasize labor rights or partisan issues. The Fraternal Order of Police generally supports Republican candidates, but it joined in the We Are Ohio effort. Organizers went out of their way to recruit Republicans in many communities to the campaign to protect local teachers, fire fighters, nurses, and police officers.

We Are Ohio gathered more than a million valid petition signatures to put reversing the legislation on the November 2011 election ballot. The measure won with 61.3 percent of the vote. This was a rare victory for the labor movement; struggles against "right-to-work" legislation were lost in the neighboring states of Michigan and Indiana. The success can be attributed to the movement's effectiveness in framing the issue as defending Ohio's teachers, fire fighters, nurses, and police officers. Cutting government spending is popular in the abstract, but not when it is framed as punishing respected, hardworking, and modestly paid local citizens.

Success and failure in social movements can be measured in different ways. Some movements focus on short-term policy objectives, others aim to raise issues and stimulate a process of cultural reevaluation and eventual change. The labor mobilizations in Wisconsin and Ohio had short-term policy objectives aimed at protecting workers' jobs. The We Are Ohio movement succeeded in doing this by carefully framing its slogans in such a way as to appeal to the widest possible base of support, taking advantage of the opportunity provided by Ohio law. The Wisconsin activists were not successful in doing this because the state constitution did not provide a way to put the issue itself on the ballot. They had to petition to recall individual politicians, a tactic that alienated some voters.

These state-level movements were very important for people in certain states, but the progressive movements needed to organize around broader issues. The Tea Party, after all, was focused primarily on federal budgetary issues, and progressives had very different views about federal policy. They wanted to use the federal government to address problems such as poverty, unemployment, and growing inequality by increasing spending on social programs and raising taxes on the wealthy. They needed a meme to crystallize their movement, much as the Tea Party meme had crystallized the opposition. They found it by focusing not on a policy goal, but on a tactic: occupying Wall Street.

The Occupy Movement

The Occupy Movement (Wikipedia 2013c; 2013d) was launched on 13 July 2011 with a blog post and a hashtag: #OCCUPYWALLSTREET (Adbusters 2011). Hashtags are simply words or phrases preceded by the number symbol (#). They are widely used on Twitter and other microblogging social networking sites as a way for users to self-organize an online discussion. Anyone can post a message that includes the hashtag and anyone can find the messages by searching for the hashtag. This method of self-organizing is especially appropriate for movements that favor egalitarian organizational structures where anyone can play a leadership role.

The use of the hashtag in this case was not accidental; it was posted by *Adbusters*, a magazine and organization that describes itself on its web site (www.adbusters.org) as "a global network of culture jammers and creatives working to change the way information flows, the way corporations wield power, and the way meaning is produced in our society." The *Adbusters* group is quite sophisticated about social theory, and makes heavy use of the meme concept (Lasn and Adbusters 2012). Kalle Lasn, the principal organizer behind *Adbusters*, observed that "*Adbusters* floated the meme of occupying the iconic heart of global capitalism." As a *New York Times* columnist reported (Sommer 2012), "spreading radically subversive memes is Mr. Lasn's avowed mission." Memes can be phrases, but they can also be pictures, videos, products, or even tunes. Some examples floated by the *Adbusters* group include "Buy Nothing Christmas" (with a picture of an empty-handed Santa Claus), "Joe Chemo" (with a picture of Joe Camel, the tobacco mascot), a "Consumer Pig" video, "Blackspot Unswooshers" (sustainable high top sneakers), and "the Year of the Snake."

Of course, not every meme goes viral. *Adbusters* has floated a lot of them, and most disappear quickly. Why did the Occupy Wall Street meme catch on? It had many of the same virtues as the Tea Party meme. It provided a focus for a large group of people who were discontented but had not found an effective theme to express their sense of grievance. These were people with an anticorporate perspective who blamed big business and big government for the economic crisis. They were not satisfied with the Democratic Party as a vehicle for their discontent, as they saw the Democrats as too moderate, too compromised, too tied to corporate financing. In an earlier historical period, these people would probably have advocated "socialism" or "anarchism" as alternative memes, but these were old and had lost their luster. Organizing a demonstration around these memes would not be likely to generate much response.

The Occupy Wall Street meme was new, and it offered something exciting to do. The *Adbusters* post, with a hashtag as its headline, was distributed widely to email lists and blogs. It cited the recent occupation of Tahrir Square in Cairo and recent encampments in Spain as models, and called on New Yorkers to descend on "Wall Street: the financial Gomorrah of America." Specifically, it said that "on September 17, we want to see

20,000 people flood into lower Manhattan, set up tents, kitchens, peaceful barricades, and occupy Wall Street for a few months" (Adbusters 2011).

They recognized that a demonstration needed to make a demand. Tahrir Square worked because the demonstrators demanded the removal of President Mubarak. What could the Occupy Wall Street demonstrators demand? The best they could come up with was a demand that President Obama convene a commission tasked with ending the influence money has on our representatives in Washington. They proposed the slogan "Democracy not Corporatocracy."

Adbusters was based in Vancouver, British Columbia, not a good location for organizing a few months' encampment in New York City. Fortunately, the encampment idea appealed to a group of organizers who were in New York City, some of whom had already staged a "Bloombergville" (named after New York's mayor, Michael Bloomberg) outside New York's City Hall to protest budget cuts (Kroll 2011). Some of them had been in Madrid on 15 May 2011 when 20,000 outraged citizens had poured into the Puerta del Sol, transforming the city's central plaza into a version of Tahrir Square. They latched on to the Occupy Wall Street meme and did the hard organizational work to make the occupation a reality.

However, they did not adopt *Adbusters'* suggestion to demand a commission to find a way to end the influence of money on politics. Campaign finance reform was not a new issue, and the Supreme Court had already vetoed it. While the protesters had long lists of complaints, they could not agree on any specific policy demands. As organizer Sarah van Gelder observed, "the system is broken in so many ways that it's dizzying to try to name them all. This is part of the reason why the Occupy movement hasn't created a list of demands. The problem is everywhere and looks different from every point of view. The one thing the protesters all seem to agree on is that the middle-class way of life is moving out of reach" (Van Gelder 2011, 4). The Occupy Wall Street meme was diffuse enough to focus their anger without tying them down to policy debates.

Wall Street symbolizes capitalism because the New York Stock Exchange is there, but the protesters did not try to occupy the stock exchange. Instead, they set up housekeeping in Zuccotti Park, a small public space a few blocks away. The park had been built by a private corporation under New York laws that require companies to build parks in exchange for permission to erect office buildings. The law required the park to be open to the public twenty-four hours a day, unlike ordinary public parks that could be closed at night or fenced off by police. This was fortuitous for the Occupy encampment.

The 17 September 2011 occupation of Zuccotti Park was successful. The park was filled with campers, and the news media descended on them. The mainstream media had been reporting on the Tea Party for two years and they needed a group to embody the other side. They seized on one of the slogans on the protesters' signs and blog posts as symbolizing the theme of the movement: "We are the 99%." The 99% meme went viral. Occupy Wall Street was defined as a movement against the increasing concentration of wealth by the most affluent 1 percent of the population. The media commentators could explore this theme in depth. It was a good counterpoint to the Tea Party's focus on debt and dependency on government.

The encampment was also intriguing from an organizational point of view (Gitlin 2012). Rather than advocating for legislative change, the protesters sought to provide a model of an alternative way of life. There was no established leadership; instead there was a general assembly where anyone could speak and decisions were made by consensus. Anyone could freeze a decision if they thought that an ethical issue was at stake. Public address systems were prohibited in the park, so organizers invented the "people's mic," whereby people would repeat the speaker's words for people who were too far back to hear. Sometimes the crowd was so large that two or three relays were needed.

This decentralized, "horizontal" decision-making took a lot of time, which was fine because it gave the protesters something to do while camping. The camaraderie was energizing, especially for people who had been depressed about not finding work in their areas of specialization or being able to maintain middle-class lifestyles. As organizer Sarah van Gelder observed:

> The Occupy Wall Street movement is not just demanding change. It is also transforming how we, the 99%, see ourselves. The shame many of us felt when we couldn't find a job, pay down our debts, or keep our home is being replaced by a political awakening. Millions now recognize that we

Ted Goertzel

are not to blame for a weak economy, for a subprime mortgage meltdown, or for a tax system that favors the wealthy
but bankrupts the government. The 99% are coming to see
that we are collateral damage in an all-out effort by the su-
per-rich to get even richer. (2011, 2)

The Occupy activists did not set themselves the goal of shutting down the
New York Stock Exchange. If the Occupy movement had occurred during
the protest cycle of the 1960s and '70s, they might have staged a sit-in at the
stock exchange around the slogan "Shut Down the Stock Exchange," just
as activists tried to shut down the Pentagon in 1967. That would have given
the police an excuse to arrest the protesters, and it would have alienated
a lot of people who would object to the protesters' methods even though
they sympathized with their goals.

In any event, this movement was not about a specific stock exchange in
New York, it was about a global economic system. The point was to propagate the meme, and the Occupy meme spread very quickly to other cities
in the United States and around the world. This was a remarkable example
of social movement diffusion. Zuccotti Park was occupied on 17 September 2011. By 9 October, Occupy movements were underway in 95 cities
in 82 countries, and in 600 communities in the United States (Wikipedia
2013b). Some of these movements actually antedated Occupy Wall Street.
A Democracy Village had been set up outside the British Parliament in
London in 2010. The Spanish movement, known as the *Indignados*, or the
Indignant, first set up camps in Madrid and elsewhere in Spain in mid-
May 2011. The General Assembly group in New York City was quite fam-
iliar with the Spanish events and with anarchist social theories and practices that have been better developed in Spain than in any other country.
The Arab Spring movement, especially the occupation of Tahrir Square in
Egypt, can also be seen as a precursor to the Wall Street occupation. These
movements differed because the problems and political structures vary
in each country, but they shared the tactic of setting up camps in public
squares.

For a few weeks, it seemed as if the Occupy movement was sweeping the globe and foretelling a major social transformation. An "instant
book" edited by Occupy Wall Street leaders (Van Gelder 2011) had the title

This Changes Everything. But what had really changed? The Wall Street traders continued with business as usual: few if any descended from the office towers to engage the protesters. The more acute conflict was with the New York City Police Department (Greenberg 2012b), who seemed happy enough earning overtime pay for managing and harassing the protesters. By the time Mayor Bloomberg arranged to have the police clear the park, some of the protesters acknowledged that they were secretly relieved (Gitlin 2012, 68–9). They did not really want to camp out in Zuccotti Park through the winter, and being driven out by the police was more dramatic than voluntarily decamping.

Protest Cycles and Electoral Politics

The first consequence of the protest cycle triggered by the economic crisis of 2007–08 was the election of Barack Obama in 2008, America's first black president. His campaign had some of the flavor of a social movement, based as it was on vaguely phrased promises such as "a future you can believe in." He was new on the scene and more charismatic than either Hillary Clinton, his challenger in the Democratic Party primary, or John McCain, his Republican opponent.

Both the Occupy and the Tea Party movements were, in part, reactions to his presidency, Occupy from the left and the Tea Party from the right. In the 2010 midterm elections, the right was resurgent and took control of Congress from the Democrats, greatly restricting what the Obama administration could do. The global protest cycle of 2011 had passed its peak, but Obama nevertheless defeated Mitt Romney, his less exciting Republican opponent in 2012.

In 2016, the country's focus was on the presidential election, and two protest movements emerged to support candidates in the election. Electoral reform engendered by earlier social movements had taken control of the nomination process away from the professional party politicians and given it to the public in primary elections. Two candidates emerged as protests against the candidates favored by the party establishments: Bernie Sanders for the Democrats and Donald Trump for the Republicans.

Bernie Sanders used themes from the Occupy movement, including an attack on "the 1 percent," and denouncing the decline of middle-class incomes and the influence of corporate money on politics. His slogan, "feel the Bern," was coined by an Occupy organizer (Heaney 2016). He appealed strongly to many middle-class white youth, both male and female, and promised free college tuition. His long commitment to socialist ideals promised a radical change, but he did not have a track record of support for black issues comparable to that of Hillary Clinton, and he was criticized by the Black Lives Matter movement that had arisen in response to police killings of black citizens in several American cities.

Sanders mounted a surprisingly effective movement for the Democratic Party nomination, but was eventually defeated by Hillary Clinton. The Republican challenger, Donald Trump, faced competition from a large number of rivals. The establishment candidate, Jeb Bush, did not have the kind of consensus support that the Democratic Party leaders gave to Hillary Clinton. He attacked international trade agreements, especially the North American Free Trade Agreement, for taking jobs from American workers. Bernie Sanders also attacked the free trade agreements in an attempt to appeal to the blue collar working class. Neither addressed automation, a primary cause of declining industrial and mining employment in the United States.

The Trump movement did adopt some of the Tea Party's policy goals: cutting taxes, repealing the Affordable Care Act, hostility to minorities and immigration, opposition to abortion rights. But Trump was not a consistent ideologue, and some of his positions, such as favoring a massive public works program to generate employment and repair the infrastructure, differed from traditional right-wing ideology. Where Trump really excelled was in the use of Internet memes to shape public discourse, something that could have been learned from Occupy as much as from the Tea Party (Marantz 2016; Nawaz 2016). Trump made heavy use of Twitter to create memes that stigmatized his opponents, such as #Crooked Hillary, #Little Marco, and #TimeToGetTough. This approach was highly effective in drawing media attention, much of which was critical, but that did not matter. Television coverage of the 2016 campaign devoted more time to Hillary Clinton's use of a private email server than to all policy issues combined (Boehlert 2016).

Conclusions

The global economic crisis of 2007–08 triggered a protest cycle in the United States as well as in many other countries. In the United States, the two most influential movements were the Tea Party and Occupy Wall Street. Both drew on a repertoire of ideas and tactics developed in previous protest cycles, especially in the 1960s and '70s. Some of the activists were old enough to have participated in those earlier cycles of activism; others were from younger generations who were creating their own traditions. The Occupy movement also drew extensively on a repertoire of tactics developed in other countries. Both were effective in using contemporary media to propagate memes that shaped public discourse.

Of the theories considered in this volume, J-curve theory best explains the emergence of these movements, while framing theory and the cultural theory of grievances best explain their impact. The two movements offered conflicting interpretations of the causes of the economic downturn and what should be done about it. Both of these conflicting interpretations were absorbed into the mainstream political dialogue in the country. The United States differs from many of the countries discussed in this volume in having a well-established electoral system that provides a legitimate channel for discontent. Much of the activism was channeled into this arena, and the issues raised by the movements were fought out in midterm elections in 2010 and 2014 and in presidential elections in 2012 and 2016.

Resource mobilization theory helps us to understand how the movements were organized. The Tea Party drew on resources long developed by right-wing activists, including wealthy foundations and publicity from conservative media. Occupy relied on support from the labor movement and from progressive political groups in New York City and around the world. Both movements made extensive use of social media and the Internet, as well as winning coverage in traditional media.

Following political process theory, Tea Party activists moved quickly to support candidates in Republican primaries. The activists who mobilized the Occupy movement were slower to respond to the mainstream political process. Many of them were disillusioned by party politics and sought a vaguely defined radical alternative. Progressive activists did become politically active in Wisconsin and Ohio, and to a lesser extent in other states, in response to antiunion initiatives. By doing so, they faced the challenge of getting more than 50 percent of the vote in actual elections, something that is more difficult than claiming to represent the 99 percent at a rally or in a blog post.

The progressive cause in 2012 was led primarily by the Obama campaign, which relied extensively on volunteer activists and used memes popularized by the Occupy movement. And Obama won with 53 percent of the vote, aided by Mitt Romney's being caught by a blogger dismissing 47 percent of American voters as hopelessly dependent on government handouts. The Tea Party's role in 2012 was largely to support right-wing primary candidates, thus weakening Romney's campaign during the general election. Both movements were very important in promoting memes that were absorbed into the mainstream party campaigns, but winning elections required putting together broader coalitions. This was also the lesson of the We Are Ohio campaign, which won a dramatic victory by appealing to a wider segment of the state's population.

In the 2016 election, the Trump campaign easily defeated well-funded and experienced Republican primary opponents, and it won an Electoral College victory in 2016, although it lost the popular vote by a substantial margin. Trump benefited from the constitutional structure in the United States, which gives disproportionate weight to small states and rural areas that had been left behind as the global economy developed.

Commentators are divided in their appraisals of both the Tea Party and the Occupy movements (Gitlin 2012; Greenberg 2011, 2012a; Kornacki 2012; Roberts 2012; Walzer 2012). Both were very successful in promoting their memes, which was their most important accomplishment. But neither became a dominant organizational force in American politics—indeed, both remained outside the mainstream. The Tea Party movement was clear about its policy proposals, but it was unable to nominate a Republican candidate that clearly shared its ideas, and its support may have done more harm than good to the Romney campaign in 2012. In 2016, Trump took more from the organizational tactics of both the Occupy and the Tea Party movements than from the Tea Party's policy agenda. Occupy never found a specific policy focus, which some commentators see as a serious flaw (Walzer 2012). However, its broad goals of lessening inequality and sustaining the middle classes were espoused by the Obama campaign, which won in 2012, and by the Bernie Sanders campaign, which came surprisingly close to winning the Democratic Party's presidential nomination in 2016. It is not at all clear that Sanders could have defeated Trump had he won the nomination; his support from minorities was weak and his focus on stigmatizing the wealthy 1 percent might not have defeated Trump's stigmatizing of minorities, the poor, and trade policies. But the demographic trends in the United States continue to favor the groups that supported Obama and Sanders, and they will certainly mount strong challenges to Trump and his base in forthcoming elections.

REFERENCES

Adbusters. 2011. "#OCCUPYWALLSTREET" (blog post). 13 July. http://www.adbusters.org/blogs/adbusters-blog/occupywallstreet.html (accessed 18 June 2018).

Barnett, Randy. 2011. "The Tea Party, the Constitution and the Repeal Amendment." *Northwestern University Law Review Colloquy* 105: 281–87.

Berg, John. 2012. "Does Changing the Story Change Voting Behavior? The Occupy Movement and the Crisis of the American Party System." *American Political Science Association 2012 Annual Meeting Paper*. http://ssrn.com/abstract=2108707 (accessed 18 June 2018).

Boehlert, Eric. 2016. "Study Confirms Network Evening Newscasts Have Abandoned Policy Coverage for 2016 Campaign." *Media Matters for America*, 26 October. http://mediamatters.org/blog/2016/10/26/study-confirms-network-evening-newscasts-have-abandoned-policy-coverage-2016-campaign/214120 (accessed 18 June 2018).

Burstein, Rachel. 2012. "How Labor Won in Ohio." *Dissent* 59, no. 3: 34–7.

Canning, Doyle, and Patrick Reinsborough. 2010. *Re:Imagining Change: How to Use Story-Based Strategy to Win Campaigns, Build Movements, and Change the World*. Oakland, CA: PM Press.

Davies, James C. 1962. "Toward a Theory of Revolution." *American Sociological Review* 27, no. 1: 5–19.

———. 1969. "The J-Curve of Rising and Declining Satisfactions as a Cause of Some Great Revolutions and a Contained Rebellion." In *Violence in America*, edited by Ted Robert Gurr, 690–730. New York: Praeger.

Dawkins, Richard. 1976. *The Selfish Gene*. New York: Oxford University Press.

Gitlin, Todd. 2012. *Occupy Nation: The Roots, the Spirit, and the Promise of Occupy Wall Street*. New York: Itbooks.

Greenberg, Michael. 2011. "Zucotti Park: What Future?" *New York Review of Books*, 8 December.

———. 2012a. "What Future for Occupy Wall Street?" *New York Review of Books*, 9 February.

———. 2012b. "New York: The Police and the Protestors." *New York Review of Books*, 11 and 25 October.

Heaney, Michael. 2016. "Bernie Sanders and the Occupy Wall Street Wing of the Democratic Party." *Mobilizing Ideas*, 29 September. https://mobilizingideas. wordpress.com/2016/09/29/bernie-sanders-and-the-occupy-wall-street-wing-of-the-democratic-party/ (accessed 18 June 2018).

Kersten, Andrew. 2011. *The Battle for Wisconsin*. New York: Hill and Wang.

Kornacki, Steve. 2012. "Triumph of the Tea Party Mindset." *Salon*, 27 December. http:// www.salon.com/2012/12/27/triumph_of_the_tea_party_mindset (accessed 18 June 2018).

Kroll, Andy. 2011. "How Occupy Wall Street really got Started." *Mother Jones*, 17 October. http://www.motherjones.com/politics/2011/10/occupy-wall-street-international-origins (accessed 18 June 2018).

Lasn, Kalle, and Adbusters. 2012. *Meme Wars: The Creative Destruction of Neoclassical Economics*. New York: Seven Stories Press.

Marantz, Andrew. 2016. "Trolls for Trump: Meet Mike Cernovich, the Meme Mastermind of the Alt-right." *New Yorker*, 31 October. http://www.newyorker.com/ magazine/2016/10/31/trolls-for-trump (accessed 18 June 2018).

Nawaz, Maajid. 2016. "Trump and the Triumphant Trolls: What's Their Secret," *Daily Beast*, 23 November. http://www.thedailybeast.com/articles/2016/11/23/trump-and-the-triumphant-trolls-what-s-their-secret.html (accessed 18 June 2018).

Nichols, John. 2012. *Uprising: How Wisconsin Renewed the Politics of Protest, From Madison to Wall Street*. New York: Nation Books.

Roberts, Alasdair. 2012. "Why the Occupy Movement Failed." *Public Administration Review* 72, no. 5: 754–62.

Skocpol, Theda, and Vanessa Williamson. 2012. *The Tea Party and the Remaking of Republican Conservatism*. New York: Oxford University Press.

Sommer, Jeff. 2012. "The War Against Too Much of Everything." *New York Times*, 22 December.

Van Gelder, Sarah, ed. 2011. *This Changes Everything: Occupy Wall Street and the 99% Movement*. San Francisco: Barrett-Koehler.

Walzer, Michael. 2012. "Social Movements and Election Campaigns." *Dissent* 59, no. 3: 25–28.

Weisburd, Andrew, Clint Watts, and J. M. Berger. 2016. "Trolling for Trump: How Russia is Trying to Destroy our Democracy." *War on the Rocks*. 6 November. https:// warontherocks.com/2016/11/trolling-for-trump-how-russia-is-trying-to-destroy-our-democracy/ (accessed 15 October 2018).

Wikipedia. 2013a. "Tea Party movement." https://en.wikipedia.org/wiki/Tea_Party_ movement (accessed 1 January 2013).

———. 2013b. "2011 Wisconsin protests." https://en.wikipedia.org/wiki/2011_Wisconsin_ protests (accessed 1 January 2013).

———. 2013c. "Occupy movement." https://en.wikipedia.org/wiki/Occupy_movement (accessed 1 January 2018).

———. 2013d. "Occupy Wall Street." https://en.wikipedia.org/wiki/Occupy_Wall_Street (accessed 1 January 2018).

PART IV:
CONCLUSIONS

9

Rethinking Protest Impacts

Moisés Arce, Roberta Rice, and Eduardo Silva

What role do social protests play in democratic change? Why do similar types of protest movements produce different kinds of outcomes? How are protest movements realigning politics around the globe? These questions stand as the final challenge for this volume. Throughout this book we have endeavored to understand the causes and consequences of the 2011 global protest cycle that began with the Arab Spring uprising in Egypt's Tahrir Square in January and concluded with the clearing of New York's Zuccotti Park in November. During that year of contention, untold numbers of citizens took to the streets and to social media to call for new forms of democratic political representation, deliberation, and decision-making. According to Tilly and Tarrow, the self-immolation of a young, college-educated Tunisian street vendor in December 2010 touched off "the most remarkable protest cycle since the movements of the 1960s in Europe and North America" (2015, 134). For the most part, the Arab Spring ended where it began—in Tunisia—in terms of its ability to precipitate democratic regime change. Nonetheless, the 2011 protest cycle marked the beginning of a new era of global politics and of a new agenda for social movement research. Two major themes have arisen out of this volume. The first theme is the important role that grievances played in fueling the 2011 protest movements. The second theme is the central role that political opportunity structures played in conditioning the impacts of social movements, if not in their emergence.

The volume's introduction sought to explain the factors driving the recent global protest cycle. In other words, we treated protest as a dependent variable. In this concluding essay, we look at protest as an independent variable by assessing its influence on political change. We begin by elaborating upon our original framework of analysis in light of the findings of our contributors. We have argued that protest movements are more likely to affect political and institutional change when they are part of a cycle of protest, when the grievances expressed by protesters resonate with the broader society, and when the political system is responsive to the demands of the protesters and the protesters are willing to engage in a process of negotiation.

The remainder of this chapter analyzes the interactive relationship between social protest and political change in the cases considered in the volume before turning its attention to the pressing question of how to assess movement impacts in a changing world.

Analyzing Movement Impacts

What happens once a protest cycle has ended? Scholars frequently lament the lack of attention to movement impacts in the social movement literature (see for instance Amenta and Caren 2007; Bosi, Giugni, and Uba 2016; Earl 2007; Whittier 2007). The existing literature does offer us some clues as to how best to assess the political consequences of social movements based on three kinds of impacts: a) direct institutional or policy impacts; b) cultural or biographical impacts on the lives of individual protesters; and c) indirect or unintended effects of social movements on contentious politics more generally. Political change is the result of continuous interactions between different actors in the political system, particularly between social movements and the state. According to Bosi,

> This changing power relation between the different actors is, more often than not, a critical catalyst for a change in the distribution of power—whether this has positive effects, or results in a backlash for the social movement and its constituency. What we surely can say is that no protest wave

leaves the power relation between the movement's constituency and the state unaffected. (2016, 338)

Clearly, protest movements have consequences at a variety of levels of analysis (micro, meso, and macro) and across a number of different areas (social, cultural, economic, and political). To advance our understanding of when these various impacts are especially heightened, our volume proposes a new framework with which to analyze social movement consequences.

The literature on political and institutional impacts takes its cue from the early work of William Gamson on social protest success (discussed in chapter 7 by Donoso and Somma). Gamson (1975) identified *new advantages* and *acceptance* as two key social movement outcomes that can be objectively assessed and measured. New advantages are said to be accrued when a state-oriented challenger's goals or demands are realized through the passage of favorable legislation or the extent to which political parties or governing agencies adopt aspects of a social movement's agenda. Acceptance relates to whether or not a social movement challenger is recognized as a legitimate representative of a sector of society through acknowledgment by governmental officials. Gamson's state-oriented assumptions about movement success are particularly problematic for gauging the 2011 protest movements that explicitly rejected established political institutions as a means of change. According to Castells, it is difficult to "assess a direct effect of social movements on the political system in accordance with the values and proposals put forward by the movements. This is because the process to translate outrage expressed in society into hope of new politics is mediated by political machines that are not prepared, and not willing, to articulate this hope" (2015, 294). A recent analysis of the latest global protest cycle surmised that "in the process, new political actors, groups, and leaderships appear to have surfaced, *some* authorities have lost office, *some* dictators have fled, and *some* reforms have been made (Davies, Ryan, and Milcíades Peña 2016, 2; emphasis in original). For the most part, social movement success indicators are not well specified in the literature, with most scholars agreeing that the direct political effects of social movements are contingent and conditioned by political context (Amenta and Caren 2007; Bosi, Giugni, and Uba 2016).

In light of the challenges of assessing external movement influences, another body of work focuses on internal dynamics by examining the personal effects of movement participation on the lives of activists. The protest movements of the 1960s, for example, inspired a series of personal or biographical studies of protest participants that pointed to a powerful and enduring impact of participation in movement activities on the political and personal lives of the participants, shaping their political orientation and behavior well into the future (Giugni 2007). At stake in this body of literature is not the direct impact of social movements on democratic politics, but the influence that these movements have on the minds of people, individually and collectively, which may influence democratic cultures and practices over time. For instance, Castells (2015) introduced the concept of a "rhizomatic revolution" in his analysis of Spain's 2011 *Indignados* or 15-M movement as a way to explain the potential culture shift that it produced. The key features of this anti-austerity movement were a refusal to adopt any political agendas, plans, or programs, and a rejection of all formal leadership and organization. The result, according to Castells (2015, 145), is a continuously growing lateral revolution that may produce a significant change in the way democracy is practiced in Spain in the years to come. Despite the inherent methodological challenges of studying self-selected individuals and long-term culture shifts, this emerging body of work serves to remind us that social movements can have impacts on different areas of human life, and that they can occur at different levels of analysis.

A final area of research on the political consequences of social protest has to do with the dynamic interaction between social movements and the field of contentious politics in general, or "mobilization outcomes" (Tilly and Tarrow 2015). A small body of work on generative effects addresses how social movements influence each other. For instance, influential movements, such as the African-American civil rights movement, can generate "spin-off" movements or spawn countermovements that can alter the protest environment (Whittier 2007). Social movements that exist alongside each other can, and often do, change how activists define themselves, frame their issues, devise their strategies and tactics, and establish their presence. Whereas spin-off movements take on a momentum of their own by borrowing from the collective action frames and protest repetoires of an influential social movement, countermovements emerge in response to the policy gains or direct political impacts of a successful social movement campaign. The 2011 global protest cycle, which generated significant political opportunities for mobilization, opened the door to countermovements and antiestablishment political reactions in Europe and the United States, the effects of which are still being felt today (see chapter 8 by Ted Goertzel for a discussion of the 2016 election of American president Donald J. Trump). In short, social movement consequences are notoriously hard to define, let alone predict. Yet this is exactly what we propose to do.

Our volume seeks to advance the literature on when social movement impacts are more likely to be especially pertinent. We have suggested that protest movements tend to influence political and institutional change when the following conditions are met: a) when they occur during phases of heightened conflict; b) when their moral and material claims evoke strong reactions from the public; and c) when their respective political system is open to negotiation with protesters. Taken together, these three claims advance our thinking on the political impacts of protest by constituting a framework for explaining movement impact or influence.

Firstly, protest cycles enhance a particular protest movement's chances at successfully promoting political change by the way in which they support new collective action frames, tactical innovation, and scale-shift. According to Ayres and Macdonald (chapter 3, this volume), the 2011 protest movements are part of a third global protest cycle against economic globalization. As reported by Tilly and Tarrow (2015), this latest cycle of contention is the largest and most influential since the classic protest cycle of the 1960s. The collective action frame that connected today's globally dispersed protest movements underscored the political and economic exclusion experienced by a new generation of highly educated and underemployed youth, oftentimes referred to as "the precariat" (Standing 2014). Instead of focusing on specific policy measures, the 2011 protest movements emphasized a general mood of discontent (e.g., "The Indignant Ones"), the extent of the public they claimed to represent (e.g. "We are the 99%"), and on the tactics they employed (e.g. "Occupy Wall Street"). Beyond occupying urban public squares, the key tactical innovations of the contemporary protest movements included the effective use of social media to broadcast their message (see Larson, chapter 4) and "scale-jumping" or making strategic use of the transnational arena rather than abandoning the local, regional, and national spheres as part of a multiscalar dynamic (see Ayres and Macdonald, chapter 3). In reference to the 1964 student protests in Berkeley, California that touched off a decade of campus revolts across much of the United States, Mason has stated: "You may have thought such days were gone—such idealism, such eloquence, such creativity and hope. Well, they're back" (2013, 4). If past experience is a guide to future possibilities, this latest protest cycle promises to leave a lasting legacy of political change.

Secondly, grievances and claims play an essential role in mobilizing public support behind protest movements and in strengthening their capacity to bring about change in the desired direction. As Simmons (chapter 2, this volume) has proposed, a meaning-based approach to understanding mobilizing grievances recognizes social movement claims as both materially and ideationally constituted, evoking emotions, images, or memories that are unique to particular times and places. For example, the global financial crisis of 2007–08 may have served as the backdrop for the 2011 global protest cycle, or what della Porta and Mattoni (2014) have termed "movements of the crisis," yet some movements began only after a catalyzing event generated the moral shock needed to draw broad-based support for change from civil society. As documented by Kingston (chapter 6, this volume), in the period leading up to the Arab Spring uprisings, arbitrary and lethal acts of state violence against ordinary citizens had surpassed threshold levels and generated intense sociopolitical scorn and disdain for most of the political regimes in the region. In this instance, the 17 December 2010 public suicide of a Tunisian fruit vendor in the face of continued police harassment served as the trigger for the popular uprisings that spread across the Arab world and resulted in democratic regime change or reform in some of the region's republican regimes. In the case of Portugal, the spark that gave rise to what is referred to as the struggle of the "Desperate Generation" or the 12-M movement occurred on 23 January 2011 at a music concert by the Portuguese group Deolinda. The band's debut song, "How Silly Am I," aimed at a generation of unpaid interns and contract workers, started a national dialogue on the precarious condition of Portuguese youth that ended with the 23 March 2011 resignation of

Prime Minister José Sócrates (Estanque, Costa, and Soeiro 2013). While there is little in common between a suicide and a song, the grievances at the core of both performances resonated with their respective societies to the extent that the protest movements that emerged had profound consequences for the political regimes in power.

Finally, domestic political institutions serve to mediate the impacts of protest movements by the way in which they absorb or resist pressures for change. In established democratic systems with strong and effective political institutions, protesters tend to "move indoors" as discontent is channeled into routinized forms of politics (Mainwaring and Scully 1995). As Donoso and Somma's study (chapter 7) of the successful Chilean Winter protests against for-profit postsecondary education in that country indicates, both the permeability of political institutions to protesters' demands and the willingness of the protesters to engage with those institutions increases the likelihood of bringing about political and institutional change. In contrast, countries with ineffective or weakly institutionalized political institutions tend to be characterized by more confrontational politics or "transgressive contention" (Tilly and Tarrow 2015). In this context, where political regimes are more likely to resist change and protesters are less willing to work with existing institutions, the direct political impacts of social movements are likely to be minimal. The work of Boulding (chapter 5, this volume) reveals the important role played by nongovernmental organizations (NGOs) in fomenting protest and political change in countries of the Global South characterized by ineffectual democratic institutions. Based on public opinion data gathered just prior to the 2007–08 global financial meltdown, Boulding found that NGOs served as mobilizing structures for protest where democratic institutions were performing poorly. In sum, protest movements may produce dramatically different kinds of political outcomes depending on the quality of representation embedded in their respective domestic political institutions.

Movements of the Crisis and their Consequences

Iceland and Tunisia proved to be the early risers of the 2011 global protest cycle (Castells 2015; Mason 2013). The first protest movements to emerge in a protest cycle are influential in reshaping political opportunities for mobilization in the social movement sector. Early risers also set the master frame of protest for subsequent movements within the cycle. For example, the African-American civil rights movement of the late 1950s established a civil rights master frame that shaped the later demands of the student movement of the 1960s as well as the women's and gay rights movements of the 1970s (Whittier 2007). The start of a protest cycle is also when newly invented forms of collective action or the novel recombination of existing tactics emerge and, if they work, are adopted by subsequent protest movements (Wang and Soule 2016). In the cases of Iceland and Tunisia, protest movements began on Internet social networks before they manifested in urban space. In both countries, protesters were highly successful in bringing about political change in the desired direction—so much so that demonstrators in Cairo's Tahrir Square in January 2011 chanted, "Tunisia is the solution," while in May 2011 Spain's *Indignados* shouted, "Iceland is the solution" (Castells 2015, 20).

The Icelandic "Kitchenware Revolution" was one of the first mass mobilizations in response to the devastating impacts of the 2008 global financial crisis on northern economies and societies (Flesher Fominaya 2014). A lone act of resistance that was recorded and uploaded to the Internet proved to be the catalyst or spark that drew thousands of protesters into the downtown core of Reykjavik with their pots and pans to demonstrate against the government's mismanagement of the economic crisis. On 11 October 2008, local singer Hordur Torfason took his guitar to the steps of the parliament building and sang about Iceland's so-called gangster bankers, or "banksters," and their corrupted allies in government (Castells 2015, 34). The protests that followed resulted in the resignation and prosecution of a number of government officials, the introduction of strict new banking and financial regulations, and the move to establish a new constitutional order. As noted by Castells (2015, 38), the Icelandic revolution was not simply about restoring the economy but about transforming a political system that was perceived as subordinated to the banks and incapable of representing the public interest. The protests lasted until new elections were held in early 2009, which saw a left-of-center governing coalition come into power. One of the most significant political outcomes of the protests was the drafting of the world's first "Wiki constitution" by way of a constituent assembly that solicited citizen feedback through social media and electronic messaging. According to Flesher Fominaya (2014, 154), even though the new constitution has yet to be legislated into law, Icelandic protesters were far more successful in getting their central demands met than their counterparts in Europe or the United States, in large part due to the willingness of Icelandic politicians to listen and respond to the will of the people.

Tunisia's "Revolution of Liberty and Dignity," which was in response to the plundering of the economy by the country's ruling elite and the repressive regime that sustained such activity, resulted in the ouster of President Ben Ali on 12 January 2011 and the shift from a one-party state to a multiparty democracy (Tilly and Tarrow 2015). The tangible political transformation that occurred in this case was facilitated, in part, by Tunisia's high rate of Internet usage and its strong culture of cyberactivism, which effectively transmitted Mohamed Bouazizi's self-immolation in front of a government building in the impoverished central region in December 2010 to a broad cross section of the Tunisian public (Castells 2015, 29). The video of what happened that day went viral and touched off a nationwide protest movement calling for regime change. Less than a month later, Ben Ali and his family had fled the country, taking refuge in neighboring Saudi Arabia. According to Kingston (chapter 6, this volume) the fall of Ben Ali marked the end of one of the Arab world's most repressive regimes and the first popular uprising to topple an established government in the Middle East since the Iranian Revolution of 1979. The 26 October 2014 parliamentary elections, the first democratic election since the uprising took place, resulted in a win by a secularist center-left party. According to Tilly and Tarrow (2015, 135) it appears, at least for the time being, that Tunisia has managed to build a democracy out of a shaky truce between secular and Islamic parties. Tunisia deservedly stands out in the region for its successful democracy protests.

The movements of the crisis in Iceland and Tunisia may have come about by way of a series of complex contextual and contingent factors, yet their concrete political and institutional gains inspired similar protest movements around the world. Weyland (2012) has suggested that protesters elsewhere were overly optimistic in assessing their own domestic opportunities for mobilization. Our volume suggests that the protest cycle that began in Iceland and Tunisia opened up opportunities for mobilization in other countries, but in the absence of broad-based social support and a political regime willing to accommodate protesters' demands, subsequent movements faltered. The centrality of political opportunity structures for explaining movement dynamics has come under increasing scrutiny in the social movement literature. As many of our contributors have noted, protesters can, in a sense, open their own windows of opportunity to mobilize through their politics of contestation. Political process theorists have long suggested that institutional conditions—such as the presence or absence of institutionalized channels of representation and state repression or tolerance of dissent—create political opportunity structures that are relatively open or closed to social mobilization (McAdam, McCarthy, and Zald 1996). A purely structural approach to political opportunities, however, risks missing contingent factors that may translate objective conditions and resources for political mobilization into significant political opportunities. Goodwin and Jasper (1999) have previously made the argument that culture and agency matter more than structures in explaining movement emergence. Our volume suggests that instead of focusing on the explanatory power of political opportunity structures for generating protest, we are perhaps best served by examining how such opportunities facilitate or inhibit movement impacts. In other words, we propose that political opportunity structures are more important to movement success than they are to movement emergence.

New Challenges: Protest and Political Change in a "Brave New World"

To date, the hard-earned cumulative knowledge about the relationship between movements and their political outcomes was based largely on studies of well-established US social movements and, to a lesser extent, European ones. As this volume highlights, however, the world of social movements is changing (again). In economically advanced countries, significant "turbulence" in global capitalism generated new protest phenomena. In Latin America, the Middle East, and Africa new waves of protest spread against neoliberal globalization, for democracy, and for ethnic, cultural, and national rights. These developments suggest promising directions for future research.

What is new in the economically advanced countries? The financial meltdown of 2007–08 and the subsequent Great Recession in the United States generated a wave of sustained protests led by Occupy Wall Street and the Tea Party. Protests similar to Occupy, such as the *Indignados* in Spain and movements against economic stabilization and economic restructuring more generally, broke out in Europe. These protests offer an opportunity to assess both the policy and broader political impact of radically different forms of movement organization, strategy, and tactics. Occupy Wall Street and the *Indignados* were spontaneous, loosely organized, and coordinated networks that prized autonomy from politics. That principle influenced their decision to embrace strategies of aggressive disengagement from institutional politics (Byrne 2012). By contrast, the Tea Party was more organized and had links to conservative think tanks and the Republican Party. Future comparisons could help us evaluate the effects of organizational structure, coalitional proclivities (and hence of more direct and indirect connections to policymaking) on agenda setting, policy formulation, and legislation. Occupy Wall Street placed a new issue on the political agenda of the 2012 US presidential campaign—growing income inequality. Before then, the question was largely invisible in the public sphere. It gave President Obama's reelection campaign momentum. However, little legislative action followed. In 2016, the issue fueled social democrat Bernie Sanders's bid for the Democratic Party's presidential nomination, which he lost to Hilary Clinton. By contrast, the Tea Party pushed a well-established issue in US political debates (taxes) and engaged full-on with the political establishment. Its electoral mobilization strategy helped to place more radical conservatives in Congress that successfully pressed for anti-tax legislation. In 2016 the Tea Party contributed to Donald Trump's election to the presidency. By contrast, it remains to be seen whether Occupy's actions initiated a longer-term politics around the issue of income inequality.

Similar questions concerning ideational foundations, organization, tactics, and strategies also apply to the near- and longer-term consequences of economic stabilization and adjustment protests for the European Union. On the one hand, like Occupy, decentralized, democratic anti-austerity movements with horizontal forms of leadership, such as Spain's *Indignados*, burst on the scene in 2011 condemning hollow forms of democracy that no longer represented the interests and welfare of a nation's citizenry as a whole. Unlike Occupy, the most lasting political legacy may have been the decision to leverage the movement into a political party, Podemos, which made significant electoral headway in 2015, transforming Spain's two-party system into a three-party system. On the other hand, globalization and austerity also fueled conservative nationalist, antiimmigration movements that have also built up political parties that have made significant electoral inroads in Europe.

Protest movements in Latin America, the Middle East, or Africa feature prominently in this book, and they are fertile ground for new directions in research on the political impacts of protest movements. The economic, political, and cultural contexts of these regions are different from those of the economically advanced democracies. In Latin America, for example, democratic institutions are often weaker and, in some cases, conceptions of democracy depart from liberal-democratic forms. Executive branches are generally stronger than legislatures. This affects the structure of opportunities and threats, as does the fact that rule of law tends to be less robust. Studies could assess the reasons for and effectiveness of movement strategies that engage the legislative and judicial branches of government in the policy process, including payoffs for efforts to establish political parties or to get representatives elected to the legislature.

By the same token, political institutions in Latin America and elsewhere in the developing world tend to be weak, brittle, and to have limited territorial reach. Laws are often poorly implemented or radically changed in their spirit in the regulatory phase of the policy process. Therefore, as is beginning to happen, it is important for research to move beyond the policy formulation and policy outcome stages of the policy process (a law, decree, or regulation) and into the study of policy implementation in order to gauge effective outcomes of movements.

Finally, we should keep in mind that in many developing countries struggles for political and socioeconomic rights are often in the embryonic stage. Hence, perhaps we should attach greater significance to symbolic victories, such as recognition of the movement's right to exist and act (public visibility) or getting issues and rights on the agenda, than we do in the case of advanced countries where many rights are already established.

Moisés Arce, Roberta Rice, and Eduardo Silva

Here, again, we have an opportunity to study the trade-offs between shorter- and longer-term perspectives on outcomes.

The Middle East and Asia are comprised of countries that have only very recently been democratized, are still democratizing, or remain authoritarian. These regions offer a chance to build on the literature on transitions from authoritarianism that sprang from the Latin American experience (1970s to early 1980s) and the velvet revolutions of Eastern Europe (late 1980s and early 1990s). Here is a rich laboratory to analyze the impact of protest and social movements on democratization. We could reassess whether movements play a greater role than the previous literature gave them credit for and, equally important, the conditions under which they do so. Studies of policy and institutional impacts of movements for democratization could be very useful as well. After all, the process of political liberalization and democratization does require authoritarian rulers to make policy decisions (Almeida 2003). Here, too, is an opportunity to advance our knowledge on the role of social movements and protest in the construction of new democratic regimes.

Last but not least, the spread of transnational governance and an international political economy driven by neoclassical economics influenced the proliferation of transnational activism. Since many movements are active in local, national, and transnational campaigns, we need more studies that assess how the interaction across scales affects the political outcomes of movements. We have solid research to build on, such as the pioneering studies of Keck and Sikkink (1998) and Tarrow (2005). Later research examined the formation, trajectory, and effects of transnational agrarian movements in various policy areas. These included land reform and food sovereignty (Borras, Edelman, and Kay 2008); transnational activism against oil development in Ecuador (Wiedener 2007); labor mobilization against export-platform manufacturing plants in Mexico (Carty 2004); and anti–Free Trade Area of the Americas campaigns in Latin America in the 1990s and early 2000s (von Bülow 2010). Others focused on transnational activism's impact on the formation of international regimes in human rights, Indigenous rights, gender rights, environmental protection, and sustainable development (Keck and Sikkink 1998; Martí i Puig 2010; Smith 2008). The fact that interactions are playing out over multiple scales complicates the issue of specifying outcomes and causality even more because it adds complexity to context and multiplies targets (Silva 2013).

This serves as a reminder that establishing causality from social movements in general is no easy task (Amenta et al. 2010). For one, the plurality of actors that may influence policy change makes it difficult to attribute impacts to social movements, which in and of themselves are complex networks of organizations raising a multiplicity of demands and following diverse strategies. Here, despite these difficulties, there is some agreement in the literature that the intertwining of organizations, strategies, and actions contributes to positive outcomes (della Porta and Diani 1999, 331). Secondly, the close relationship between multiple related variables makes it difficult to disentangle cause and effect. Mobilization by itself often is not sufficient to cause observed changes. Third, and closely related, other actors and conditions frequently mediate outcomes. Indeed, we can expect that most political outcomes of movements will be mediated by other actors or factors rather than direct, or that they will be indirect, meaning that movements start a process of change that other actors or factors complete without movement involvement.

A fourth major question regarding causality in the political impact of social movements involves a temporal dimension. As della Porta and Diani (1999, 232) point out, social movements seek to bring about long-term change. However, the height of mobilization and protest usually results in short-term, incremental reforms. This dovetails with a further issue: judging short-term versus long-term goals. The evidence shows that movements tend to have greater impact in obtaining their goals in the early phases of collective action and less in later periods as pushback develops against their achievements. This affects the longer-term implementation and feedback stages of the policy process. By the same token, sometimes the early phases of protest lead to small concessions, which in turn incentivize more protests in the hope of obtaining greater concessions. So the cycle sometimes follows a pattern of protest, concessions, more protest, more concessions. This gives us another angle on how movements may have to adjust their short- versus long-term goals.

We have a variety of methodological tools at our disposal to think more rigorously about the effects of protest and social movements, especially in relation to teasing out causal connections. Ecological data gathering on movements, their organization, strategy, goals, and political effects is the logical starting point for analysis (Amenta et al. 2010, 300). That data can then be applied to qualitative historical and comparative case studies that are especially useful for understanding causal relationships (Mahoney 2008). In these studies, we should use process tracing to establish connections between causes (movements, protest, and others) and effects. Where policymaking is concerned, analysis must show that a) action altered agendas and plans of authorities and targets; b) that challengers caused changes in the content of proposals by state actors and legislative representatives; c) that influential legislators changed their votes on bills; or d) that movements affected the speed or nature of policy implementation (Amenta 2006). Comparative case studies employing the methods of difference and similarity (or most similar systems and dissimilar systems) are especially useful for teasing out causal linkages in cases of mediated effects (Amenta et al. 2010, 301).

Quantitative analysis tends to dominate US studies of the relationship between social movements and their political outcomes. Multivariate quantitative methods that include interaction effects are useful for analyzing the contingent nature of protest outcomes, especially for establishing the net effect of social mobilization (Bosi and Uba 2009). Several methods are useful for analyzing temporal dimensions. These include time series for individual cases, hazard-rate models for multiple case studies, and generalized linear regression models in cases where the outcome is continuous (Amenta et al. 2010). Some studies have begun to combine quantitative with qualitative methods. Again, these have been conducted mainly in studies of US movements. This leads to calls for more analyses that combine the two in order to more fully understand the complex causal relationships between social movements and the policy and broader political outcomes of their contentious action.

If indeed the global protest cycle of 2011 was the most important cycle since the 1960s, what political changes or trends might it have contributed to in the current juncture? One noticeable change was the emergence of new types of movements along the Occupy-*Indignados* model, decentralized, eminently democratic and horizontal in leadership structure, and explicitly not interested in engaging with the political process. This is not just a European phenomenon, as it was also present in the Arab Spring and in citizens' movements in Latin America, such as Mexico's #YoSoy132 student movement in search of greater freedom of the press (Castells 2015). Their appearance opens questions about the characteristics of such movements, with some suggesting that they are more akin to episodic protest events. Their significance lies in their mass quality; they are the multitude, a new phenomenon generated by the contemporary phase of globalized capitalism. Do their consequences differ appreciably from those we might attribute to more traditionally defined social movements?

At the core of the 2011 global protest cycle were demands for greater democracy, more responsive and accountable democracy. In economically advanced democracies, and in Latin America, democracy seemed hollowed out, responsive only to the demands of globalized capital and generally unresponsive or unaccountable to the needs of the citizenry. In the Middle East, the demand was more basic—democracy instead of authoritarian rule. Future research could track the effects these movements may have had on party systems, broader socioeconomic policies, interest intermediation regimes, mechanisms for holding elected representatives accountable, democratization, or liberalization of authoritarian regimes. A key question might be: Is a new democratic ethos flourishing that can underpin changes in political culture?

The current juncture also offers a cautionary note. Not all movements are progressive. Reaction is setting in. This is all too evident with the rise of conservative populism, nationalist, and anti-immigration (if not outright racist) sentiments flourishing all around us in the advanced capitalist countries. In addition to tracking their development, it could be interesting to see if, and how, more progressive movements handle, corral, and/or otherwise seek to contain them.

Conclusion

This volume has attempted to shed new light on the relationship between protest and democracy in the era of free markets. The financial crisis of 2007–08 that began in the northern economies has had dramatic consequences for the established democracies of Europe and the United States as well as for diverse political regimes in the Global South. The massive protest movements that emerged in response to the economic downturn captured headlines around the world and caught many analysts by surprise. The 2011 protest movements have since garnered significant analytical attention due to their innovative nature, geographical spread, and widespread attention to political and economic inequality and uncertainty (Davies, Ryan, and Milcíades Peña 2016). It is clear from our current vantage point that the movements of the crisis were part of a new global protest cycle, the impacts and implications of which continue to reverberate throughout the world's political regimes as they spawn countermovements and upend electoral contests for established political actors. As Tilly and Tarrow (2015, 229) remind us, all cycles of contention must come to an end, but what matters is the process of political change that they help to set in motion. We hope this book contributes to an understanding of what future scholars may deem to be a critical turning point in global contentious politics.

References

Almeida, Paul. 2003. "Opportunity Organizations and Threat-Induced Contention: Protest Waves in Authoritarian Settings." *American Journal of Sociology* 109, no. 2: 345–400.

Amenta, Edwin. 2006. *When Movements Matter: The Townsend Plan and the Rise of Social Security*. Princeton, NJ: Princeton University Press

Amenta, Edwin, and Neal Caren. 2007. "The Legislative, Organizational, and Beneficiary Consequences of State-Oriented Challengers." In *The Blackwell Companion to Social Movements*, edited by David A. Snow, Sarah A. Soule, and Hanspeter Kriesi, 461–88. Malden, MA: Blackwell.

Amenta, Edwin, Neal Caren, Elizabeth Chiarello, and Yang Su. 2010. "The Political Consequences of Social Movements." *Annual Review of Sociology* 36: 287–307.

Borras, Saturnino, Marc Edelman, and Cristóbal Kay. 2008. "Transnational Agrarian Movements: Origins and Politics, Campaigns and Impact." *Journal of Agrarian Change* 8, no. 2–3: 169–204.

Bosi, Lorenzo. 2016. "Incorporation and Democratization: The Long-Term Process of Institutionalization of the Northern Ireland Civil Rights Movement." In *The Consequences of Social Movements*, edited by Lorezno Bosi, Marco Giugni, and Katrin Uba, 338–60. New York: Cambridge University Press.

Bosi, Lorenzo, Marco Giugni, and Katrin Uba. 2016. "The Consequences of Social Movements: Taking Stock and Looking Forward." In *The Consequences of Social Movements*, edited by Lorezno Bosi, Marco Giugni, and Katrin Uba, 3–37. New York: Cambridge University Press.

Bosi, Lorenzo and Katrin Uba. 2009. "Introduction: The Outcomes of Social Movements." *Mobilization* 14, no. 4: 409–15.

Byrne, Janet, ed. 2012. *The Occupy Handbook*. New York: Back Bay Books.

Carty, Victoria. 2004. "Transnational Labor Mobilizing in Two Mexican Maquiladoras: The Struggle for Democratic Globalization." *Mobilization* 9, no. 3: 295–310.

Castells, Manuel. 2015. *Networks of Outrage and Hope: Social Movements in the Internet Age*, 2nd ed. Malden, MA: Polity.

Davies, Thomas, Holly Eva Ryan, and Alejandro Milcíades Peña. 2016. "Protest, Social Movements and Global Democracy since 2011: New Perspectives." *Research in Social Movements, Conflicts and Change* 39: 1–29.

della Porta, Donatella, and Mario Diani, eds. 1999. *Social Movements: An Introduction*. Oxford: Blackwell.

della Porta, Donatella, and Alice Mattoni. 2014. "Patterns of Diffusion and the Transnational Dimension of Protest in the Movements of the Crisis: An Introduction." In *Spreading Protest: Social Movements in Times of Crisis*, edited by Donatella della Porta and Alice Mattoni, 1–21. Colchester, UK: ECPR Press.

Earl, Jennifer. 2007. "The Cultural Consequences of Social Movements." In *The Blackwell Companion to Social   Movements*, edited by David A. Snow, Sarah A. Soule, and Hanspeter Kriesi, 508–30. Malden, MA: Blackwell.

Estanque, Elísio, Hermes Augusto Costa, and José Soeiro. 2013. "The New Global Cycle of Protest and the Portuguese Case." *Journal of Social Science Education* 12, no. 1: 31–40.

Flesher Fominaya, Cristina. 2014. *Social Movements and Globalization: How Protests, Occupations and Uprising are Changing the World*. New York: Palgrave Macmillan.

Gamson, William. 1975. *The Strategy of Social Protest*. Homewood, IL: Dorsey Press.

Giugni, Marco G. 2007. "Personal and Biographical Consequences." In *The Consequences of Social Movements*, edited by Lorezno Bosi, Marco Giugni, and Katrin Uba, 489–507. New York: Cambridge University Press.

Goodwin, Jeff, and James M. Jasper. 1999. "Caught in a Winding, Snarling Vine: The Structural Bias of Political Process Theory." *Sociological Forum* 14, no. 1: 27–54.

Keck, Margaret, and Kathryn Sikkink. 1998. Activists Beyond Borders: Advocacy Networks in International Politics. Ithaca, NY: Cornell University Press.

Mahoney, James. 2008. "Toward a Unified Theory of Causality." *Comparative Political Studies* 41, no. 4/5: 412–36.

Mainwaring, Scott, and Timothy R. Scully. 1995. "Introduction." In *Building Democratic Institutions: Party Systems in Latin America*, edited by Scott Mainwaring and Timothy R. Scully, 1–34. Stanford, CA: Stanford University Press.

Martí i Puig, Salvador. 2010. "The Emergence of Indigenous Movements in Latin America and their Impact on the Latin American Political Scene." *Latin American Perspectives* 37, no. 6: 74–92.

Mason, Paul. 2013. *Why It's Still Kicking Off Everywhere: The New Global Revolutions*. London: Verso.

McAdam, Doug, John D. McCarthy, and Mayer N. Zald. 1996. *Comparative Perspectives on Social Movements: Political Opportunities, Mobilizing Structures, and Cultural Framings*. New York: Cambridge University Press.

Silva, Eduardo, ed. 2013. *Transnational Activism and Domestic Movements in Latin America: Bridging the Divide*. New York: Routledge.

Smith, Jackie. 2008. *Social Movements for Global Democracy*. Baltimore, MD: Johns Hopkins University Press.

Standing, Guy. 2014. *The Precariat: The New Dangerous Class*. New York: Bloomsbury.

Tarrow, Sidney. 2005. *New Transnational Activism*. New York: Cambridge University Press.

Tilly, Charles, and Sidney Tarrow. 2015. *Contentious Politics*, 2nd ed. New York: Oxford University Press.

von Bülow, Marisa. 2010. *Building Transnational Networks: Civil Society and the Politics of Trade in the Americas*. Cambridge: Cambridge University Press.

Wang, Dan J., and Sarah A. Soule. 2016. "Tactical Innovation in Social Movements: The Effects of Peripheral and Multi-Issue Protest." *American Sociological Review* 81, no. 3: 517–48.

Weyland, Kurt. 2012. "The Arab Spring: Why the Surprising Similarities with the Revolutionary Wave of 1848?" *Perspectives on Politics* 10, no. 4: 917–34.

Whittier, Nancy. 2007. "The Consequences of Social Movements for Each Other." In *The Blackwell Companion to Social Movements*, edited by David A. Snow, Sarah A. Soule, and Hanspeter Kriesi, 531–51. Malden, MA: Blackwell.

Wiedener, Patricia. 2007. "Benefits and Burdens of Transnational Campaigns: A Comparison of Four Oil Struggles in Ecuador." *Mobilization* 12, no. 1: 21–36.

Contributors

MOISÉS ARCE (Frederick A. Middlebush Professor and Chair of the Political Science Department at the University of Missouri) has been with the department since 2006. He received his PhD in 2000 from the University of New Mexico. He is the author of *Market Reform in Society* (Pennsylvania State University Press, 2005), *Resource Extraction and Protest in Peru* (University of Pittsburgh Press, 2014), and numerous articles in such journals as *Comparative Political Studies, Comparative Politics, European Political Science Review, International Organization, Journal of Politics, Journal of Politics in Latin America, Latin American Politics and Society, Latin American Research Review, Party Politics, Political Research Quarterly, Social Science Quarterly, Studies in Comparative International Development*, and *World Politics*. His research has been funded by grants from the National Science Foundation and the Social Science Research Council. He previously taught at Louisiana State University. Professor Arce has served as a visiting Fulbright lecturer at the Pontificia Universidad Católica del Perú (2003), and as a visiting professor at the University of Tokyo (2014). From 2004 to 2006, he served as cochair of the Peru Section, an interdisciplinary organization of the Latin American Studies Association.

JEFFREY AYRES is a professor in the Department of Political Science, Saint Michael's College in Vermont. He is coeditor with Peter Andrée, Michael Bosia, and Marie-Josée Massicotte of *Globalization and Food Sovereignty: Global and Local Change in the New Politics of Food* (University of Toronto Press, 2014), and with Laura Macdonald of *North America in Question: Regional Integration in an Era of Political Turbulence* (University of

Toronto Press, 2012). He is also coeditor with Laura Macdonald of *Contentious Politics in North America: National Protest and Transnational Collaboration under Continental Integration* (Palgrave Macmillan, 2009), and author of *Defying Conventional Wisdom: Political Movements and Popular Contention Against North American Free Trade* (University of Toronto Press, 1998).

CAREW E. BOULDING is associate professor of political science at the University of Colorado Boulder. Her research examines the role of nongovernmental organizations in local politics in developing democracies. Boulding is the author of *NGOs, Civil* Society *and Political Protest* (Cambridge University Press, 2014). Her work has appeared in numerous journals, including *Comparative Politics, World Development, Party Politics, Journal of Politics, Latin American Research Review,* and *Studies in Comparative International Development.*

SOFIA DONOSO holds an MPhil and a PhD in development studies from the University of Oxford. She is an assistant professor at the Universidad Mayor and a research fellow at the Centre for Social Conflict and Cohesion Studies. She is coeditor with Marisa von Bülow of *Social Movements in Chile: Organization, Trajectories and Political Consequences* (Palgrave Macmillan, 2017). Her research has been published in the *Journal of Latin American Studies, Research in Social Movements, Conflicts and Change,* as well as in several chapters in edited volumes.

TED GOERTZEL is professor emeritus in the Department of Sociology at Rutgers University. He is author of *Brazil's Lula: The Most Popular Politician on Earth* (BrownWalker Press, 2011), *Fernando Henrique Cardoso: Reinventing Democracy in Brazil* (Lynne Rienner, 1999), and *Turncoats and True Believers* (Prometheus, 1992). He is coauthor with Guy Burton of *Presidential Leadership in the Americas since Independence* (Lexington,

2016) and coauthor with Ben Goertzel of *The End of the Beginning: Life, Society and Economy on the Brink of the Singularity* (Humanity Plus, 2015).

PAUL KINGSTON is professor of political science and director of the Centre for Critical Development Studies at the University of Toronto Scarborough. Kingston is interested in the politics of power that underpin the dynamics of development. He is the author of *Reproducing Sectarianism: Advocacy Networks and the Politics of Civil Society in Postwar Lebanon* (SUNY Press, 2013) and of *Debating Development: Britain and the Politics of Modernization in the Middle East: 1945–1958* (Cambridge University Press, 1996). He is coeditor with Ian Spears of *States within States: Incipient Political Entities in the Post–Cold War Era* (Palgrave Macmillan, 2004). Kingston is also the author of numerous articles and book chapters on the politics of the Middle East.

JENNIFER M. LARSON is associate professor of political science at Vanderbilt University. Her research is on social networks, ranging from sets of interactions in online social media to fully offline personal connections in word-of-mouth communication networks. She is coauthor with Terry Clark, Joshua Potter, John Mordeson, and Mark Wierman of *Applying Fuzzy Mathematics to Formal Models in Comparative Politics* (Springer, 2008). Larson's work has appeared in numerous journals, such as *American Political Science Review, American Journal of Political Science, Journal of Politics, World Politics, Journal of Peace Research,* among others.

LAURA MACDONALD is a professor in the Department of Political Science and the Institute of Political Economy at Carleton University. She is the author of *Supporting Civil Society: The Political Impact of NGO Assistance to Central America* (Macmillan Press and St. Martin's Press, 1997) and coauthor with Jane Bayes, Patricia Begne, Laura Gonzalez, Lois Harder, and Mary Hawkesworth of *Women, Democracy, and Globalization in North America: A Comparative Study* (Palgrave Macmillan, 2006). She is coeditor with Jeffrey Ayres of *North America in Question: Regional Integration in an Era of Economic Turbulence* (University of Toronto Press, 2012) and *Contentious Politics in North America: National Protest and Transnational Collaboration under Continental Integration* (Palgrave Macmillan, 2009). Macdonald is also coeditor with Arne Ruckert of *Post-Neoliberalism in the Americas: Beyond the Washington Consensus?* (Palgrave Macmillan, 2009).

ROBERTA RICE is associate professor of Indigenous politics in the Department of Political Science at the University of Calgary. Her research focuses on Indigenous politics in Latin America. She is the author of *The New Politics of Protest: Indigenous Mobilization in Latin America's Neoliberal Era* (University of Arizona Press, 2012), which was nominated for the 2014 prize in comparative politics by the Canadian Political Science Association. She is the coeditor with Gordana Yovanovich of *Re-Imagining Community and Civil Society in Latin America and the Caribbean* (Routledge, 2016). Her work has appeared in *Bolivian Studies Journal, Comparative Political Studies, Canadian Journal of Latin American and Caribbean Studies, Latin American Research Review,* and *Party Politics.* She is also the author of several chapters on Latin American politics in *The Paradox of Democracy in Latin America* (University of Toronto Press, 2011). Her research has been funded by the Social Sciences and Humanities Research Council of Canada.

EDUARDO SILVA holds the Friezo Family Foundation Chair in Political Science and is professor of political science and a research associate of the Center for Inter-American Policy and Research at Tulane University. He is the author of *Challenging Neoliberalism in Latin America* (Cambridge University Press, 2009) and *The State and Capital in Chile* (Westview, 1996). Silva is editor of *Transnational Activism and National Movements in Latin America: Bridging the Divide* (Routledge, 2013). He is coeditor with Francisco Durand of *Organized Business, Economic Change, and Democracy in Latin America* (North-South Center Press, 1998) and with Paul W. Drake of *Elections and Democratization in Latin America, 1980–95* (University of

California San Diego Press, 1986). Silva has published extensively in journals and edited volumes on social mobilization, environmental politics, and business-state relations.

ERICA S. SIMMONS is an associate professor of political science and international studies at the University of Wisconsin–Madison. She is the author of *Meaningful Resistance: Market Reforms and the Roots of Social Protest in Latin America* (Cambridge University Press, 2016). She is the author of numerous articles on contentious politics and qualitative methods in such journals as *PS: Political Science and Politics, World Politics, Comparative Politics,* Theory *and Society, Qualitative and Multi-Method Research and Comparative Political Studies.*

NICOLÁS M. SOMMA is an associate professor of sociology at the Pontificia Universidad Católica de Chile and a research fellow at the Centre for Social Conflict and Cohesion Studies. His areas of expertise include social movement theory and political sociology. His research has appeared in *Sociological Quarterly, Sociological Perspectives, Latin American Politics and Society, Party Politics, Journal of Historical Sociology,* and *Acta Sociologica,* among others.

Index

A

Abdelfattah, Mohamed, 80
Adbusters, 181–83. *See also* Lasn, Kalle
Affordable Care Act, US, 178, 187
Africa, 2, 204, 206. *See also* Algeria; Egypt;
    Libya; Tunisia
agency-oriented approaches, 36
aggrieved groups. *See* grievances
al-Assad, Bashar, 123. *See also* Ba'ath Party,
    Syria
Aleppo, Syria, 123
Alexandria, Egypt, 87
Algeria, 126
Ali, Ben, 86, 137, 203
Alinsky, Saul, 177
Alliance for Responsible Trade (ART), 62
American Revolution, 176
antidemocratic trends, 66–67
anti-free-trade coalitions, 61, 63, 65–66
antiglobalization, 49–50, 56, 204. *See also*
    globalization
anti-government sentiments, 10, 84, 178, 182
anti-nuclear movement, 29
anti-slavery movements, 53
anti-tax legislation, 205
anti-war movement, 150
APEC, 64
Aquino, Benigno, 29
Arab world, 119–21, 124, 126–28, 130–31,
    135, 137–38, 140, 200, 203; rates of
    Internet connectivity, 130; youth, 126.
    See also Algeria; Arab Spring; Bahrain;
    Egypt; Iraq; Libya; Middle East;

Palestine; Saudia Arabia, Syria; Tunisia;
    Yemen
Arab Spring, 1, 13, 76–77, 85, 119–22, 126–38,
    140, 185, 195, 200, 209; dynamics, 128;
    early phases, 131; mobilizations, 135;
    movement, 185; outbreak, 119, 126–28,
    130; protests, 76, 127–30, 135; timing,
    131; uprisings, 77, 127, 135; years
    leading up to the, 132, 200. *See also*
    Bouazizi, Mohamed
Argentina, 7, 9, 64, 109
armed resistance, 26
Asia, 48, 56, 207. *See also* China
associational life and membership, 14, 93, 94,
    97, 99, 101, 108–9, 113
austerity, 52, 206. *See also* neoliberalism
authoritarianism, 62, 88, 120–21, 125,
    127–28, 131–32, 140, 152, 156, 207, 210;
    liberalization of, 210; political context,
    62; regimes, 88, 121, 125, 132, 152, 210;
    resilience of, 120, 127, 131; reversal, 156;
    rule, 152, 210; structures, 121; systems
    of governance, 120, 127–28, 131,
    139–40; transitions from, 207
autocratic states, 84

B

Ba'ath Party, Syria, 123–24, 132. *See also* al-
    Assad, Bashar
Bachelet, Michelle, 146, 155–57, 163, 167
Bahrain, 127, 136–37, 139

banksters, 202
Bertelsmann Transformation Index, 103
bilateral aid, 97, 122
bilateralism, 64, 65
Black Lives Matter, 51, 187
Bloomberg, Michael, 183, 186
Bolivia, 7, 9, 26, 38, 97, 99. *See also*
    Coordinator for Water and Life, Bolivia
Boric, Gabriel, 164–65
Bouazizi, Mohamed, 1, 136, 203. *See also*
    Arab Spring
boycotts, 101, 108
Brazil, 55, 57, 64, 71, 97, 99, 101
British Columbia, 48, 183
British Parliament, 185
Broad Front. *See* Frente Amplio, Uruguay
Bush, George W., 175
Bush, Jeb, 173, 187

C

Cairo, Egypt, 80, 87
California, 200
Canada, 48, 60, 61–62, 64–65, 150; Action
    Canada Network (CAN), 61–62;
    activists, 48, 61–62; government, 60,
    64; Pro-Canada Network, 61; social
    movements, 62. *See also* British
    Columbia; Canada-US Free Trade
    Agreement (CUSFTA); Council of
    Canadians; North American Free
    Trade Agreement (NAFTA); New
    Democratic Party, Canada; Progressive
    Conservative Party, Canada; Security
    and Prosperity Partnership of North
    America; Quebec, Canada; United
    States-Mexico-Canada Agreement
    (USMCA)
Canada-US Free Trade Agreement
    (CUSFTA), 60–61
capitalism, 183, 210
charitable organizations, 26, 96
Chicago boys, 153
Chicago Mercantile Exchange, 176

Chicago Tea Party, 176
Chile, 1, 15, 29, 146–47, 150–51, 154,
    156, 159, 161–63, 165–67; Agency
    of the Quality of Education, 157;
    constitutional change, 161; high
    school, 154; media, 155; political
    parties in, 151–52, 156, 203; school
    inspectorate, 157; student protests in,
    147; tertiary education expenditures
    in, 159; test of university selection,
    154; Valparaiso, 165; voucher system,
    153, 161; youth, 156. *See also* Bachelet,
    Michelle; Boric, Gabriel; Chicago boys;
    Chilean student movement; Chilean
    Winter; Communist Party, Chile;
    Coalition of Parties for Democracy,
    Chile; Communist Party, Chile;
    Constitutional Law of Education,
    Chile; Crédito con Aval del Estado
    (CAE), Chile; Figueroa, Francisco;
    Humanist Party, Chile; Jackson,
    Giorgio; La Moneda, Chile; Lagos,
    Ricardo; Ministry of Education,
    Chile; Movimiento Autonomista,
    Chile; National Socioeconomic
    Characterization, Chile, Nueva
    Democracia, Chile; New Majority,
    Chile; Party for Democracy, Chile;
    Piñera, Sebastián; *Pingüinos*; Pinochet,
    Augusto; Presidential Commission
    on Education, Chile; Revolución
    Democrática, Chile; Sharp, Jorge;
    Socialist Party, Chile; Vallejo, Camila;
    voting—in Chile
Chilean student movement, 146, 161, 166;
    political impacts of the, 145–46, 161
Chilean Winter, 13, 15, 158, 201
China, 30
christianity, 150, 157, 162–64, 167; and
    the political right, 150; and the US
    Democratic Party, 157, 162–64, 167
Chrysler, 175
churches, 61, 95, 96
citizen participation, 156

Citizens' Trade Campaign, 62
civil rights movement, 11, 24, 28, 50, 198,
    202; emergence of, 24, 28; legislation, 28
civil society, 5, 8, 10, 13, 15, 63, 94–95, 97–98,
    109, 111, 113, 131, 156, 167; actors,
    156; activities, 15, 111, 113; African-
    American, 198, 202; claims, 5; conflict,
    120; demobilization, 8; membership
    in, 100, 112–13; organizations, 5, 97,
    108–9, 112–13; strengthening of, 97;
    representatives, 128
claims, 11–12, 14, 24–25, 28, 33–36, 39–40,
    60, 88; content of 11, 24, 34; transfer of,
    60; variety of, 39
climate change, 35
Clinton, Bill, 63
Clinton, Hillary, 173–74, 186–87, 205
clubs, 26
coalitions, 10, 146–47, 150, 164; center-left,
    146–47; creation of new, 146; formation
    of, 10; government, 164
Coalition of Parties for Democracy,
    Chile, 151–55, 157, 159, 161–63, 167;
    consecutive governments of, 159, 162;
    parties in, 157, 163
collective action, 4, 5, 6, 8, 11–12, 23–27,
    30–33, 36–37, 39, 50, 52, 55, 57, 71, 80,
    94, 119, 120, 126, 135, 148–49, 160, 166,
    176, 198, 199, 202, 208; activity, 49,
    126; claims-making, 50; class-based, 4;
    context of, 31; cycles of, 52; "defensive,"
    5; early phases of, 208; frames, 55, 57,
    198–99; identity, 32–33, 55; invented
    forms of, 202; new forms of, 149;
    problem of, 80; protest, 27; puzzle of,
    23; theorizing on, 39; type of, 135
Communist Party, Chile, 147, 152, 163–64,
    167
community, 9, 38, 47, 56, 95, 99; bartering,
    56; based activities, 9; based
    organizations, 38, 95, 99; perceptions
    of, 38; supported agriculture (CSA), 47;
    types of, 95
Connecticut, US, 28

Congress, US, 62, 178, 186, 205; control of,
    186; Republicans in, 178, 205, role of, 62
Constitutional Law of Education, Chile, 146,
    156, 157
connective structures, 26
contention, 6, 11, 29, 34, 40, 51–52, 60, 178,
    195, 199, 201, 211; cycles of, 51, 199,
    211; dynamics of, 34, 40; forms of, 11;
    multi-scalar processes of, 52; political
    opportunities for, 6; processes of, 50;
    repertoires of, 60, 178; study of, 29;
    transgressive, 201
contentious politics, 2, 10, 14, 16, 28, 48–54,
    58, 60, 65, 94, 98, 101, 109, 111, 113,
    146, 196, 198, 209; and claims-making,
    54, 58; historical process of, 52; and
    political outcomes, 209; protests,
    48–49, 52, 60, 109. See also
    transnational contentious politics
co-optation, 27
Coordinator for Water and Life, Bolivia, 27
corporations, 47–48, 50, 52, 58, 124, 133, 177,
    182, 187; and industrial agricultural
    practices, 47; and power, 52; and their
    interests, 133, 177. See also Monsanto
    corporation
Council of Canadians, 48, 61
countermovement, 198–99, 200, 211
counterrevolution, 119
Crédito con Aval del Estado (CAE), Chile,
    159, 160
cross-border issues, 48–51, 54, 59;
    characteristics, 49–50; collaboration,
    51; networks, 59; organizing summit,
    48; permanence and connections, 54.
culture, 24, 27, 30–33, 35, 36–37, 39,
    61, 119, 176, 181; approach to, 35;
    conceptualization of, 36; context,
    26, 37; dynamics, 32; identity, 61;
    norms, 119; pluralism, 30; practices,
    30; processes, 32; resources, 27; re-
    evaluation processes, 181; symbols, 176;
    turn in the social movement literature,
    24, 31–33, 36, 39

D

Damascus, Syria, 123
Damascus Declaration, 129
Davies, James C., 5, 24, 174
demobilization, 4
democracy, 1–9, 11, 23, 37, 48, 49, 57, 58, 66, 84, 93, 97, 103, 108–9, 147, 151–52, 166, 203, 204, 206, 210; advanced, 9, 11, 98, 206, 210; conceptions of, 206; developing, 98, 206, 210; economic globalization and, 57; effects of protest on, 8; era of, 23; expectations for, 152; political limitations on, 57; protests in, 3, 6; pursuit of, 84; quality of, 3, 103, 108; reinstatement of, 147, 152; schools for, 93; shift from a one-party state to a multiparty, 203; threats to, 7; transition to, 6; variation of parties and party systems in, 3
Democracy Village, 185
Democratic Party, US, 150, 173, 178–80, 182, 186, 190, 205. *See also* christianity—and the US Democratic Party; Clinton, Bill; Clinton, Hillary; Obama, Barack; Obamacare; Sanders, Bernie
democratic politics and process, 2, 7–9, 13–15, 29, 52, 56–58, 66, 83–84, 94, 98, 102, 105, 109, 111, 113, 139, 151–52, 156, 158, 164, 166–67, 173, 195, 198, 200–201, 206, 210; action, 58; actors, 66; breakdown, 152; change, 195, 200; citizenship, 14; cultures, 198; decline, 52; deficits, 57; elections, 94, 102, 105; ethos, 210; governance, 98; governments, 83, 164; institutions, 13–14, 109, 113, 201, 206; openness, 7; participation, 66; politics, 7, 29, 198; protests, 2; reform, 2, 15; regimes, 7, 8, 83, 139, 195, 200; restoration, 166; rule, 151, 156, 158; stability, 151; states, 9, 84; system, 109, 201; transitions, 2, 8–9, 58, 158, 167

democratization, 3, 8, 16, 23, 207, 210; context of widespread, 3; early stages of, 8; social movements and, 207
demographic factors, 58, 102
demonstrations, 93, 100–101, 106, 108, 113, 128; authorized, 93; participation in, 108; peaceful, 106; unauthorized, 93
depoliticization, 49
deprivation, 25
Deraa, Syria, 123
deregulation, 52, 57
desperate generation, 1, 200
developing world, 3, 48, 52, 57, 93–95, 97, 99, 108–9, 112, 124, 206
dictators, 119, 197
dictatorship, 37, 156–57. *See also* authoritarianism
diffusion, 11, 51, 54, 60, 62–65, 67, 129
disaffected radicalism thesis, 7, 9
discontent, 25, 34, 156, 164, 167, 175, 182, 199, 201; constancy of, 25; different types of, 34
discrimination, 35
dynastic succession, 122, 125, 129

E

ecological concerns, 150, 208; data, 208; movements, 150; parties, 150; sustainability, 47. *See also* environmentalism
economic policies and concerns, 2–6, 10, 24, 28, 34, 47–58, 60–61, 63, 65–66, 122, 173–75, 178, 182, 186, 202, 205; cleavage, 28; conditions, 4, 5, 34; crisis, 2, 173–75, 178, 182, 186, 202; development, 24; globalization, 4, 47–54, 56–57, 60–61, 63, 65–66; growth, 122; inequality 4–6, 10; insecurity, 52; liberalization, 3–6, 10; stabilization, 205; threat, 34. *See also* neoliberal economics
economic threats, 5, 34, 49

Ecuador, 7, 207

education, 1, 15, 95, 102, 146–47, 151,
153–54, 158–59, 161–62, 164; cost of,
153; policies, 151, 161, 164; private,
153–55, 157–59; privatization of, 1, 15,
158; public, 153–54, 160–61; public
expenditure on, 154; quality of, 146,
162; system, 147, 151, 159, 161–62, 166.
See also Chile

educational reform, 15, 146, 153–58, 160,
163, 165

Egypt, 1, 26, 71, 78, 80, 83, 87, 122–30,
132–34, 136, 139, 185; April 6
Movement in, 129; Gross National
Product, 134; Internet in, 83; Kefaya
movement in, 129; labor market, 123;
military, 133–34; Mubaraks of, 125;
National Democratic Party in, 132;
pre-Arab Spring in, 130; politics, 129;
police and security forces, 134; post-
uprising period in, 132; protests in,
26, 71, 78, 83, 128; repression in, 133;
Revolutionary Fire, 71; ruling coalition,
133–34; US alliance with, 134; youth
unemployment in, 123; uprising, 127.
See also Alexandria, Egypt; Cairo,
Egypt; Facebook Revolution; Mafhouz,
Asmaa; Mubarak, Gamal; Said, Khaled;
Tahrir Square, Egypt

elections, 39–40, 94, 98–99, 102–3, 105,
109, 112–13, 145, 147–49, 161, 163–65,
178–79, 186, 188–89, 202–3; confidence
in, 112; disputing power in, 164;
effectiveness of, 102; general, 189; midterm, 186, 188; municipal, 165; national,
147; parliamentary, 147, 161, 165, 203;
presidential, 147, 163, 165, 186; primary,
186; second round of, 148

Electoral College, US, 174, 189

electoral politics, 8, 12, 14, 39, 94, 98, 111,
149–50, 152, 162, 173–74, 186, 205, 211;
campaigning, 149; contestation, 8, 12,
211; defeat, 162; fraud, 39, 94, 98, 111;
irregularities, 39; mobilization, 149,
205; outcomes, 98; participation, 14, 98;
process, 98; reform, 186; system, 152,
188. *See also* party systems, analysis of

elites, 6, 31, 50, 61, 124, 131–33, 156, 203;
corporate and professional, 124;
cultural, 61; political and military, 133;
ruling, 4, 131

employment, 5; insecurity, 10;
underemployment, 52; unemployment,
52, 122–24, 181

emotion, 29–33

environmentalism, 11, 48, 55, 59, 61, 63, 207

Erdogan, Recep Tayyip, 84

Europe, 51, 56, 66, 97, 105, 130, 150, 195, 199,
203, 205–7, 209, 210; electoral politics
in, 206; established democracies of, 210;
Velvet Revolution, 207. *See also* Greece;
Paris, France; Portugal; Spain; Soviet
Union

European Union (EU), 57, 64, 66, 205

F

Facebook, 71–73, 77, 81, 84, 130–31. *See also*
Facebook Revolution; social media

Facebook Revolution, 71

factionalism, 134

farmer's organizations, 56–57, 61, 63

farms and farming, 10, 47–48, 54–59, 63,
122. *See also* farmer's organizations;
Harvey, Peter

Figueroa, Francisco, 158

finance and financial resources, 26, 52, 95,
122, 133, 146, 152–54, 158–59, 163, 180

financial crisis, 2007–08, 15, 51, 124, 174–75,
182–83, 188, 200, 202. *See also* Occupy
Wall Street; Lehman Brothers

financial markets, 2–5, 38, 56–57, 122–23;
reform of, 2–5, 122–23

Flickr, 73. *See also* social media

food and food security, 50, 54–59, 66, 207;
activists, 55; cooperatives, 54; industry,
59; sovereignty, 54–59, 66, 207; systems,
55

foreign aid, 97

foreign direct investment, 3

Foster, John, 61–64

frame model, 25, 30–32, 34, 35–37, 40, 51, 66, 175; alignment, 30; analysis, 30, 32; concept of, 36; resonance, 32, 35. *See also* framing process

framing process, 23, 30, 36–37, 55, 188; literature, 36–37; and symbols, 31, 35–37, 55, 59, 60; theory, 188

France. *See* Paris, France

Fraternal Order of Police, 180

free markets, 2–4, 6, 23, 210; era of, 23, 210

free trade, 53, 57, 61, 62, 64–65, 188; agenda, 64; agreements, 57, 188; deals, 64; opponents, 61; policies, 64; zones, 64. *See also* Free Trade Area of the Americas (FTAA); North American Free Trade Agreement (NAFTA)

Free Trade Area of the Americas (FTAA), 52, 64; campaign against, 207

freedom, 37

Freedom House, 103

Frente Amplio, Uruguay, 147, 150, 165, 167

Friedman, Milton, 153

Full Moon Farm, 47

G

Gamson, William, 29, 145, 148, 197

gay and lesbian activism, 33

gay rights movement, 11, 35, 202

gender, 102, 207

General Motors, 175

generic drugs, 48

genetically modified organisms (GMOs), 47, 54

Genoa, Italy, 50

Gezi Park, Turkey, 73, 85

global protest cycle, 2, 3, 4, 11–14, 16, 47, 49–52, 54–55, 59, 65–66, 72, 82, 88, 129, 135, 138, 182, 186, 195–97, 199–201, 203, 209, 210–11

Global South, 2–3, 14, 93, 201, 210; countries of the, 201; democracies in the, 93; political regimes in the, 210

globalization, 2–4, 6, 14, 23, 34, 47–53, 56–58, 61, 63–66, 121, 124, 174, 185, 188–89, 199, 200–201, 204, 206, 209–10. *See also* antiglobalization

governments: attacks on, 10; and globalization, 58; and NGOs, 95, 97; and protests, 7, 53, 82–84, 86, 88, 137, 178, 184–85, 206; structure and performance of, 7, 98, 109, 111, 137, 149, 181, 189, 206; trust in, 102, 104–5, 107, 109, 181–82, 189

grassroots movements, 56, 58, 62, 97, 129, 177

Greece, 1, 150. *See also* Syriza

grievances, 2–3, 5, 6, 11–12, 14, 23–25, 33–40, 51, 74–76, 79, 88, 120, 126, 134–35, 137–38, 155, 156–57, 160, 166, 173–75, 182, 188, 195–96, 200–201; material and ideational, 2, 12, 14; meanings of, 35–36; meaning-laden approach to, 34–35, 39; renewed attention to, 33–34; sets of, 135; socioeconomic and/or political, 138; student, 156; types of, 34, 37–38

guerrilla movements, 26

H

Hama, Syria, 123

Harvey, Peter, 59

Hemispheric Social Alliance, 64

historical memory and experiences, 31, 36

Homs, Syria, 123

human rights, 10, 27, 207

Humanist Party, Chile, 165

I

Iceland, 201–3. *See also* banksters

ideation, 34, 37

identity-based movements, 31–32

income levels, 3. *See also* wealth
Indiana, US, 180
Indigenous peoples and rights, 10, 48, 55, 57, 207
Indignados, 185, 198–99, 202, 205, 209
individuals, 7, 9, 11, 25, 30, 74, 101, 103, 109, 111
inequality, 1, 23, 34, 52, 58, 75, 124, 126, 153–54, 160, 181, 205, 211; income, 1, 58, 75, 205; reproduction of, 154; rising levels of 52, 124, 126
informal workers, 10
information age, 71, 88
Instagram, 72. *See also* social media
institutions, 3, 6–8, 10–13, 15, 28–29, 82, 121, 201; and institutional access, 6; and institutional change, 11–13; mechanisms of, 12; politics of, 15; processes of, 10; structure of, 28; weakening of, 7
Inter-American Development Bank, 50, 102
intergovernmental organizations, 50, 52, 57, 59. *See also* Inter-American Development Bank; United Nations (UN); World Trade Organization (WTO)
international financial institutions, 50, 52, 57, 97, 102. *See also* International Monetary Fund (IMF); World Bank
International Monetary Fund (IMF), 50, 52, 57. *See also* international financial institutions
international trade agreements, 48, 52–53, 57, 60, 187. *See also* Canada-US Free Trade Agreement (CUSFTA); free trade; Free Trade Area of the Americas (FTAA); North American Free Trade Agreement (NAFTA); Maastricht Treaty of the European Union; Trans Pacific Partnership (TPP); United States-Mexico-Canada Agreement (USMCA);

International Telecommunications Union, 87
Internet access and activism, 1, 14, 72, 81–83, 85, 87–88, 127, 130, 174, 176, 187–88, 202–3
interpersonal trust, 102, 104–5
investor-state, 48
inward-oriented models of growth, 3
Iran, 71, 76, 81–83. *See also* Iranian Revolution; Twitter Revolution
Iranian Revolution, 203
Iraq, 128
irrigator organization, 26; dissidents in, 82
Islamic parties, 203
Israel, 84, 134

J

Jackson, Giorgio, 164–65, 167
J-curve theory, 5, 24, 174–75, 188

K

Kasich, John, 180

L

La Moneda, Chile, 164
La Vía Campesina, 56-59. *See also* National Family Farm Coalition
labor groups and movements, 4, 9, 48, 50, 61, 150, 179, 180, 188. *See also* unions
Lagos, Ricardo, 159
Lasn, Kalle, 182
Latin American politics and movements, 5–6, 26, 56, 93–94, 99–100, 105–6, 108–9, 111–12, 150, 204, 206–7, 210
Latinobarómetro, 93–94, 101, 103, 105, 110, 112
land occupations, 10, 93, 101
land reform, 122
language, 31, 36–37
Lebanese Independence Intifada, 128
Lehman Brothers, 175
Libya, 133, 137
local movements and focus, 1, 27, 32, 35, 51, 55–56, 58–59

M

Maastricht Treaty of the European Union, 52
Mafhouz, Asmaa, 78, 80
marginalized groups, 55, 58, 132
markets. *See* financial markets
marketization, 23, 38
McCain, John, 186
meaning-making, 12, 30-31, 34-40, 200; and
    meaning laden-claims, 34-35, 38-40
media, 1, 60, 71, 76, 155, 177, 184; freedom
    of, 37, 210. *See also* news media;
    newspapers; social media
Mexico, 38, 48, 60, 62-64, 99, 207, 210;
    activists from, 48; anti-Mexico rhetoric,
    65; export manufacturing plants in,
    207; government, 62; protests over
    corn in, 38; social movements in, 62.
    See also Mexico City; North American
    Free Trade Agreement (NAFTA);
    Red Mexicana de Acción Frente al
    Libre Comercio (RMALC); Security
    and Prosperity Partnership of North
    America; United States-Mexico-
    Canada Agreement (USMCA);
Mexico City, 38, 62
Michigan, US, 180
Middle East, 1, 2, 6, 15, 120, 122-24, 126,
    131, 139, 203-4, 206-7, 210; context of,
    131; neoliberalism in the, 122; post-
    Arab Spring, 139. *See also* Arab World;
    Bahrain; Egypt; Iran; Iraq; Israel;
    Palestine; Saudi Arabia; Syria; Turkey;
    Yemen
middle-classes, 124, 183-84, 186, 187
migrants, 55
military and protestors, 133, 136-37
military equipment and guerilla movements,
    26
military institutions and power, 132-37, 139,
    146-47, 151-54, 158-59, 164
Ministry of Education, Chile, 153
mobilization, 3, 4, 6-10, 15, 26, 28, 32, 52,
    55, 65, 79, 113, 119-21, 126-28, 130-31,
    135-36, 138, 200, 203, 208; agents of,

126; campaigns, 7, 55; height of, 208;
    nature of, 65; opportunity for, 8, 203;
    oppositional, 121, 137; processes, 136;
    rise of, 3; scale and intensity of, 8;
    source, 120; strategies, 32; types of, 113;
    wave of popular, 119-21, 135. *See also*
    mobilizing structures
mobilizing structures, 26-27, 32
Monsanto Corporation, 47
morality, 27, 33, 135-36, 139; and moral
    claims, 33; and moral outrage, 33,
    135-36, 139
movements, 7, 13-14, 24-25, 27-29,
    31-34, 36, 39, 150, 152, 198, 209; and
    characteristics of, 32; composition
    of, 34, 36; core of, 24; dynamics of,
    14, 25; emergence of, 13-14, 28, 34,
    39; emergence of new types of, 209;
    framing process for, 31; identities, 150,
    152; organization of, 25; outcomes of,
    13; participation in, 33, 198; society, 7;
    trajectory of, 34
Movimiento Autonomista, Chile, 165
Mubarak, Gamal, 125, 131-32, 134, 137, 183
Multilateral Agreement on Investment, 52
multinational corporations. *See* corporations

N

nation-states, 28, 53
National Family Farm Coalition, 58. *See also*
    La Vía Campesina
National Socioeconomic Characterization,
    Chile, 159
nationalism, 50-51, 53, 61, 63, 65, 121, 132,
    174, 206, 210
natural resources, 5
negative inducements, 5
neighborhood associations, 26
neoclassical economics, 207
neoliberalism, 5, 52, 122, 124, 134, 152, 155,
    167, 204; anti-austerity contention,
    48, 51, 198, 205; economic policies,
    122; education model, 155; elites, 134;
    globalization, 204; model, 167; policies,

124; principles, 152; projects, 52; reforms, 5

networks, 26, 39

New Democratic Party, Canada, 61

New Majority, Chile, 163–64, 167

New York, New York, 179, 182–83, 185, 188. *See also* New York City Police Department; New York Stock Exchange; Occupy Wall Street and Occupy movement; Wall Street, New York; Zuccotti Park, New York

New York City Police Department, 186

New York Stock Exchange, 183, 185

New Zealand, 48

News media, 127; *Al Jazeera*, 127; *BBC*, 73; *CBS News*, 177; *Fox News*, 177

Newspapers, 78; *Guardian*, 80; *New York Times*, 78, 177, 182; *New Yorker*, 85; *Time*, 1; *Washington Post*, 78; *Washington Times*, 82

nongovernmental organizations (NGOs), 13–15, 50, 93–95, 97–101, 103, 105–6, 108–9, 111–13, 201; activity, 93, 100–101; contact with, 100, 105–6, 108, 111, 113

nonviolence, 127

normalization thesis, 7, 9

North America, 14, 48, 50, 56, 60, 62–64, 66, 105, 195; trinational activities, 48, 63–65. *See also* Canada; Mexico; North American Free Trade Agreement (NAFTA); United States; United States-Mexico-Canada Agreement (USMCA); Security and Prosperity Partnership of North America

North American Free Trade Agreement (NAFTA), 52, 57, 62–65, 187; institutional framework established by, 64; legislative campaign against, 62; ratification of, 64; renegotiation of, 65. *See also* Citizens' Trade Campaign

Northeast Organic Farming Association of Vermont (NOFA-VT), 54

Nueva Democracia, Chile, 165

O

Obama, Barack, 15, 64, 150, 173, 175–78, 183, 186, 189, 205; campaign of, 15, 189; election of, 178; presidency of, 64, 150, 176–77, 183, 205

Obamacare, 178, 187

Occupy Wall Street and Occupy movement, 1, 13, 15, 48, 51, 71, 75, 77, 173, 181–89, 199, 205, 209; encampment, 184; event, 77; leaders, 185; meme, 182, 183, 185; movement, 71; Democracy not Corporatocracy (slogan), 183. *See also* Tumblr Revolution; We Are the 99%

Ohio, US, 178, 180–81, 188. *See also* Kasich, John; We Are Ohio

oil revenue, 122

Organization for Economic Cooperation and Development (OECD) countries, 159

organizational structures and networks, 25–26, 51, 147, 181

P

Palestine, 84, 128

Paris, France, 85

Party for Democracy, Chile, 157

party systems, analysis of, 3, 8–9, 12, 15–16, 29, 102-3, 105, 106–7, 111-13, 149, 150–52, 210

patriotism, 30

peasants, 55, 57

People's Summit, 59

petitions, 99, 101, 106, 108, 149, 161, 179–80

Philippines. *See* Aquino, Benigno

Piñera, Sebastián, 158, 161–62, 164, 167

Pingüinos, 155–57, 164, 166; movement, 155–56; protests, 164. *See also* Chilean student movement

Pinochet, Augusto, 29, 151–52, 156, 166

plebiscite, 152

Podemos, Spain, 150, 206

polarization, 15, 146, 147, 151–52, 161, 164, 167, 175

political opportunities, 4, 5, 6, 23, 27–29, 32,
34, 66, 119–21, 126, 130–31, 133, 135–39,
179–80, 199–201, 204; approach, 27;
concept of, 29; dimensions of, 4–6;
emergence of, 126; extent of, 133;
nature of, 131; paucity of, 66; structural
approach to, 204; theorists, 28
political opportunity structures, 10, 13, 15,
27, 62, 64, 119–21, 128, 130–31, 137–40,
146–47, 151, 156, 195, 204; centrality of,
204; concept of, 119, 138–39; contingent
nature of, 139; ebbing and flowing of,
119–20; existence and salience of, 139;
explanatory power of, 204; openings in,
121; permeable nature of, 62; shifts in,
147, 151; types of, 139
political participation, 7–9, 14, 62, 66, 80, 93–
95, 97–100, 102, 109, 111, 125–26, 156
political process theory and model, 4–5,
23–25, 32, 35, 50, 53, 188, 204
politicians, 10, 28. *See also* names of
individual politicians
populism, 173–74, 210
Portugal, 1, 200. *See also* Sócrates, José
poverty, 3, 63, 97, 111, 120, 122–24, 126, 181;
levels, 122, 126; pro-poor movement,
105; rates, 120, 123–24; reduction, 97;
Presidential Commission on Education,
Chile, 156
privatization, 52, 57, 123
procurement, 48
Progressive Conservative Party, Canada, 61
protests, 1–2, 4–16, 23, 27–29, 33–34, 38,
48–54, 60–61, 63, 65–66, 71–79, 82–88,
93–94, 97, 99–100, 103, 105–6, 108–9,
111–13, 128–29, 138, 146–47, 149, 154,
157–58, 160–62, 164, 173–76, 179,
185–86, 188, 195–96, 198–99, 201–6,
208–11; actions, 1, 10, 14, 49, 52, 54;
activities, 2, 4–6, 8–9, 14–15, 49–50,
53, 60–61, 63, 65–66, 94, 105, 128–29;
attendance, 79; behavior, 10, 12, 108,
113; campaigns, 65; character of, 72, 74,
82, 86; comparison of, 38; coordination

of, 65; cycles, 16, 48, 51–53, 173, 175,
185–86, 188, 195, 199–202; demands,
12–13, 15; democracy's effects on, 8, 34,
94, 112, 203; dynamics, 2, 6, 23; early
phases of, 208; events, 14, 51, 87, 160,
164; explanations for, 23; frequency
of, 77; impacts, 12; mechanisms, 13,
54, 113; mobilizing structures of, 201;
momentum of, 76; movements, 4, 6–8,
10–16, 76, 173, 186, 195, 196–201, 203,
206, 210–11; nonviolent and mass
nature of, 138; outcomes, 14, 72, 74, 86,
88, 209; participation, 76, 78, 85, 100,
103, 109, 160; political impacts of, 49,
199, 206; politics, 7, 9, 16, 28; predictor
of, 106, 109; processes, 13; public
acceptance of, 160; rates, 99–100; rise
of, 3; role of social media in, 73; size of,
78, 82; stage of, 74, 87; success, 71–72,
80, 86, 88; tools, 72; types of, 195;
visibility, 72, 78, 82; waves of, 2, 15, 82,
87, 146–47, 154, 158, 160–62, 164, 196,
204. *See also* global protest cycle; names
of individual protest movements; riots
public opinion, 148, 201
public transportation, 160

Q

Quebec, Canada, 50, 61

R

rebellion, 33, 51
Red Mexicana de Acción Frente al Libre
Comercio (RMALC), 62
relative deprivation, 24–25, 34
repoliticization, 4–5, 49
repression, 6, 29, 39, 120–21, 129–30, 133,
136, 204
Republican Party, US, 150, 173–75, 177–80,
186, 188–89, 205. *See also* Bush, George
W.; Bush, Jeb; Kasich, John; McCain,
John; Romney, Mitt; Trump, Donald;
Walker, Scott

resistance, 33, 38–39, 60

resource mobilization, 23, 25–27, 127, 130, 188

resources, 26, 34–35, 39–40, 95, 133–34, 137–38

revolutions, 24, 37, 76, 86, 119; rhizomatic, 198

Revolución Democrática, Chile, 165

right-wing activism and ideology, 177, 187–88

riots, 10, 52, 93, 101, 161

Romney, Mitt, 175, 186, 189

rule of law, 109, 206

rural communities and society, 59, 122–23

S

Said, Khaled, 1, 136

Saleh, Ali Abdullah, 125, 134–35

Sanders, Bernie, 173, 186–87, 190, 205

Santelli, Rick, 176

Saudi Arabia, 78, 203

scale jumping, 14, 53, 66

scale shift, 53–54, 146

Scandinavia. See Iceland; Stockholm, Sweden

Seattle World Trade Organization Ministerial, 50

Security and Prosperity Partnership of North America (SPP), 64

semiotic practices, 33, 36

Sharp, Jorge, 165

slacktivism, 81

social media, 10, 12–14, 71–88, 120, 129, 160, 174, 188, 195, 199–200, 203; access to, 82, 84; activism, 71–72, 76, 83; activity, 86–88; *Adbusters*, 182–83; campaign, 160; content on, 84; effect of, 72, 74; effective use of, 199–200; era of, 85; government responses to, 84; nature of, 72; platforms, 72, 76; presence of, 72, 78–79, 81. See also Facebook; Facebook Revolution; Flickr; Instagram; Twitter; Twitter Revolution; YouTube

social mobilization, 2, 7, 13, 26, 35, 38–39, 79, 120–21, 131–33, 135–39, 152, 155;

consequence of, 2; nonviolent strategies of, 136; oppositional, 137; politically transformative, 131,133; processes of, 121, 137, 139

social movements, 2–4, 6–8, 10–15, 23–36, 39, 49–51, 53, 61, 63, 71–72, 85, 88, 93, 119–20, 135, 138, 145–53, 162, 165–66, 174–77, 181, 185–86, 195–202, 204, 207–9; acceptance of, 148; activity, 35, 49; agents, 119; approaches, 27; approaches to analyzing, 53; campaigns, 199–200; challengers, 197; claims, 39, 200; comprehensive research agenda on, 148; consequences, 2, 13, 196–97; contextual aspects of, 119; decline, 34; development, 34, 145; diffusion, 185; dynamics, 27, 32; emergence, 13, 34–36, 51; emotional dimensions of, 32; entrepreneurs, 138; framework, 120, 131; leaders, 176; memes, 176; organizations, 147, 149; organizing, 53, 61; outcomes, 36, 197; political effects of, 10, 196–98; political outcomes of, 3, 145; political impacts of, 145–49, 151, 195, 208; principal causes of, 39; relationships between, 209; repertoires, 200; role of, 207; types of, 145; understandings of, 34; resources, 27; sector, 202; success, 197; theory, 24–25, 31, 34, 39, 72, 135; trajectories, 27

Social Security, US, 177

socialism, 150, 182, 187

Socialist Party, Chile, 162

socioeconomic conditions and policies, 120–21, 123, 139, 210

Sócrates, José, 200

South America. See Argentina; Bolivia; Brazil; Chile; Ecuador; Latin American politics and movements

sovereignty, 57

Soviet Union, 56

Spain, 1, 150, 182, 185, 198, 206; 15-M movement of, 198. See also *Indignados*; Podemos, Spain

W

Walker, Scott, 179–80
Wall Street, New York, 181–83, 185–86
Washington, US, 183
Washington Fair Trade Coalition, 48
water, 26–27, 29, 38; collection practices, 38; privatization, 26, 38; wars, 26–27, 29
We Are Ohio, 180–81, 189
We Are the 99%, 184, 199. *See also* Occupy Wall Street and Occupy movement
wealth, 58, 122, 124, 184; concentration of, 58, 122, 124, 184; distribution of, 124
Wisconsin, US, 178–81, 188. *See also* Walker, Scott
white supremacist movement, US, 30
women, as participants in protest, 105
women's movement, 11, 202
women's organizations, 10, 26, 61, 96, 149
women's rights, 58, 61, 63, 149, 165, 202
World Bank, 50, 52, 57, 97, 102. *See also* international financial institutions
World Trade Organization, 50, 52, 57. *See also* intergovernmental organizations
World Values Survey, 94, 100–101, 103, 106, 110–12

Y

Yemen, 123, 125, 127, 133–34, 136, 139. *See also* Saleh, Ali Abdullah
YouTube, 73, 78, 80. *See also* social media

Z

Zuccotti Park, New York, 76, 183–84, 186, 195. *See also* Occupy Wall Street and Occupy movement